Abraham Willett

(c1735–c1805)

of

Onondaga County
New York

Albert James Willett, Jr.

HERITAGE BOOKS
2015

HERITAGE BOOKS
AN IMPRINT OF HERITAGE BOOKS, INC.

Books, CDs, and more—Worldwide

For our listing of thousands of titles see our website
at
www.HeritageBooks.com

Published 2015 by
HERITAGE BOOKS, INC.
Publishing Division
5810 Ruatan Street
Berwyn Heights, Md. 20740

Copyright © 2000 Albert James Willett, Jr.

All rights reserved. No part of this book may be reproduced or transmitted in any form or by any means, electronic or mechanical, including photocopying, recording or by any information storage and retrieval system without written permission from the author, except for the inclusion of brief quotations in a review.

International Standard Book Numbers
Paperbound: 978-0-7884-5614-5
Clothbound: 978-0-7884-1542-5

DEDICATION

To Herbert Lockwood, III,
who has provided encouragement
to see this project to its completion

ACKNOWLEDGEMENTS

Margaret Ernest, Seattle, Washington, always doing the tedious work of researching census records on request. Her help and friendship extends far beyond this volume.

Judy Gorham, Muskegon, Michigan, has provided data on the Consider Heath Willett family down to the present day.

Ruth Z. Lewis, Lansing, Michigan. One example of the level of her help is that she copied every mention of the Willett surname in the 1900, 1910, and 1920 Michigan census record. Copying literally hundreds of census records from microfilm is one of the most tedious chores of family history, but the results of that effort have been extremely helpful over the years and have contributed much to this volume.

H. Whitwell Wales, Foster City, California, for data on the Carlotta Willett family, and extracts from Consider H. Willett Furniture Company Catalogs for 1941, 1942, and 1958-1959.

Diane Willett, Topping, Virginia, wife, companion, photographic scanner, and typist who provides technical help and moral support.

Herbert Lockwood Willett, III, Falmouth, Massachusetts, provided the privately printed family histories *The Corridors of the Years* and *Further Corridors*. Herbert Lockwood Willett also provided support and encouragement in seeing this volume to completion.

James Willett, Laurinburg, North Carolina, who is my computer expert and son. On call at all hours to answer questions on how to keep the computer up and running.

Robert and Donna Willett, Cocoa Beach, Florida. Donna for proofreading the entire manuscript, making numerous grammatical corrections, insightful comments and suggestions concerning style and format. Robert and Donna made their collection of original family documents, photographs, diaries, and extensive Civil War era collection of family letters available to the author to quote in this volume.

George Willits of Woodstock, Ontario, Canada, provided proof reading and insight. A kindred spirit and dear friend. Has provided enormous encouragement for me to continue researching and preserving family history.

TABLE OF CONTENTS

DEDICATION

PREFACE i

1 Abraham Willett (c1735-c1805) of Onondaga County, New York 1

2 William Willett (1769-1844) of Onondaga County, New York 4

3 Permelia Willett (1793-1854) of Onondaga County, New York 11

4 Abraham Willett (1793-1859) of Onondaga County, New York 13

5 Hannah Willett (1805-1874) of Onondaga County, New York 18

6 Interlude: The Civil War, From Soldier to Sutler 25

7 Alfred Milan Willett (1829-1906) of Ionia County, Michigan 99

8 Floyd Abram Willett (1833-1868) of Steuben County, New York 106

9 Gordon Arthur Abram Willett (1835-1898) of Ionia County, Michigan 111

10 Abigail Jane Willett (1837-1864) of Kalamazoo County, Michigan 148

11 James W. Willett (1839-1906) of Montcalm County, Michigan 150

12 Anna Willett (1813-1874) of Ionia County, Michigan 168

13 William Willett (1809-1853) of Onondaga County, New York 170

14 Consider H. Willett (1840-1912) of Chicago, Illinois 174

15 The Consider H. Willett Furniture Company 218

Bibliography 227

Index 229

PREFACE

Just a few words about this work.
Expect errors. In a work of this scope and size, with numerous sources for data, there are bound to be mistakes. The editor does not apologize for doing the impossible, but offers the following work as a reasonable outline of the William Willett family from its earliest traditional ancestry to the present. Every effort has been made to compare data and note discrepancies by circulating the original drafts of various sections of this volume to those most interested and often most directly descended from a particular branch of the family. Every census record was consulted which seemed even remotely possible to be connected to this extended family. Every census record that was found to pertain to this extended family has been extracted and cited. Published works, whether newspaper articles, obituaries, or biographies, have been consulted and abstracted. Every effort has been made to ascribe data taken from previously published sources. But in some cases, either in the distant past, or more recent but careless present, a citation has been lost while the quote or data has been retained. It has been felt more important to present the data that has been collected than to exclude data because it was not fully documented or properly cited. The goal of this volume is to point a future researcher to the records or locale where further information can be found thus saving them time and effort to fully document their own line. In this respect, I believe the following work will be found useful.

The index is not an every-name index. The index is abbreviated and lists only those names as listed in CAPITAL and BOLD letters in the "Heading" of a narrative section, and those names which have the surname CAPITALIZED and BOLD under the "List of Children" section. This index leads the researcher only to descendants of the subject of this volume or to those who married into the Willett family. Also it has the advantage of never listing the same person more than twice, once as a child, and then again as the adult head of a family. This way, anyone searching for information is led only to data that is connected to the genealogical purpose of this volume.

Accuracy: this work does not present itself as perfect. At the same time, what is presented is not "plausible" genealogy, but the results of numerous contributors both living and deceased. Information has been gleaned from numerous printed, manuscript, Bible Record, Vital Record, and oral history sources and thus each source will have to be weighted to determine its degree of accuracy and trustworthiness.

As best as type can reproduce the written word, each census record, abstract, or transcript is as close to the original as type permits. Brackets [ ] are used when information has been inserted in an original record, usually to clarify what is being said.

Italics are used for the 1790-1840 census records where only the name of the head of the household is listed in the original record. These early census records cite only the sex and approximate age of those being counted. Whenever other sources, such as, later census records, Bible Records, family history, oral history make it possible, the name of the wife and children are listed beside the age and sex groupings.

If there is a Question Mark (?) behind a date, the date is estimated.

If there is a Star (*) behind a date, the date does not agree with the year range as applied to certain census records.

PREFACE

Any year date, which is not prefaced by a month and day, can be expected to be correct with +/- one year. Do not expect all dates as recorded to agree with each other. Even those dates graven in stone are notorious for the errors graven into the stone. This is because such dates are only as accurate as the memory of the person who provided the information. Particularly when the elderly outlive their contemporaries such dates are often the best guess of the person writing the obituary or providing the stone carver with information. The dates as recorded in the various records need to be balanced against the sum total of all known and available data.

Underlining is used to bring attention to the fact that a particular surname is "as written" in an original record. This has the same meaning as the Latin "sic" which is also used to denote that a record is "as" originally written. Usually this is used for the surname where one record will spell Willet with only one "t" while another record concerning the same individual or family will spell the surname Willett with two "tt"s.

Nicknames are generally listed after the Christian name from which they derive. However, some nicknames have no relationship to a given name and are normally listed after the first Christian name.

Abbreviations have been kept to a minimum. The only abbreviations used are:

B = born
M = married
D = died
Sic = Latin for "as it is written"

The meaning of some abbreviations within some citations has been lost over the years, but it is thought better to list a citation completely as originally recorded, even when some of the meaning of that citation is not obviously apparent. Page 16 has two instances of this type of transcription where X-482 and 61-93 are not further identified. Hopefully, should a researcher consult the original deed books of Cortland County, New York, these notations would make sense.

There is a "Heading" for each family listing the names of the spouses in capital letters. If a person has been married more than once, then each marriage has its own "Heading".

There is a "Narrative" section below each "heading".

Short references are quoted within the body of the text. There is a "Reference List" immediate after the "Narrative" section which lists general references which are not otherwise cited in the body of the text.

Finally, there is a "List of Children". The surname in the list of children is capitalized, and is found in the index.

"See next..." refers readers to additional information on descendents.

The editor of this volume recommends that you use this study of the Willett family with caution and verify with original sources your direct line. Having said that, the editor has taken as much caution and diligence as can be expected in a work of this magnitude. As often as possible every pertinent census record has been consulted, considered and quoted. The main purpose of this volume is to identify the sources from which this family history was constructed so future researchers can verify the research on which this volume is based and hopefully come to the same conclusions.

The editor takes responsibility for any errors of omission or commission. In a work of this size, coming from many diverse sources, there are bound to be errors. However, every effort has been made to keep errors to an absolute minimum. As many census, birth, marriage, death records have been cited as were found during the compilation of this volume. In the final instance, a researcher should return to the original source to verify the accuracy of any data which might be suspect. Towards this end, citations refer to original sources as often as possible.

CHAPTER ONE

ABRAHAM WILLETT (C1735-C1805)

OF ONONDAGA COUNTY, NEW YORK

I.1
ABRAHAM WILLETT
Of Onondaga County, New York

Abraham Willett was born about 1735, in New Jersey? This branch has a family tradition of descent through a New Jersey Willett family. Samuel Willett Comstock, writing in correspondence, dated March 16, 1943, stated, "Abraham ... was either a son of William or one Samuel, only known sons of Samuel Willett and Hannah, his wife, who lived in Middletown Township, Monmouth County, New Jersey, the earliest Willett of New Jersey." However, there must be at least one generation missing, and Comstock offered no proof of this allegation. There were several Willett families who could be the ancestor of this branch. Most likely, Abraham Willett is the parent of the William Willett who is the ancestor of the children listed next. Also, this Abraham Willett could be connected to one of the Pennsylvania Willett families and perhaps the names listed in this chapter are the children of a second marriage.

Some Hunterdon County, New Jersey, court records that might pertain to this Abraham Willett are listed below:

    No. 31460 May 17, 1758:
    No. 7021 filed December 8, 1759

Abraham Willett was a resident of Hunterdon County, New Jersey (1758), but by August, 1762 (1763), and February, 1764 (1765), he was described as late of Hunterdon County.

    No. 34657 August 3, 1762 (1763)
    No. 14592 filed November 26, 1763
    No. xxxx February 8, 1764 (1765]
    No. 9755 May Term 1764
    No. 31346 dated May 2, 1764
    No. 7902 filed July 23, 1764
    No. 33809 May 22, 1765 (1766]

No. 7617 filed July 26, 1765 (1766)
No. 28036 February Term 1768
No. 34956 October 27, 1768 (1769]
No. 6909 filed December 15, 1770
No. 33951 February 3, 1773 (1774)
No. 34379 August 3, 1773 (1774)

FOR THE RECORD: None of the above can be linked directly to the Abraham Willett of this sketch. The above citations are only mentioned for the record.

It is not proven that this Abraham Willet, of Readington (1765), Tewksbury (February 1768), and New German Township (October 1768, October 1770) is the progenitor of the following Willett family. What is known is that most of the Willett families living in Hunterdon County, New Jersey, can be accounted for, and none of those Willett families have ever claimed the following children as part of their heritage.

This Abraham Willett must have been born about 1740? (By tradition in New Jersey) and married about 1765? (Wife's name is unknown).

If the tradition is true, then Abraham Willett had come to Onondaga County, New York, about 1799 or 1800, with his wife. And there is no known reason why he may not have been there even earlier, perhaps before 1791. In the 1800 Onondaga County, census, Abraham Willett is listed with a male child who is under 10 years of age. This may be a grandson (age 7 in 1800) or could be Abraham's child born late in life.

In 1800, Abraham Willett and family were enumerated in Cicero, Onondaga County, New York census, page 209, as follows:

1 male   45-up   bef. 1755   *Abraham   age 60? b 1740?*
1 female   45-up   bef. 1755   *(wife)*
1 male   0-10   1790-1800   *(son/possibly a grandson)*

J. E. Bookstaver (1907) found this family in Onondaga County, New York, whose descendants trace (by tradition) to New Jersey and Flushing, Long Island. Actually, in 1800, there were two (2) Willett families living in Onondaga County.

WILLIAM WILLETT (1769-1844)

There was also a William Willett (presumed son of Abraham Willett) family in the 1800 Cicero, Onondaga County, New York census, page 208, as follows:

1 male	26-45	1755-1774	William	age 31	b 1769
1 female	16-26	1774-1784	Hannah	age 25	b 1775
1 female	16-26	1774-1784	[Susannah Lesley?]		
1 female	10-16	1784-1790	Permelia	age 7	b 1793
1 male	0-10	1790-1800	Abraham	age 6	b 1794
1 female	0-10	1790-1800	Jane	age 3	b 1797
1 female	0-10	1790-1800	Experience	age 1	b 1799
1 female	45-up	bef. -1755	mother-in-law / Sarah Foster?		

William Willett's age was listed as being between 26 and 45; within his household was a female, probably his mother-in-law, who was over 45. It is the assumption of the editor of this volume that William Willett is most likely the son William Willett who had married Hannah Foster.

Presumably, this Abraham Willett had died about 1805 in Onondaga County, New York. At least, he is not noted in the 1810 Onondaga County, New York census, even though his son William Willett and family are listed.

1. **William WILLETT**: b 1769 perhaps in Tewksbury, Hunterdon County, New Jersey; m first abt 1792, Hannah Foster (b 1775, Argyle, Washington County, New York; d May 28, 1831, New York); m 2d his widowed sister-in-law, Mrs. Susannah [Foster] Lesley (d October 10, 1852, New York); d January 22, 1844, Onondaga County, age 74, and is buried in the Pine Ridge Cemetery, Navarino, Onondaga County, New York. See next I.1.1.

2. **(daughter) WILLETT**: b abt 1775.

3. **(daughter) WILLETT**: b abt 1777.

4. **(son/grandson) WILLETT**: b 1793 (1800 Onondaga County census). This individual is deduced from the 1800 Onondaga County, New York census record.

CHAPTER TWO

WILLIAM WILLETT (1769-1844)

OF ONONDAGA COUNTY, NEW YORK

I.1.1a
WILLIAM WILLETT and HANNAH FOSTER
Of Cicero, Onondaga County, New York

William Willett was born in 1769, perhaps in Tewksbury Township, Hunterdon County, New Jersey, the son of Abraham Willett (Comstock, letter dated March 5, 1943, address: 104 City Island Avenue, City Island, New York).

Usually, William Willett and Hannah Foster are claimed as the parents of Abraham, William, Hannah, and the other children, listed below.

FOR THE RECORD: It is not likely that he is the William Willett, the miller of Potterville, New Jersey.

Until further discovery is made, William Willett born in 1769, in Tewksbury Township, Hunterdon County, New Jersey, will be assumed to be the ancestor of this branch.

William Willett must have removed to Argyle, Washington County, New York, by 1791.

William Willett married first in Argyle, Washington County, New York, about 1792, Hannah Foster (b 1775, Argyle, New York; d May 28, 1831, buried in the Pine Ridge Cemetery, Onondaga County, New York, along with her husband, William, and sister, Susan [Foster] Willett). Mrs. Hannah (Foster) Willett was the daughter of Captain Jonathan Foster and Sarah. Jonathan Foster was a Revolutionary War soldier from Massachusetts.

The William Willett family was living in Washington County, New York, in 1793, when their son Abraham was born.

FOR THE RECORD: The following notes are made so future researchers can differentiate between the two William Willett families, i.e., William Willett of Albany with wife Isabel, and William Willett of Onondaga County with wife Hannah Foster, the subject of this volume.

WILLIAM WILLETT (1769-1844)

NOTE: In 1790, the William Willett of Albany County, New York, is known to have a wife Isabella. This listing does not belong to the William Willett of this volume. The 1790, William <u>Willet</u> listing in the Albany County, New York census, page 41, is reconstructed as follows:

1 male	16-up	bef. 1774	*William*
1 female			*Isabella*

NOTE: At the death in 1792 of William Willett, Senior of Albany, his widow was listed as Isabel/la. This death date for William Willett is now confirmed by the following. On September 4, 1792, Isabella Willett, wife of William Willett, deceased, renounced administration of William's estate. Benjamin Phillips and John Laing performed the Estate Inventory on November 23, 1792. Samuel Willett, Archibald McNaughton, John Vannorthwyche, and John Laing made Bond on September 4, 1792, as a guarantee of performance of the inventory. The estate amounted to 108 pounds, 9 shillings, ten pence, and was insolvent.

NOTE: In the 1792 inventory of the Estate of William Willett, of Saratoga, New York, is the mention of one half a leased mill and 75 acres of leased land in Saratoga, New York (Comstock, 1927, page 8).

In 1790, a Jonathan Foster was living close to [our] William Willett in Argyle, Washington County, New York.

On February 18, 1798 ("Twenty-first Year of Our Independence"), the Court of Washington County, New York, ordered the sheriff to arrest George Lesley and William Willett of Argyle in a case of debt concerning a promissory note of June 1, 1796, Nine Pounds due to Ebeneezer Allen before the June 15 (then next), and "which said George Lesley is in custody and the said William Willett is returned not found." Lesley and Willett had previously refused to pay the plaintiffs when payment was demanded, and the court ordered an inquiry and found for the plaintiffs. The only other record found of William Willett in Washington County after this date, is his signature on the February 23, 1798, will of Jonathan Foster. It can be assumed that by 1798, William Willett had moved westwards in search of a new beginning.

In 1798, Jonathan Foster of Argyle, Washington County, New York, wrote his will (proved 1801) and mentioned by name a William <u>Willet</u>. The will of Jonathan Foster also mentions daughter Hannah (Foster) wife of William Willett.

> I Jonathan Foster of Argyle and in the County of Washington and state of New York ...
>
> ... my loving Daughter Hannah Willet, Mary Foster, Nancy Foster, and Experience Foster twenty five Pounds apiece to be paid by my Executor one year after my Decease or as they come to be Eighteen years old. Also, I do give and bequeath to my loving daughter Susannah Lesley one hundred and fifty dollars ...

The will was dated February 23, 1798, and below the signature of Jonathan Foster are the further names of "Sarah Foster, Allen Foster, Amos Foster, Experience Foster, Wm. Willet, Benj. Teft/t, William Teft/t. This 1798 will of Jonathan Foster of Argyle, Washington County, New York is conclusive proof that William Willett, husband of Mrs. Hannah (Foster) Willett was living at that time, and thus not the same as the William Willett who died in 1792 in Albany, New York. Jonathan Foster left property to his wife, (Mrs.) Sarah Foster, and to eight children, including daughters (Mrs.) Hannah Willett, and (Mrs.) Susannah Lesley (William Willett's second wife and also sister-in-law). His daughter Mary Foster (b August 3, 1781; d September 22, 1850) had married Benjamin Tefft (b October 16, 1773; d May 2, 1847, Greenwich, Washington County, New York). Daughter Nancy Foster (b October 3, 1782; d June 13, 1857, Galesville, Washington County, New York) had married William S. Tefft (b c1780; d May 3, 1827).

In 1800, William Willett and family were listed in the Cicero, Onondaga County, New York census, on page 208 (his parents were listed on the next page).

1 male	26-45	1755-1774	William	age 31	b 1769
1 female	16-26	1774-1784	Hannah	age 25	b 1775
1 female	16-26	1774-1784	[Susannah Lesley?]		
1 female	10-16	1784-1790	Permelia	age 7	b 1793
1 male	0-10	1790-1800	Abraham	age 6	b 1794
1 female	0-10	1790-1800	Jane	age 3	b 1797
1 female	0-10	1790-1800	Experience	age 1	b 1799
1 female	45-up	bef. 1755	mother-in-law/ Sarah Foster?		

The female, age over 45, was probably his mother or mother-in-law. Then there were 2 females, age between 16 and 25 (one of whom would have been his first wife Hannah, born 1775, the other possibly a sister to either himself or

Hannah, or more likely a servant girl living in his household).
It should be noted that in 1800, there was a Samuel Willett living at Cambridge, Washington County, New York, and a William Willett living in Argyle, Washington County, New York. Washington County, New York, is the county that William Willett, the subject of this sketch, has just departed.

On August 12, 1808, William Willett of Onondaga County sold for $500.00 "part of lot 217" to H.i....g (name unreadable) (Onondaga County Court House Land Record, Syracuse, New York, Book H, page 470).

In 1810, William Willett and family are listed in the Onondaga County, New York, census page 8, as follows:

1 male	26-45	1765-1784	William	age 41	b 1769
1 female	26-45	1765-1784	Hannah	age 35	b 1775
1 male	16-26	1784-1794			
1 male	16-26	1784-1794			
1 male	16-26	1784-1794	Abraham	age 16	b 1794
1 male	10-16	1794-1800			
1 female	10-16	1794-1800	Jane	age 13	b 1797
1 female	10-16	1794-1800	Patience	age 7*	b 1803*
1 female	10-16	1794-1800	Hannah	age 5*	b 1805*
1 female	0-10	1800-1810	Ann	age 3	b 1807

In 1820, William Willet and family are listed in the Onondaga, Onondaga County, New York census, page 108, as follows:
1-0-0-1-0-1 2-1-2-0-1

1 male	45-up	bef.-1775	William	age 51	b 1769
1 female	45-up	1765-1784	Hannah	age 45	b 1775
1 male	16-26	1794-1804			
1 female	16-26	1794-1804	Patience	age 17	b 1803
1 female	16-26	1794-1804	Hannah	age 15*	b 1805*
1 female	10-16	1804-1810	Ann	age 13	b 1807
1 male	0-10	1810-1820	William	age 9	b 1811
1 female	0-10	1810-1820			
1 female	0-10	1810-1820			

Listed separately in the 1820 Onondaga County, New York census, are William Willett's son, Abraham Willet, and family, as follows:
1-0-0-0-1-0 0-0-1-0-0

1 male	26-45	1775-1794	Abraham	age 26	b 1794
1 female	16-26	1794-1804	Betsey	age 29*	b 1791*
1 male	0-10	1810-1820	Enoch F	age 5	b 1815

On March 28, 1821, William Willett of the town of Onondaga sold for $600.00 part of lot 217 (late Onondaga Reservation) containing 42 acres and 32 rods of land to Abraham Willett (Onondaga County Court House Land Record, Syracuse, New York, Deed Book 56, page 234). In 1830, William Willit (sic) and family are listed in the Onondaga, Onondaga County, New York census, page 180, as follows:

1 male	60-70	1760-1770	*William age 61*	*b 1769*
1 female	50-60	1770-1780	*Hannah age 55*	*b 1775*
1 male	20-30	1800-1810		
1 male	20-30	1800-1810	*William age 19**	*b 1811**
1 female	20-30	1800-1810	*Patience age 27*	*b 1803*
1 female	15-20	1810-1815	*Ann age 17*	*b 1813*
1 female	15-20	1810-1815		
1 male	0-5	1825-1830		

Listed separately is his son, Abraham Willet (page 182).

Mrs. Hannah (Foster) Willett died on May 28, 1831, age 56, and is buried in the Pine Ridge Cemetery, Navarino, Onondaga County, New York, along with her husband, and Susanna, her sister, William's second wife.

Children of William Willett and his first wife, Hannah Foster:

1. **Permelia WILLETT**: b 1793 (possibly a twin), Greenwich, Washington County, New York. Permelia Willett married abt 1822, Asher T. Cummings (b 1799, New York/Connecticut; d 1875, Kalamazoo County, Michigan). Mrs. Permelia (Willett) Cummings died in 1854 in Onondaga County, New York. See next I.1.1.1.

2. **Abraham WILLETT**: b 1793, Washington County, New York, according to the 1855 Virgil, Onondaga County, New York State census (possibly a twin); m abt 1814, Betsey Bugsby (b 1791 in Connecticut; d December 22, 1871, Cortland County, New York); in 1832, removed to Virgil Township, Cortland County, New York; d April 5, 1859, Virgil, Cortland County, New York. See next I.1.1.2.

3. **(Betsey) WILLETT**: b 1796. Possibly married about 1820, Amos Skinner (b 1793, New Hampshire). Perhaps the Betsey Skinner, age 54, in the 1850 Town of Onondaga, Onondaga County, census, who has Susan Willett, age 73,

born New York, living with her. This most likely is William Willett's widow, Mrs. Susannah (Foster) Willett.

4. **Jane WILLETT**: b 1797, New York; d January 1, 1851, and is buried in the Pine Ridge Cemetery, Navarino, Onondaga County, New York, in the same area as her father, William Willett, her mother, Mrs. Hannah (Foster) Willett (first wife), and her stepmother, Mrs. Susannah (Foster) Willett (William's second wife).

5. **Experience WILLETT**: b 1799, New York.

6. **Patience WILLETT**: b 1803, Onondaga County, New York.

7. **Hannah WILLETT**: b January 18, 1805, Navarino, Onondaga Township (Otisco), Onondaga County, New York; m at Onondaga, Onondaga County, New York, April 18, 1827, Alfred Floyd Smith (b January 14, 1804, Brookhaven, Long Island, Suffolk County, New York; d August 11, 1844, Vesper, New York, buried Pine Ridge Cemetery, Navarino, Onondaga County, New York); d December 28, 1874, North Plains, Ionia County, Michigan. See next I.1.1.7.

8. **Ann WILLETT**: b 1813, Onondaga County, New York; m abt 1830, George Case; removed to Michigan about 1848; d April 28, 1874, age 59 years, 4 months, 7 days, in Ionia County, Michigan. See next I.1.1.8.

9. **William WILLETT** (Jr.): b 1811, Onondaga County, New York; m abt 1836, Triphosa (Tryphena) Jackson (b 1817; d August 4, 1895, buried Pine Ridge Cemetery, Navarino, Onondaga County, New York); resided Onondaga County, New York; d August 27, 1853, age 42, buried Pine Ridge Cemetery, Navarino, Onondaga County, New York. See next I.1.1.9.

I.1.1b
WILLIAM WILLETT and MRS. SUSAN (FOSTER) LESLEY
Of Cicero, Onondaga County, New York

William Willett married 2d about 1835, Mrs. Susannah (Foster) Lesley (b 10 April, 1777, New York; d October 10, 1852, buried in the Pine Ridge Cemetery, Navarino, Onondaga County, New York), widow. Susannah was William Willett's sister-in-law, and the daughter of Captain Jonathan Foster and his wife Sarah.

On April 18, 1836, William Willett [Senior] of the town of Onondaga sold for $1,500 "lot 209 (late Onondaga Reservation) and part of lot 217" (bordered on south and west by land owned by William Willett, Junior) to William Willett, Junior (Onondaga County Court House Land Record, Syracuse, New York).

In 1840, William Willet and family are listed in the Onondaga County, New York census, page 105, as follows:

1 male	60-70	1770-1780	*William*	age 71	b 1769
1 female	60-70	1770-1780	*Susan*	age 63	b 1777
1 male	20-30	1810-1820	*William*	age 29	b 1811
1 female	20-30	1810-1820	*Triphosa*	(d-i-l)	b 1817
1 male	10-15	1825-1830			
1 female	0-5	1835-1840	*Elizabeth*		(granddaughter)

William Willett died on January 22, 1844, age 74, and is buried in the Pine Ridge Cemetery, Navarino, Onondaga County, New York, beside his first and second wives and near his daughter Jane Willett.

In 1850, (Mrs.) Susan Willett, age 73, was enumerated with Amos Skinner (b 1793, New Hampshire) and family, Onondaga, Onondaga County, New York census, page 262, dwelling 566-587, as follows:

Skinner Amos		57	m	NH	wagon maker, $500
	Betsey	54	f	NY	
	Marinda	29	f	NY	
	Seymour	18	m	NY	laborer
Willett	Susan	73	f	NY	

Mrs. Susannah (Foster-Lesley) Willett died on October 10, 1852, aged 75, and is buried in the Pine Ridge Cemetery, Navarino, Onondaga County, New York along with her husband, William Willett and her sister Hannah.

Although the parents and the birth place of William Willett can not be confirmed, we can be reasonably certain that the children listed below are the children of William Willett and Hannah (Foster) of Onondaga County, New York. This statement is fully supported by vital records, census records and "favor" biographies of the late 1800s.

(Bookstaver, 1907, pages 65-66; *The Willett Families*, 1985, page 165).

CHAPTER THREE

PERMELIA WILLETT (1793-1854)

OF ONONDAGA COUNTY, NEW YORK

I.1.1.1
PERMELIA WILLETT and ASHER T. CUMMINGS
Of Onondaga County, New York

Permelia Willett was born in 1793 (1790-1800) (possibly a twin), Greenwich, Washington County, New York. In the *Biographical Review of Calhoun County, Michigan*, 1904, page 134, Permelia Willett's father is named as William Willett.

Miss Permelia Willett married about 1822, Asher T. Cummings (b 1799, Connecticut; d 1875, Kalamazoo County, Michigan). The *Biographical Review of Calhoun County, Michigan*, Chicago, pub. By Hobart and Mather, 1904, page 134, says, "He wedded Permelia Willett, whose family also came from Connecticut (sic), the father being William Willett".

Another reference stated,

He [Asher Cummings] married Permelia Willett, who was born in Greenwich, Washington County, N. Y., and was a daughter of <u>James</u> [sic] Willett, a native of the same county as herself. Mrs. Cummings died in 1854, in Onondaga County, N. Y. ... *(Portrait Biographical Album of Calhoun County, Michigan*, 1891, Chicago, Chapman Bros., page 922).

In 1830, Asher Cummings and family are listed in the Onondaga County, New York census, page 183, as follows:

1 male	30-40	1790-1800	*Asher*	age 31	b 1799
1 female	30-40	1790-1800	*Permelia*	age 37	b 1793
1 female	5-10	1820-1825	*Lydia*	age 5?	b 1825?
1 male	0-5	1825-1830	*George*	age 2	b 1828
1 male	0-5	1825-1830	*James R.*	age 0	b 1830

In 1840, Asher Cummings and family are listed in the Onondaga County, New York census, page 105, as follows:

1 male	40-50	1790-1800	*Asher*	*age 41*	*b 1799*
1 female	30-40	1800-1810	*Permelia*	*age 47**	*b 1793**
1 female	15-20	1820-1825	*Lydia*	*age 15?*	*b 1825?*
1 male	10-15	1825-1830	*George*	*age 12*	*b 1828*
1 male	10-15	1825-1830	*James R.*	*age 10*	*b 1830*
1 male	5-10	1830-1835	*Willard*	*age 5*	*b 1835*

In 1850, Asher Cummings and family are listed in the Onondaga County, New York census, page 265, dwelling 618-640, as follows:

Cummings	Asher	head	51	NY	farmer
	Permelia	wife	57	NY	
	James R.	son	20	NY	
	Willard T.	son	15	NY	
McMannis	Maria	NR	14	CAN	
Powers	John	NR	23	IRE	laborer
Willett	Jane	NR	22	NY	

Mrs. Permelia (Willett) Cummings died in 1854 in Onondaga County, New York (*Portrait Biographical Album of Calhoun County, Michigan*, 1891, Chicago, Chapman Bros., page 922).

1. **Lydia CUMMINGS**: b abt 1825; d in Kalamazoo, Michigan, before 1881.

2. **George O. CUMMINGS**: b June 15, 1828, Onondaga Township, Onondaga County, New York; m 1st in November, 1848, Jeannette Wood (d 1876), of Onondaga County, New York; removed to Calhoun County, Michigan in 1860; m 2nd Miss Harriet Huggett; resided [1881] in Lansing, Michigan.

2. **James R. CUMMINGS**: b March 10, 1830, Town of Onondaga, Onondaga County, New York; m 1st in Syracuse, Syracuse County, New York, in March, 1856, Abigail Jane Smith (b October 1, 1837 at Sterling, New York; d December 9, 1864 at Augusta, Kalamazoo County, Michigan, of consumption, age 27 years, 2 months) (they were first cousins); m 2nd on April 16, 1867, Miss Harriet E. Christie, the daughter of James and Ann Christie; resided [1881] Kalamazoo, Michigan.

3. **Willard T. CUMMINGS**: b 1833, New York; resided [1881] Kalamazoo, Michigan.

CHAPTER FOUR

ABRAHAM WILLETT (1793-1859)

OF ONONDAGA COUNTY, NEW YORK

I.1.1.2
ABRAHAM WILLETT and BETSEY BUGSBY
Of Virgil Township, Cortland County, New York

Abraham Willett was born in 1793 in Washington County, New York (according to the 1855 Cortland County New York State census). In deciding on the birth year of Abraham Willett, the 1850 New York State federal census gives an age of 57 (b 1793) while the 1855 New York state census says age 63 (b 1794). His tombstone says Abraham Willett died at age 66 in 1859, thus also giving 1793 as the year of his birth. This is also the birth year calculated for his sister, Permelia. Perhaps Permelia and Abraham were twins, or less likely, they were born in the same year, one early the other late, or the data given in their fifties (in 1850) is slightly inaccurate for any number of possible reasons.

Abraham Willett married, most likely in Onondaga County, New York, in 1814, Betsey Bugsby (b 1791, Connecticut; d December 22, 1871 in Virgil, Cortland County, New York).

From 1814 until 1832, they resided in Onondaga County, New York.

In 1820, Abraham Willet and family are listed in the Onondaga, Onondaga County, New York census, page 108, as follows:
1-0-0-0-1-0 0-0-1-0-0

1 male	26-45	1775-1794 *Abraham*	age 27	b 1793
1 female	16-26	1794-1804 *Betsey*	age 29*	b 1791*
1 male	0-10	1810-1820 *Enoch F*	age 5	b 1815

Listed separately is his father, William Willet (page 108).
On March 28, 1821, William Willett of the town of Onondaga sold for $600.00 part of lot 217 (late Onondaga Reservation) containing 42 acres and 32 rods of land to Abraham Willett (Onondaga County Court House Land

Record, Syracuse, New York, Deed Book 56, page 234). William Willett was Abraham's father.

In 1830, Abraham Willet (sic) and family are listed in the Onondaga, Onondaga County, New York census, page 180, as follows:

1 male	30-40	1790-1800	Abraham	age 37	b 1793
1 female	30-40	1790-1800	Betsey	age 39	b 1791
1 male	15-20	1810-1815	Enoch F	age 15	b 1815

Listed separately is his father, William Willit (page 180).

On March 5, 1832, Abraham Willett of the town of Onondaga sold for $1,000.00, "lot 217 (late Onondaga Reservation) to William Willett, Junior and Alfred F. Smith containing 42 acres and 32/100 of an acre" (Onondaga County Court House Land Record, Syracuse, New York, Deed Book 134, page 375). Abraham Willett's wife Betsey released her dower rights in the sale and deed. In 1840, Mrs. Betsey Willett again acknowledged that she willingly signed the original deed. The original deed was not recorded until 1854.

In 1832, Abraham Willett and family removed to Virgil Township, Cortland County, New York.

On November 7, 1834, Abraham Willet (sic) purchased 104 acres of land, known as Lot No. 7, in Virgil for $520.00 (*Cortland County Grantee Index April 18, 1808, to December 29, 1877,* Book V-35).

On February 1, 1835, Abraham Willet (sic) purchased 2 acres of land, known as Lot No. 7, in Virgil for $16.00 (Cortland County Grantee Index April 18, 1808, to December 29, 1877, Book W-96).

The 1835 Virgil, Cortland County, New York State census lists Abraham Willet (sic) as follows:

2 males including head	Abraham
	son, Enoch
1 female	wife, Betsey
1 person entitled to vote	himself

In 1840, Abraham Willett and family are listed in the Virgil Township, Cortland County, New York census, page 3, as follows:

1 male	40-50	1790-1800	Abraham	age 47	b 1793
1 female	40-50	1790-1800	Betsey	age 49	b 1791
1 male	15-20	1820-1825			

In the 1850 Virgil Township, Cortland County, New York Federal census, page 400, dwelling 1094-1134, is listed Abraham Willet and family, as follows:

Willet	Abraham	head	57 m	NY	farmer
	Betsey	wife	59 f	CN	

The 1855 Virgil, Cortland County, New York State census (V-237) lists Abraham Willet (sic), farmer, 23 years resident of Virgil, as follows:

Willet	Abraham	age 63	b Washington County, NY
	Betsey	age 65	b CT

Abraham Willet died on April 5, 1859, age 66, at Virgil, Cortland County, New York, and is buried in the Forest Hills Cemetery, Town of Cortlandville.

In 1860, Betsey Willett, age 70, was enumerated with her son, Enoch F. Willett, of East Virgil, Cortland County, New York.

Mrs. Betsey Willett died on December 22, 1871, age 77, at Virgil, Cortland County, New York, and is buried in the Forest Hills Cemetery, Town of Cortlandville, Cortland County, New York.

(Bookstaver, 1907, page 67; *The Willett Families*, 1985, page 166).

1. **Enoch Furman WILLETT**: b 1815, at Onondaga County, New York; m abt 1838, Sophia Davis (b 1818, Lisle, Broome County, New York; d May 7, 1903, Cortland County, New York); resided Onondaga County, New York; d March 2, 1874, age 59, in Cortland County, New York. See next I.1.1.2.1.

2. **(male) WILLETT**: b abt 1822, (1820-1825) New York; possibly died young adult, or alternatively a relative, servant or choreboy instead of a blood relative.

I.1.1.2.1
ENOCH FURMAN WILLETT and SOPHIA DAVIS
Of Virgil Township, Cortland County, New York

Enoch Furman Willett was born 1815 in Onondaga County, New York.

In 1832, as a teenager, Enoch came to Virgil, Cortland County, New York, with his parents.

On December 3, 1836, Enoch F. Willet (sic) purchased for $180.00, 30 acres in Virgil, known as Lot No. 8 (X-482, sic).

Enoch Furman Willett married about 1838, Sophia Davis (b 1818, Lisle, Broome County, New York; d May 7, 1903, Cortland County, New York). He was a farmer (1855, 1860).

In 1840, Enoch F. Willett and family are listed in the Virgil Township, Cortland County, New York census, page 3, as follows:

1 male	20-30	1810-1820	*Enoch F*	*age 25*	*b 1815*
1 female	20-30	1810-1820	*Sophia*	*age 22*	*b 1818*
1 male	0-5	1835-1840	*Charles A*	*age 1*	*b 1839*

On September 25, 1841, Enoch F. Willet (sic) purchased for $30.00, 1 acre in Virgil, known as Lot No. 8 (61-93, sic).

In the 1850 Virgil Township, Cortland County, New York Federal census, page 400, dwelling 1095-1135, is listed Enoch Willet and family, as follows:

Willet	Enoch	35	m	NY	farmer, $2,600
	Sophia	32	f	NY	
	Charles	10	m	NY	
Ketchum,	Roma	69	f	CN	
Davis	Eliza A	18	f	NY	

In 1855, E. F. Willet (sic) and family are listed in the Virgil, Cortland County, New York State census.

In the 1860 East Virgil Township, Cortland County, New York Federal census, dwelling 91, is listed Enoch F. Willett and family, as follows:

Willett	Enoch F	45	m	NY	farmer
	Sophia	42	f	NY	
	Chas	20	m	NY	
	Hellen	13	f	NY	
	Betsey	70	f	NY	

On April 1, 1867, Enoch F. Willett (sic) purchased for $3,500.00 a 60 foot strip in Cortland Village (this is the house and lot on Mill Street, Cortland Village) (45-170, sic). Enoch Willett died on March 2, 1874, age 59, in Cortland County, New York (*Cortland County File X-7888*).

E. F. Willett was an intelligent and estimable citizen. He acquired a good property, the main part of which he left to his son, and removed to Cortland. He was once chosen Supervisor of Virgil, and was also Captain in the Militia. He died a few months since, much respected and lamented (*Festal Gathering of the Early Settlers and Present Inhabitants of Virgil, Held on Thursday, the 25th of August, 1853* [sic], *also Supplementary Letters, on the History of the Town down to July, 1876, with an Account of the Centennial Celebration*, Nathan Bouton, 1878, page 52).

Mrs. Sophia (Davis) Willets (sic), widow, married second in Cortland County, New York, on November 18, 1876, Jacob Price of Cortland.

(Bookstaver, 1907, page 67; *The Willett Families*, 1985, page 166; 1855 Virgil, Cortland County, New York State census, V-236).

1. **Charles Adrian WILLETT:** b 1839, Virgil, Cortland County, New York; m abt 1865, Helen M. Sperry (b 1841, New York; d March 1, 1924); resided Cortland, Cortland County, New York; no issue; d July 15, 1896 (*Cortland County File X-6569*); will probated September 30, 1896 (*Cortland County Surrogate's Court*, Will of Charles A. Willett of Cortland County, March 18, 1879, probated by wife, Helen M. Willett, September 30, 1896) (Bookstaver, 1907, page 67; 1870 East Virgil, Cortland County, New York census, page 911 [9], dwelling 76-72). Will left all to wife, Helen M. Willett, if she survives him, otherwise one thousand dollars to Helen M. Waters [sister of Charles Willett], and remainder to legal heirs equally.

2. **Hellen M. WILLETT:** b 1852, New York (adopted); m in Cortland, New York, on September 5, 1870, Geo. L. Waters.

CHAPTER FIVE

HANNAH WILLETT (1805-1874)

OF ONONDAGA COUNTY, NEW YORK

I.1.1.7
HANNAH WILLETT and ALFRED FLOYD SMITH
Of Onondaga County, New York,
And Ionia County, Michigan

Hannah Willett was born on January 18, 1805, at Otisco (or Navarino, Onondaga Township), in Onondaga County, New York, the daughter of William and Hannah Willett (born Otisco according to Bible Record). Miss Hannah Willett is always described as being the daughter of William Willett and Hannah Foster (Comstock, letter dated March 5, 1943, 104 City Island Avenue, City Island, New York).

Miss Hannah Willett married at Onondaga, Onondaga County, New York, on April 18, 1827, Alfred Floyd Smith (b January 14, 1804, at Brookhaven, Long Island, New York; d August 11, 1844, in Vesper, Onondaga County, New York, age 40), the son of William Smith (b July 19, 1774, Fairfield, Connecticut) and Abigail Cole (b March 14, 1777, Long Island, New York).

In 1830, Alfred Smith and family are listed in the Onondaga County, New York census, as follows:

1 male	30-40	1790-1800 *Alfred*	*age 26* b 1804**
1 female	20-30	1800-1810 *Hannah*	*age 25 b 1805*
1 male	5-10	1820-1825 *Milan*	*age 1 b 1829*
1 female	0-5	1825-1830 *Jane*	*age 0 b 1830*

On April 12, 1836, Alfred F. Smith and wife, Hannah, sold for $671.00 "Lot 217 in the Onondaga Reservation now in the town and County of Onondaga ... 42 acres and 32/100 of an acre", to William Willett, Junior (the brother of Mrs. Hannah [Willett] Smith) (Onondaga County Deed Book 63, page 208).

In 1840, Alfred Smith and family are listed in the Onondaga County, New York census, as follows:

1 male	40-50	1790-1800	Alfred	age 36* b 1804*
1 female	20-30	1810-1820	Hannah	age 35* b 1805*
1 male	15-20	1820-1825	Milan	age 11* b 1829*
1 male	5-10	1830-1835	Abraham	age 7 b 1833

Missing from the 1840 Alfred Smith census are 3 or 4 of his children. The other three (presuming this is the correct census) may be residing with their aunt, Mrs. Permelia Cummings.

Mr. Smith was a tanner, currier, farmer, shoemaker, and taught school in the winters. They first lived in Oswego County, New York, where he farmed. Then the family moved to Auburn, New York, where Alfred Smith was a keeper at the prison for 4 or 5 years. In 1842, they moved to Otisco for 2 years. Then the Smiths moved to the little town of Vesper, in Tully Township, at the south end of Lake Otisco, in Onondaga County, New York, where they resided until the death of Alfred Floyd Smith on August 11, 1844.

The last will and testament of Alfred E. Smith late of the town of Tully was dated 1844, and stated,. "To my dear and beloved wife, Hannah, one-sixth part of all my estate, to Milan W., 1/6, to Abram, 1/6, to Gordon 1/6, to James W. 1/6, and to Jane A. 1/6, when they reach age of 21". Wife Hannah was executrix and Enoch F. Willett was executor.

At a later date, Isaac F. Minard was appointed guardian to Alfred F. Smith's minor children (all five listed; actual date not noted).

Shortly after the death of their father, Milan went to Skaneateles to learn the joiner's trade. Abram went to Cortland to learn the printer's trade and made his home with his uncle Abram at Blodgetts Mills, 5 miles out of town. Gordon went, in 1845, to live with Robert Earl, a dealer of produce, sheep and cattle hides, meat, eggs, and shipper in Vesper.

In 1844, the father died, and the mother was left with the care of her young children and a very slender competence. During the next few years two of her sons, Milan, born in 1829, and already married (1852), and Gordon, born in 1835, decided to try their fortunes in the new West ... (*The Corridors of the Years*, Herbert Lockwood Willett, page 3).

It was a period in which people in the Eastern States were excited by stories of the new opportunities for farming and business in those new territories that were as yet little known but seemed inviting enough to lure ambitious young people from New York and New England. Population was growing increasingly dense in the older sections of the country, competition was keener, the timber was disappearing, and much of the land was stony and difficult to cultivate. Those adventurous spirits who had gone on earlier expeditions sent back glowing reports of the opportunities offered by rich soil, abundant timber, plenty of room, and land offered by the government at prices as low as a dollar and a half an acre (*The Corridors of the Years*, page 1).

In 1850, (Mrs.) Hannah (Willett) Smith, as head of household, and her family were listed in the Onondaga County, New York census, page 265, dwelling 619-641. Immediately preceding Mrs. Hannah (Willett) Smith's census listing is that of her sister's family household. The 1850 census record (in its original) order is transcribed as follows:

Cummings	Asher	head	51	NY farmer
	Permelia	wife	57	NY
	James R.	son	20	NY
	Willard F.	son	15	NY
McMannis	Maria	NR	14	CAN
Powers	John	NR	23	IRE laborer
Willett	Jane	NR	22	NY
Smith	Hannah	head	45	NY
	Jane	daughter	13	NY
	James	son	11	NY

In 1855, Hannah Willet (sic) is listed in the Marcellus, Onondaga County, New York State census (not copied).

When the older Alfred Smith children removed to Michigan, "They brought their mother with them, and she continued to live with the Milan Willetts until her death in 1874." (*The Corridors of the Years*, Herbert Lockwood Willett, 1967, page 3).

All of Mrs. Hannah (Willett) Smith's children eventually immigrated to the counties of Ionia, Montcalm, and Gratiot in Michigan except Floyd Abram Willett.

On January 19, 1859, Mr. Tower gave notice to the Michigan Senate that he would on some future day ask leave to introduce "A bill to change the name of Gordon Smith, Hannah Smith, M. W. Smith, James W. Smith, Julia Smith, Eva M. Smith, and Carrie Smith, to Gordon Willett, Hannah Willett, M. W. Willett, James W. Willett, Julia Willett, Eva M. Willett, and Carrie Willett".

On January 22, 1859, A. B. Turner, entered to the Speaker of the House of Representatives of Michigan, "A bill to change the name of Hannah, Milan W., Gordon A., James W., Julia, Eva, and Carrie Smith; Which have passed the Senate by a majority vote of all the Senators elect. In which the concurrence of the House is respectfully asked. Very Respectfully, A. B. Turner".

On January 25, 1859, Charles V. DeLand, Clerk of the House of Representatives was instructed to return to the Senate the following: "A bill to change the name of Hannah, Milan W., Gordon A., James W., Julia, Eva, and Carrie Smith, in which the House have concurred by a majority vote of all the members elect, and have ordered the first named bill to take immediate effect by a vote of two-thirds of all the members elect. Very Respectfully, Charles V. DeLand".

On January 28, 1859, Mr. Grosvenor, from the committee on enrolled bills, reported the following bills, "A bill to change the name of Hannah, Milan W., Gordon A., James W., Julia, Eva, and Carrie Smith. The bills were signed and presented to the Governor".

In 1859, By an Act of the Michigan Legislature, Mrs. Hannah (Willett) Smith, widow of Alfred Floyd Smith, and three of her sons, one daughter-in-law, and two granddaughters, changed their surname to Willett. Later Abraham Willett Smith changed his name. Two of the sons chose to honor their dead father by adopting parts of his name.

Act No. 31 of the Laws of Michigan of 1859.

An Act to change the names of Hannah, Milan W., Gordon A., James W., Julia, Eva, and Carrie Smith.

Section 1. The people of the State of Michigan enact, that the names of Hannah Smith, Milan, Gordon A., James W., Julia, Eva, and Carrie Smith, be and the same are hereby changed as follows: Hannah Smith, to Hannah Willett, Milan W. Smith to Alfred Milan Willett, James W. Smith to James W. Willett, Julia Smith to Julia Willett, Eva Smith to Eva Willett, and Carrie Smith to Carrie Willett.

Approved January 29, 1859.

[all the above citations are from *Acts of The Legislature of the State of Michigan, passed At the Regular Session of 1859, With an Appendix*, Lansing, 1859, Hosmer and Kerr, Printers to the State].

One family tradition has it that the name change was "probably related to the ownership of property" (*Further Corridors*, page 9). However, there is no family tradition of property owned by any branch of the Willett family that would account for such a belief. At the time of the decision to change their names, the Smiths had already been located for nearly a decade in Ionia County, Michigan, and, Alfred Smith had been dead 15 years. By 1861, Abram Smith in New York State had also legally changed his name to Floyd Abram Willett.

There were three rumored Willett inheritances current during that time period which might have come to the attention of Mrs. Hannah (Willett) Smith.

First and foremost was a Townsley-Lawrence inheritance in England that went back to a Sir Richard Townsley, son of Charles Townsley who fell at Marston Moors. Mrs. Elizabeth Lawrence had nine children by her first husband; remarried a second time to Captain Philip Carteret, and lastly to Sir Richard Townsley. All Willett claims to this inheritance come through her Lawrence descendants.

Granddaughter Elizabeth Lawrence, daughter of William Lawrence, married in 1737, John Willett.

Granddaughter Deborah Lawrence, daughter of Obadiah Lawrence, married Jonathan Willett.

Granddaughter Elizabeth Lawrence, daughter of Samuel Lawrence, married Samuel Willett.

Her great-granddaughter Hannah Lawrence, daughter of Richard, and granddaughter of Joseph Lawrence, married Samuel Willett.

However, this Townsley-Lawrence fortune was not real - yet other Willett families spoke of the Townsley-Lawrence inheritance in personal letters as late as the 1880s as though a substantiated and legitimate claim of kinship would result in being awarded a portion of this fortune. No Townsley-Lawrence-Willett fortune existed, yet the rumors persisted and discussions are on record in letters of the New Richmond, Quebec, Canada, Willett family as late as 1917! However, whether or not Mrs. Hannah (Willett) Smith knew of or might have thought she was a claimant to this fortune is unknown at this time.

A second Willett fortune was both very real and very substantial but applied only to the relatives of Miss Elizabeth (Willett) Catt who left a considerable fortune to her Catt relatives who would take the name and arms of Willett. This inheritance is based at Brighton, Sussex County, England, and there is no known connection to any Willett family in the United States.

A third claim of fortune was very spurious. It concerned those Willett descendants related to the Bogardus family of New York City. Only Elbert Willett of Albany, New York, is known to have a kinship to this family. However, unscrupulous lawyers advertised this claim extensively, and collected fees for providing the supposed claimant with legal representation.

In 1860, Hannah Willet was listed in the household of her son, Alfred M. Willet in the Lyons, Ionia County, Michigan census, as follows:

Willet	Alfred M.	head	31	NY	carpenter
	Julia	wife	29	NY	
	Eva M.	daughter	6	NY	
	Carrie	daughter	2	MI	
	Gordon A.	brother	25	NY	clerk
	Hannah	mother	50	NY	

Mrs. Hannah (Willett-Smith) Willett died of pneumonia on December 28, 1874, age 69 years, 11 months, 10 days, at North Plains, Ionia County, Michigan (1874 "Hannah Willett" Death Certificate No. 1788; Bible Record; "Returns of Deaths, Ionia County, 1874; brief obituary notice in "The Ionia Sentinel" newspaper, Friday, January 1, 1875, page 5). In the "Returns of Deaths 1874" Hannah was noted as the daughter of William Willett and Hannah Willett of North Plains, Ionia County, Michigan.

(Bookstaver, 1907, page 68; *Portrait and Biographical Album*, 1891, pages 771-772; *The Corridors of the Years*, Herbert Lockwood Willett, 1967, privately published; *The Willett Families*, 1985, pages 166-167).

1. **Milan Willett SMITH** (changed in 1859 to **Alfred Milan WILLETT**): b April 18, 1829, at Volney, Oswego County, New York; m first in Skeneateles, Onondaga County, New York, on September 8, 1852, Julia Yager (b 1832, New York; d January 16, 1894, Ionia County, Michigan), the daughter of Wendel Yager; entered service as Captain of Company I, 1st U. S. Sharpshooters, on February 5, 1862; resigned his commission on November 8, 1862; m second in Saginaw County, Michigan, on April 30, 1895, Harriet J. Northrup; d March 14, 1906, Ionia County, Michigan. See next I.1.1.7.1.

2. **Jane SMITH**: b 1830, Sterling, New York; probably died in infancy. Actual date of death is unknown.

3. **Abraham Willett SMITH** (changed in 1859 to **Floyd Abram WILLETT**): b November 29, 1833, in Onondaga County, New York (Bible Record); m in Tully, Onondaga County, New York, on August 31, 1861, Anna Howell Miner (b March 30, 1836, at New York City, New York; d August 13, 1918); commissioned on August 21, 1861, as a First Lieutenant with Company C, 1st U. S. Sharpshooters (Berdan's Sharpshooters); resigned on June 7, 1862; d June 8, 1868, at Keuka, Steuben County, New York, age 34 years, 6 months, 7 days. See next I.1.1.7.3.

4. **Gordon Arthur SMITH** (changed in 1859 to **Gordon Arthur WILLETT**): b August 23, 1835, at Onondaga County, New York; m at Ionia County, Michigan, on January 2, 1862, Mary Elizabeth Yates (b January 23, 1839; d June 9, 1909); served with the Sanitary Commission during the Civil War; resided at Ionia County, Michigan; d July 18, 1898, at the home of his son Arthur Willett, at Petoskey, Emmett County, Michigan. See next I.1.1.7.4.

5. **Abigail Jane SMITH**: b October 1, 1837 at Sterling, New York; m in Syracuse, Syracuse County, New York, in March, 1856, James R. Cummings (b 1830); d December 9, 1864 at Augusta, Kalamazoo County, Michigan, of consumption, age 27 years, 2 months. See next N.1.1.7.5.

6. **James Willett SMITH** (changed in 1859 to **James W. WILLETT**): b March 13, 1839, at Sterling, New York; m at North Plains, Ionia, County, Michigan, on July 4, 1864, to Mary Annette ("Nettie") Germain(e) (b June 18, 1845, New York); during Civil war served with the 1st U. S. Sharpshooters (Berdan's Sharpshooters); resided Stanton, Montcalm County, Michigan; d October 17, 1906, at Bruce Crossing, Ontonagon County, Michigan. See next I.1.1.7.6.

CHAPTER SIX
INTERLUDE: THE CIVIL WAR
FROM SOLDIER TO SUTLER

The Civil War stirred up passions of patriotism which are hard to envision today. When the war began, all four of Mrs. Hannah Willett's sons attempted to enlist in the 1st US Sharpshooters (1st USSS), Berdan's Sharpshooters.

Floyd Abram Willett, age 27, of Kalamazoo County, Michigan, answered President Lincoln's call for volunteers, and was commissioned on August 21, 1861, as a First Lieutenant with Company C, 1st U. S. Sharpshooters (Berdan's Sharpshooters). He mustered on August 26, 1861, and was promoted to Adjutant on October 18, 1861. He resigned on June 7, 1862 (*Michigan Volunteers, 1861-1865*, page 120).

On October 12, 1861, Captain A. Milan Willett, age 33, mustered I Company, 1st Regiment USSS.

On October 28, 1861, Private James W. Willett enrolled in Company I, 1st Regiment of U.S. Sharpshooters Volunteers.

In April, 1862, the fourth brother, Gordon Arthur Willett, age 27, went to Washington, D. C. expecting (or hoping) to be appointed Quarter Master in Berdan's Sharpshooters. His application was refused, most likely because of his fragile health. Gordon then applied and received employment on trial with the US Sanitary Commission. His organizational talents were quickly recognized and he became a de facto Quarter Master on the *S. R. Spaulding*, a Steam Ship used primarily as a hospital ship. The *S. R. Spaulding* carried the sick and wounded from the Battle of Williamsburg to Washington, D. C., returned and took a second load of wounded to New York. It returned again to the York River as the Seven Days Battle was commencing.

The following narrative covers the military careers of the four Willett brothers during the Civil War.

THE BEGINNING

On May 3, 1861, President Lincoln made his second call for volunteers. This was a request for three year volunteers which was answered by numerous volunteer regiments. The Union soldier joined to save the Union. The reason the majority of the Confederate soldiers joined the Confederacy was to expel the northern aggressor and invader of his home soil; perhaps the more educated and political element southerner joined to defend States Rights. Soon after

Lincoln's call, on June 10, 1861, the first engagement of Federal troops against Confederate troops took place at Big Bethel, near Hampton, Virginia.

Major John Baytop Cary, had enlisted May 5, 1861, as Major, and served on General Magruder's staff at Big Bethel on June 10, 1861 (*32d Virginia Infantry*, page 177). The Confederate participants at Big Bethel were Montague's Battalion, Stuart's Battalion, three cavalry companies, including the Old Dominion Dragoons, and the Wythe Rifles (later Company A, 32d Virginia Infantry). Colonel J. Bankhead Magruder had 1,800 troops. He was attacked by 4,000 federal soldiers under General Pierce, with New York and Massachusetts Infantry.

The Federal infantry included the 1st, 2nd, 3rd, 5th, 7th New York, and 4th Massachusetts. They came across Hampton River, to Sawyer's Swamp, turned towards Little Bethel and then followed the road towards Big Bethel. As they approached Big Bethel, the Union forces forced their way across the swampy creek immediately before the Confederate position, and the artillery emplacement was taken by the Union troops. However, the 1st North Carolina charged the advancing Federal troops, driving the blue coats back across the creek. From that point. the battle turned into an artillery duel, which lasted from 9:00 A.M. until 1:30 P.M. The Confederate Artillery fired ninety-eight cannon shots with deliberation.

Finally, Union Major Winthrop tried to deceive the Confederate forces by having a heavy federal column cross the creek wearing a "white band around the cap" and crying out repeatedly, "Don't fire!" The ruse partially worked, as Confederate uniforms were often captured Union clothing, and in the hot Virginia summer sun, dust had settled onto all the combatant's uniforms giving them the appearance of a dusty gray coloring. As soon as the Union troops were across the creek, they began to rush the Confederate artillery emplacement. The North Carolina Infantry realized their mistake and opened fire. Major Winthrop's charge was broken before the troops could reach the artillery emplacement and Major Winthrop died in the charge in a gallant effort to capture the Confederate artillery. Even the Confederates that were being attacked acknowledged Winthrop's bravery. Colonel D. H. Hill, C. S. A., mentioned Winthrop's desperate charge, bravery, and death in the Confederate report of the battle sent to Richmond.

The Union force lost sixteen killed in action, and thirty-four were wounded. Confederate losses were one dead, and 7 wounded. By later standards this was a mere skirmish - but on June 10, it was the first time Union troops faced Confederates in a distinctly hostile attempt to force the Confederates to surrender control of some of their territory. The June 10, 1861, battle at Big Bethel was soon eclipsed by the (First) Battle of Bull Run in northern Virginia between General McDowell's Union forces and Confederate Generals Beauregard's and Johnston's soldiers on the Southern side.

On June 15, 1861, the Federal government accepted Col. Berdan's offer to raise a regiment of sharp shooters. The marksmen thus raised were required that "no man be accepted who cannot, at 200 yards, put 10 consecutive shots in a target, the average distance not to exceed five inches from the center of the bulls-eye." (Stevens, page 2).

On August 14, 1861, Floyd A. Willett wrote to his brother Gordon:

Kalamazoo, Mich.
August 14, 1861

Dear Gor,
... I would be glad to meet in Detroit, Friday of this week when our Company will meet to elect officers and arrange to proceed to Weehawken, N. J. opposite New York City. Shall probably leave Detroit Monday or Tuesday of next week ... I shall not go unless I get a commission though I suppose I shall not have much trouble getting it. The 6th Reg are going into camp here at present and makes it lively times to what it was before ... If you can meet me at Detroit at Michigan Exchange or Company's Room.

In Haste, Yours
F. A. Willett

On August 21, 1861, Floyd A. Willett mustered into service with Company C, 1st Regiment USSS, ("Berdan's Sharp Shooters"), at Detroit, Michigan. In command was Captain Benjamin Deusler of Quincy, First Lieutenant Floyd A. Willett, of Kalamazoo, and Second Lieutenant James H. Baker of Lansing. Floyd was the first of the Willett brothers to join the 1st USSS.

The rendezvous for the regiment was at Weehawken, New Jersey.

CAMP INSTRUCTION/PATROLLING

On September 24, 1861, the newly raised 1st Regiment,

Berdan's Sharpshooters, proceeded to Washington, D. C., and went into Camp Instruction.

On September 27th, Company C, 1st USSS, crossed the chain bridge from the Washington, D. C., side and for the first time invaded Virginia and attacked a Rebel cavalry patrol who were foraging. George D. Sanford of Company C was wounded in this foray. Company C then continued its patrol going further into the Virginia countryside until reaching Munson's Mill where they were engaged after in a skirmish after midnight, September 29. The night-time engagement caused a good deal of fratricide in Union units. Fratricide is a much later military term used to describe "friendly" fire casualties. The 1st USSS were fortunate in having only one additional wounded. The Confederates left the field at Munson's Mill to the Union forces. By September 30, the Sharpshooters were back at Camp Instruction.

Campaigning and soldiering skills were being learned, albeit slowly and painfully. The original Camp Instruction had tents lined up with military precision and orderliness and staked to the ground. This preciseness led to sickness, as floors and drainage were not taken into consideration - perhaps were considered by a disciplinarian as contrary to good order. However, the effect of the lack of good drainage and no flooring in the tents was one that increased sickness from sleeping on the damp ground. Even the initial method of preparing food could cause illness. Americans tended to fry their rations, while Germans tended to boil theirs. It became obvious that boiling decreased the incidence of sickness in camp - and as the soldiers learned to combat not just the Rebel enemy, but sickness and disease, boiling food became more common among the Union soldiers.

On October 12, 1861, Captain A. Milan Willett mustered I Company.

On October 28, 1861, Private James W. Willett enrolled in Company I, 1st Regiment of US Sharpshooters.

1st Lieutenant Floyd Abram Willett received $134.50 for pay in full from October 31, 1861, until November 30, 1861.

On December 12, 1861, Floyd A. Willett, the first Willett brother to volunteer, was promoted into the position of Regimental Adjutant when Major William S. Rowland left the regiment after a dispute with Colonel Berdan.

On December 24, 1861, a Leave of Absence for ten days was granted to 1st Lieutenant Floyd A. Willett, Berdan's Sharpshooters (Special Orders No. 198, by Command of Major General McClellan).

On January 16, 1862, Gordon Willett married Mary Yates at Ionia, Ionia County, Michigan.

The Civil War was not one of glory for Gordon's brothers on duty with the Army of the Potomac. The physical side of just staying alive and free of a variety of communal diseases that ran through camps was a real challenge. The harsh weather was often devastating to weakened soldiers who were not accustomed to living out of doors for extended periods of time. Sickness and disease could kill, as well as actual warfare. Often "fever and chronic diarrhea" was more of a life-threatening event than actual battle wounds to the soldier who was not used to cold rains and damp grounds.

On January 28, Charles S. Tripler, Surgeon and Medical Director of the Army of the Potomac, wrote a scathing report on the plight of Federal troops bivouacked near Washington, D. C. He noted unsanitary condition of the just-arriving recruits, and their bouts with typhus, pneumonia, measles, and malarious fevers. He cites as causes such conditions as:

...foul air, bad clothing, imperfect shelters, exposure to cold and moisture, and imperfectly drained and badly policed camps. As a remedy I suggest good shelter, good clothing, good food, good water, dry camp grounds, and an abundant supply of pure air.

Specifically regarding Berdan's men, Surgeon Tripler said:

The Berdan Sharpshooters are in a bad sanitary condition, and not improving. Their camp is badly located, and I shall visit this regiment personally. This regiment is suffering from measles, and lately severe lung complications have accompanied the disease. A fresh and dry camp is necessary for the command. If a suitable ground is selected and the tents put up in the way I have suggested, then I should look for favorable results (Marcot, page 41).

These unsuitable camp conditions probably contributed to the breakdown of health and subsequent sicknesses that plagued Floyd Abram Willett and A. Milan Willett during the Peninsula campaigns. Later, James Scott would attested that, A. Milan Willett, " ... previous to his enlisting into the U. S. service in October, 1861 (sic), he was a sound and healthy man free so far as I knew of rheumatism or any other disabilities ... " ("General Affidavit" of James Scott, dated June 10, 1892; in the Civil War Pension File of A. Milan Willett).

Colonel Hiram Berdan's Regiments "were to be armed with the most reliable rifle then made and to be employed as sharpshooters and skirmishers ... Each Applicant had to pass a shooting test, no men were enlisted who could not put ten bullets in succession within a ten-inch circle at 200 yards at rest and 100 yards off hand." ("Berdan Sharpshooters" undated newsletter).

On February 5, 1862, A. Milan Willett, age 33, entered service as Captain of Company I, 1st U. S. Sharpshooters, at organization, for three years service. He mustered on March 4, 1862. Albert Richardson wrote the following: "Indeed Albert Ariel Richardson was my grandfather. He served in Company I starting in November, 1861, The Company received their basic training in Muir, Michigan, at Capt. Willett's home. It was mustered in to the Army of the Potomac in Detroit in February 1862. They left for Washington, D. C., shortly afterward."

On March 8, 1862, came news that the *CSS Virginia* (formerly the *USS Merrimac*) had steamed out into Hampton Roads and destroyed the wooden hulled Federal warships *USS Congress* and *USS Cumberland*. The very next day the great battle was fought between the *USS Monitor* and *CSS Virginia*. Each side claimed victory. But the *USS Monitor* would not again leave the protection of the naval cannons at Fortress Monroe.

The 1st USSS remained in Camp Instruction until Gen. McClellan began his ill-fated Peninsula Campaign (letter signed Albert Richard, to Arthur, undated, letter courtesy Arthur Ruitberg).

CAMP CALIFORNY

On March 12, 1862, the Sharpshooters received their orders to report to General Fitz-John Porter who was encamped near Alexandria, Virginia. The start was less than encouraging. A hard rain was falling; the distance to be covered was 15 miles. A sea of mud fatefully awaited their tramping feet before they reached Camp Californy. Less than two weeks later, on March 21 the loading of the transports commenced at Old Town Alexandria, and early the next morning on a beautiful day the 1st USSS departed for the Virginia Peninsula and the Federal bastion of Fortress Monroe. As they were leaving Alexandria, all the steamships passed in review before General Porter's flagship. Cheers, saluting cannon, and spectacle were everywhere present as the steamships turned down stream and soon passed out of sight of Washington and Alexandria, rounded the bend at Fort Washington and passed Mount Vernon. On March 23, the Sharpshooters disembarked from the steamship *Emperor* at Fortress Monroe. The first sight they saw must have been very similar to that described six weeks later by the war correspondent, George Townsend.

The quay itself was like the pool of a mass of spears, smoke stacks, ensigns and swelling hills. The low and quaint cupola of the famous *Monitor* appeared close to shore, and near at hand rose the thick body of the *Galena*. Long boats and flat boats went hither and thither across the blue waves; the grim ports of the men of war were open and the guns frowned darkly from their coverts; the seamen were gathering for muster on the flagship [*USS Minnesota*] and the drums beat from the barracks on shore; the Lincoln Gun, a fearful piece of ordinance, rose like a sphinx from the Fortress sands, and the sodded parapet, the winding stone walls, the tops of brick quarters – within the Fort, were some of the features of a strangely animated scene, that has yet to be perpetuated on canvas and made historic (Townsend, page 64).

The Lincoln Gun was a huge naval cannon that faced the rip-raps and Sewell's Point. The rip-raps were natural rocks, which barely projected above the water's surface. The large volume of water moving over the rip-raps created whirl pools and strong currents that were a hazard to navigation. Later military construction created an island out of this natural rocky outcrop and permitted the rip-raps to be manned. The man made island created on top of the rip-raps was named Fort Wool.

Although no more inexperienced in war than their Confederate counterparts, these Union volunteers streaming towards the Port of Hampton were soon to meet the face of war.

The port of Hampton was another spectacle with Federal vessels of all sizes and descriptions sailing into and out of Hampton River and Sunset Creek. The Union Army had delayed the Peninsula campaign until the threat posed by the ironclad *CSS Virginia* was no more - but who in the Union forces that day could be sure the Confederate navy did not have other surprises awaiting? The *USS Monitor* was riding peacefully at anchor - the sole ironclad thwarting Confederate designs on the great Union wooden fleet that was disembarking the largest army ever assembled on American shores.

HAMPTON

On the morning of the March 24, 1862, the 1st USSS disembarked on the Virginia Peninsula. The port of Hampton presented a sad foreboding of the scope and breadth the war would become. The Rebels under Gen. Magruder had burned Hampton in August, 1861. This was the home of many of the men who actually fired the town; in some cases the men fired their own homes. The fiery destruction was ordered simply to keep Hampton from being of use to the Union forces who at that time had been encamped at Fortress Monroe at what would become known as Mill Creek (much later renamed Phoebus). Perhaps the Confederate military leadership had been misled by a rumor that Union Commander Ben Butler was going to turn Hampton over to the contrabands. The rumor was not true – or was it?. Nothing remained of Hampton except charred walls, blackened chimneys, and desolation. The burning of Hampton was an early indication of the terrible price that the nation would have to pay during the course of the what the Union claimed was a War of Rebellion, while contemporary Southerners were convinced it was a War of Northern Aggression. Only later would the term Civil War become the accepted term for this conflict between one sovereign nation and another.

Confederate cavalry still patrolled the western bank of Hampton River and the sole road leading to Yorktown and Williamsburg. A Confederate outpost was still maintained at Big Bethel. Confederate pickets were at the village of Poquoson looking over the west side of the Poquoson River into Fox Hill. The Warwick River had been turned into a defensive line by a Rebel army that was rumored to contain 100,000 Southern soldiers. The rumor was false - but even Gen. McClellan was being misled, so who could fault the common soldier for thinking he faced a determined, numerous Rebel foe? A few hours of wading for shell fish and other river delicacies in the Hampton River and Sunset Creek soon ended as the 1st USSS were moved into camp at a corn field four miles west of Fortress Monroe (Stevens, page 31).

Three Confederate lines of defense protected the Virginia Peninsula. One line, perhaps nothing more than a skirmish line, with its left protected Ships Point on Chisman's Creek and anchored on Harwood's Mill, at the head of the Poquoson River, in York County. The line then stretched across the Peninsula in a series of outposts and batteries extending to Young's Mill on the Confederate right in Warwick County. General Magruder also had forward independent unsupported posts at various times, the main forward outpost being the artillery battery at Big Bethel across the York-Hampton Road. Frequently, Confederate cavalry patrols ventured forward to Little Bethel and then onward to within sight of Hampton. At the time, the Hampton-York Road was the only ground avenue of movement from Hampton to Yorktown, as the Virginia Peninsula was intersected with swamps, marshes and creeks which made any other ground route difficult. And to call the single route a road was a misnomer, as the route meandered from farm to settlement, around swamps, and head of creeks, with little regard to its final destination, Yorktown.

The second Confederate line of defense was anchored by the fortification of Yorktown, and utilized the old British defense redoubt and embankment defensive system which had remained virtually intact from the American Revolution. Gloucester Point batteries, on the north side of the York River, provided additional protection to keep Union warships sufficiently distant from Confederate held Yorktown. This Confederate defense line extended eight miles through dense woods, often three lines deep in defense, and was anchored at Wynne's Mill at the head of the Warwick River and then in a southern direction to the James River. On the streams that fed the Warwick River, the Confederates kept five dams full of water and that water barrier created an additional obstacle to troop movement. Redoubts on Mulberry Point and Mulberry Island completed this second line of defense.

The Williamsburg line created the main line of defense with 14 mutually supporting redoubts running from Queen's Creek on the north to Tutter's Neck on the south and anchored in the center with Fort Magruder. Batteries at Jamestown Island, Spratley Farm, and across the James River were designed to protect the James River from Federal gunboats attempting to pass up the James River.

RECONNAISSANCE IN FORCE

But Gen. McClellan had brought his Army to the Peninsula for a purpose, and at an early hour on March 27, before the dawn, the Sharpshooters left their camp [in East Hampton] and began moving west over the only road which snaked its way towards Yorktown. Recent rainfall had made the fields muddy, and perhaps the Sharpshooters were lucky in that they had led the way as skirmishers out of Hampton, past Sawyer's Swamp, Little Bethel, and onward towards Big Bethel. A few Rebel cavalry watched their progress, exchanged a few shots and then fell back a safe distance. The Rebel cavalry continued a retrograde movement towards the west and the Confederate outpost at Big Bethel. At Big Bethel, a small infantry detachment, perhaps a forward picket and a few cavalry, fired a few desultory shots at the advancing Union Army. The 1st USSS attacked the outpost across the marshy ground to the redoubt which was now devoid of cannon and several Confederates were made prisoner as the remainder of the small Confederate detachment fell back toward Half Way House. A few miles farther on the Yorktown Road, the Sharpshooters were halted and ordered to return back to Camp Porter.

After this excursion, the Federal army fell back to the safety of the east side of the Hampton River. Once again, the west bank of the Hampton River was Rebel territory. On April 3, Gen. McClellan arrived by steamship at Fortress Monroe.

ADVANCE!

On April 4, the time for Union reconnaissance and maneuvering was over. Again, the 1st USSS led the advance, this time leading Gen. Fitz-John Porter's entire division - 58,000 men and 100 cannon in trail behind them. Their objective was a place called Cockletown, a little over half-way between Hampton and Yorktown, and farther along the York-Hampton Road than they had been previously. McClellan's opponent was Prince John Magruder, the Virginian general who had kept the Federal forces hemmed in at Fortress Monroe while he created a defensive system for his meager Rebel army. Magruder had also paraded his troops in full view of the Union forces, shifted them back and forth to create the illusion that he had more soldiers under his command than he actually had available. The ruse was successful and led in part to the apprehension on Gen. McClellan's part that he was facing a numerically superior foe.

Some of the hardship that every soldier must have shared can be imagined from the contemporary account left by the Rev. J. J. Marks, in the *Peninsula Campaign in Virginia*. Writing in his diary on April 4, 1862, Rev. Marks wrote:

> We left Hampton on the 4th of April (1862) and reached Great Bethel about two P. M. This was the scene of a disastrous battle fought the 10th of June, 1861 ... The land was swept of fences, grain, horses, cattle, and everything they raised during the summer. There was none to till the fields, and no means of protecting what the women and old men had planted; and in the Peninsula, during the summer, hundreds of families were destitute and in want. There was nothing

left in the country on which they could live. (*Tabernacle History*, page 40, Tabernacle Church, Poquoson, York County, Virginia)

This was what the Willett brothers saw as they were in advance of McClellan's Army as skirmishers and passed first Little Bethel and then Big Bethel on the Hampton-Yorktown road. Behind the Willett brothers, "The road [between Hampton and Big Bethel] were very poor, and muddy with recent rains, and were crowded with the indescribable material of the vast army which was slowly creeping through the mud over the flat, wooded country." (Gross, page 30)

This time, little Rebel opposition was presented, as the Union Army was massed and their numbers were overwhelming. The Union army passed Little Bethel, Big Bethel and the abandoned redoubt that was there. A northern newspaper reporter, Mr. Goss, who was traveling with the rear of the gigantic Union army was a day behind the Willett brothers, left this account of the site called Big Bethel.

During our second day's march it rained, and the muddy roads, cut up and kneaded, as it were, by the teams proceeding us, left them in a state of semi-liquid filth hardly possible to describe or imagine. When we arrived at Big Bethel the rain was coming down in sheets. A dozen houses of very ordinary character, scattered over an area of a third of a mile, constituted what was called the village. Just outside and west of the town was an insignificant building [church] from which the hamlet takes it name. It did not seem large or of sufficient a consequence to give name to a place as small as Big Bethel. Before our arrival it had evidently been occupied as officers' barracks by the enemy, and it looked very little like a church.

There was a rude but very significant drawing on the plaster of the walls, which if not complimentary was amusing.

A hotel was depicted, and on its sign was inscribed 'Richmond'. Jeff Davis was standing in the doorway, and with an immense pair of cowhides was booting McClellan from the door, and underneath the sketch was the inscription, 'Merry Mack'.

It was significant only so far as it proved a prophecy.

I visited one of the dwelling houses just outside of the fortifications (if the insignificant rifle pits could be called such) for the purpose of obtaining something more palatable than hard-tack, salt beef, or pork, which with coffee, were the marching rations. The woman of the house was communicative, and expressed surprise at the great number of Yanks who had come 'down to invade our soil'. She said she had a son in the Confederate army, or, as she expressed it, 'in our army', and tearfully said she would tremble for her boy every time she heard of a battle. I expressed the opinion that we should go into Richmond without much fighting. 'No!" saids she, with the emphasis of conviction, 'you alls will drink hot blood before you alls get thar!' (Goss, pages 31-32)

The skirmishers continued a few miles to Half Way House where the road forked eastward to Poquoson; then continued on the main road, which turned northward and paralleled the east bank of the Poquoson River. The skirmishers, among who were the Willett boys, finally arrived at where the tidal marsh ended and Howard's Bridge crossed the marshy stream that drained into the Poquoson River. Another Confederate redoubt was on the western side of Howard's Bridge, this time manned by 400 Mississippi Infantry and two pieces of Confederate artillery. The 1st USSS deployed and advanced on the Confederates. The skirmishers were ahead of the 14th New York, 4th Michigan, 9th Massachusetts, and 62nd Pennsylvania. After a few shots from the Federal artillery, and a volley of rifle fire from each side, the vastly-outnumbered Confederates retired (Stevens, page 36). Cockletown was just a mile further. No further contact was made, except for videttes, pickets, and the occasional cavalry patrol, which had all fallen back as the Union Army advanced. All forward Rebel detachments and companies had fallen back on the main Confederate force, and were firmly entrenched behind the Rebel main defensive line that was anchored on the north by a fortified Yorktown, and the York River, and thence southerly along the Warwick River to the James River.

Again, the words of the reporter George Townsend are best for describing the scene at Yorktown as encountered by the Willett brothers.

[Speaking about his first glimpse of the Confederate defenses at Yorktown] Miniature mountain ranges they seemed, deeply ditched, and revetted, with sods, fascines, hurdles, gabions, or sand bags. Along the York riverside there were water batteries of surpassing beauty, that seemed at a distance, successions of gentle terraces. Their pieces were likewise of enormous caliber and their number almost incredible. The advanced line of fortifications, stretched from the mouth of the Warwick Creek, on the South, to a point fifteen miles distant on the York; one hundred and forty guns were planted along this chain of defenses; but there were two concentric lines, mounting each, one hundred and twenty, and one hundred and forty guns. The remote series consisted of six forts of massive size and height, fronted by swamps and flooded meadows, with frequent creeks and ravines interposing' sharp 'fraise' and 'abattis' planted against scarp and slope, pointed cruelly eastward. There were two water batteries, of six and four thirty-two columbiads respectively, and the town itself, which stands upon a red clay bluff, was encircled by a series of immense rifled and smoothbore pieces. Including a powerful pivot gun. (Townsend, pages 68-69, account actually written on May 14, 1862)

THE BATTLE OF YORKTOWN

The Battle of Yorktown took place on April 5, 1862. As the Federal army neared Yorktown and its fortification of extensive earthworks, a Confederate artillery shell came screaming over Company G, 1 USSS. In unison, Company G "ducked" away from the screaming shell, as did other nearby companies. The next moment, "loud hurrahs and laughter at each other, they rushed to the double quick." (Stevens, page 37) Charging and pressing the Rebel pickets back, the company came into view of Yorktown and its protecting earthworks. The main part of McClellan's Army stopped at the 1,800 yard mark, spread out from Lee's Mill on the right to Yorktown on the left. McClellan didn't know it at the time, but he was in for an extended stay. The Sharpshooters moved forward about 800 yards into a peach orchard and began a concerted effort to drive the forward Confederate pickets back behind the earthworks. Rebel cavalry came out into clear sight and threatened to ride down the Union skirmishers. However, a well placed Union artillery shell and a volley from the skirmishers discouraged such fool-hardiness. The 1st USSS had some wounded, and a very close call when a Rebel artillery shell threw a few of the Sharpshooters menacingly but harmlessly into the air. That night the Rebel band serenaded the Union Army with "Dixie" followed by a cannonade. 1st USSS casualties on the 5th, after ten hours on the firing line, were three dead, six wounded, and numerous narrow scrapes. About 9:00 PM, the 44th New York relieved the forward deployed Sharpshooters who retired a mile to the rear into a thick copse of woods.

April 5, 1862, established the 1st USSS in their role as skirmishers and sharpshooters. The Sharpshooters were before Yorktown as skirmishers and that's what was their role for the duration of the siege. They came under direct fire; as Berdan put it, their mission was to "guard the road against enemy cavalry; guard the right and left wings against enemy flankers, and watch the movement of the enemy; and to pick off enemy gunners." (Marcot, page 49)

The Confederates held General McClellan at bay with the fortifications at Yorktown and the Warwick River defensive line made up of redoubts and swamp, as well as misinformation about the size of the defending force. The Battle of Yorktown convinced Gen. McClellan that a frontal assault against a determined enemy who was in strength and behind heavily fortified earthworks would result in an undue loss of life. Always unwilling to waste his soldier's lives when other ways would produce the same results, McClellan decided upon siege and investment. Unfortunately for McClellan, President Lincoln mistook this care for the common soldier's life as a case of "the slows".

THE SIEGE OF YORKTOWN

Then came several more days of rain, with roads churning into ever deeper quagmires. This delayed the delivery of rations along the only road from Hampton to Yorktown. The delay caused the Union soldiers to begin to prey on Rebel cattle. But the soldiers quickly learned that Rebel cattle without salt were garlicky flavored and unpalatable. The garlic flavor came from the wild onions that grew in every field and flavored the local meat and milk products heavily.

On April 6, Gen. McClellan opened a forward commissary and depot at Ship's Point, the nearest safe place he could bring his steamers for unloading to the battlefront. The lane leading from Ships Point to Cockletown quickly became a quagmire. McClellan had a corduroy road built from Ships Point to Cockletown. From there it was a short trip to supply his Army, which was spread out in fields and woods on the high ground to the north and west. For all of Gen. McClellan's supposed "slowness", McClellan was well-liked by the men whose lives he refused to waste even under

Presidential pressure. (McClellan's deliberation was an attempt to minimize unnecessary deaths of the soldiers under his command who had to do the actual work of assaulting positions defended by a Rebel foe determined not to relinquish Southern soil to Northern invaders).

On April 10, the Sharpshooters moved back a half-mile and made camp closer to the Moore House on the York River. This was in sight of the Rebel batteries and their defensive works at Gloucester Point. The rest of the Army of the Potomac withdrew towards Cockletown, while the work of the Federal engineers proceeded with slow deliberation in the creation of revetments, parallels, and redoubts. The *CSS Virginia* (formerly the *USS Merrimac*) was still afloat. Rumors abounded of the *CSS Merrimac* steaming out of the Elizabeth River, destroying the Federal Fleet at Fortress Monroe and the shipping at Ships Point, leaving McClellan's Army stranded, unsupported and unsupplied deep in enemy territory. The defenders of Yorktown had limited ammunition to expend and would lob only ten or twelve cannon shots at the encircling Federal Army each day. A few Northern warships would steam up the York River, throw a few shells at Yorktown and depart back to the safety of Fortress Monroe and her naval cannon. But, mostly the Federal ships were kept close to Fortress Monroe, under her cannon, with the *USS Monitor* ready to defend the Union fleet from the Confederate ironclad. Everywhere there was a lookout posted to watch for the daily-expected return of the *CSS Virginia*.

The Sharpshooters furnished daily details of 60 men who were moved into forward rifle pits before daylight in advance of the rest of the Army. Behind the thin line of the Sharpshooters, fatigue parties and engineers advanced the siege lines of parallels, berms, and roads necessary to support the attack (Stevens, page 45). It was Brigadier General Fitz-John Porter's responsibility to lay the great lines of parallels and redoubts, and forward artillery positions necessary for the final stage of the attack. Being so far forward, it was not uncommon for the Sharpshooters to be close enough to the Rebels to do a little communicating. It is a well-documented fact that pickets often arranged a truce across opposing sides and communicated rather freely across the hostile space separating the armies. Tobacco, newspapers, and banter were freely traded. That is, until some officer (Yankee or Rebel) came along and stifled the exchange.

The northern reporter George Alfred Townsend left an account of an event that must have been witnessed by the Willett brothers. Professor Lowe was an aeronaut who had tendered his services to the Federal government to develop a tethered-balloon as an observation platform. Under normal conditions the balloon was tethered to the earth by a long cable.

On 11th of April, at five o'clock, an event at once amusing and thrilling occurred near our (Federal) quarters. The commander-in-chief had appointed his personal and confidential friend, General Fitz-John Porter, to conduct the siege of Yorktown. Porter was a polite, soldierly gentleman, and a native of New Hampshire, who had been in the regular army since early manhood. He fought gallantly in the Mexican War, thrice promoted and once seriously wounded, and he was now forty years of age – handsome, enthusiastic, ambitious, and popular. He made frequent ascensions with Lowe, and learned to go aloft alone. One day he ascended thrice, and finally seemed as cozily at home in the firmament as upon the solid earth. It is needless to say that he grew careless, and on this particular morning leaped into the car and demanded the cables be let out with all speed. I saw with some surprise the flurried assistants were sending up the great straining canvas with a single rope attached. The enormous bag was only partially inflated, and the loose folds opened and shut with a crack like that of a musket. Nosily, fitfully, the yellow mass rose into the sky; the basket rocking like a feather in the zephyr; and just as I turned aside to speak to a comrade, a sound came from overhead, like the explosion of a shell, and something striking me across the face laid me flat on the ground.

Half blind and stunned, I staggered to my feet, but the air seemed full of cries and curses. Opening my eyes rudefully, I saw all faces turned upwards, and when I looked above, - the balloon was adrift.

The treacherous cable, rotted with vitriol, had snapped in twain; one fragment had been the cause of my downfall, and the other trailed, like a great entrail from the receding car, where Fitz-John Porter was bounding upward upon a Pegasus that he could neither check nor direct.

The whole army was agitated by the unwonted occurrence. From battery No. 1, on the brink of the York, to the mouth of the Warwick River, every soldier and officer was absorbed. We heard the enemy's alarm-guns, and directly the signal flags were waving up and down our front.

The general appeared directly overhead the edge of the car. He was tossing his hands frightenedly, and shouting something that we could not comprehend. 'O-pen – the valve!' called Professor Lowe, in his shrill tones; 'climb – to – the netting – and reach – the calve – rope.'

The valve! – the valve!' repeated a multitude of tongues, and all gazed with thrilling interest at the retreating hulk still kept straight upward, swerving neither to the east or west.

It was a weird spectacle, - that frail, fading oval, gliding against the sky, floating in the serene azure, the little vessel swinging silently beneath, and a hundred thousand martial men watching the loss of their brother in arms, but powerless to relieve or recover him. Had Fitz-John Porter been drifting down the rapids of Niagara, he could not have been so far from human assistance. But we saw him directly, no bigger than a child's toy, clambering up the netting and reaching for the cord.

'He can't do it,' muttered a man beside me; 'the wind blows the valve rope to and fro, and only a spry, coolheaded fellow can catch it.'

We saw the general descend, and appearing again over the edge of the basket, he seemed to be motioning to the breathless hordes below, the story of his failure. Then he dropped out of sight, and when we next saw him, he was reconnoitering the Confederate works through a long black spy-glass. A great laugh went up and down the lines as this cool procedure was observed, and then a cheer of applause ran from group to group. For a moment it was doubtful that the balloon would float in either direction; it seemed to falter, like an irresolute being, and moved reluctantly southeastward, towards Fortress Monroe. A huzzah, half muttered, quivered on every lip. All eyes glistened, and some were dim with tears of joy. But the wayward canvas now turned westward, and was blown rapidly towards the Confederate works. Its course was fitfully direct, and the wind seemed to veer often as if contrary currents, conscious of the opportunity, were struggling for the possession of the daring navigator. The south wind held mastery for a while, and the balloon passed the Federal front amidst a howl of despair from the soldiery. It kept right on, over the heights of Yorktown. The cool courage, either of heroism or despair, had seized upon Fitz-John Porter. He turned his black glass upon the ramparts and masked cannon below, upon the guns at Gloucester Point, and upon distant Norfolk. Had he been reconnoitering the moon, he could not have been more vigilant, and the Confederates probably thought this some Yankee device to peer into their sanctuary in spite of ball or shell; but there were some discharges of musketry that appeared to have no effect, and finally even these demonstrations ceased. Both armies in solemn silence were gazing aloft, while the imperturbable mariner continued to spy out the land.

The sun was now rising behind us, and roseate rays struggled with the zenith, like the arcs made by showery bombs. They threw a hazy atmosphere upon the balloon and the light shone through the network like the sun through the ribs of the skeleton ship in the 'Ancient Mariner'. Then as all looked agape, the aircraft 'plunged, and tacked, and veered,' towards Federal lines again.

The allelujah that now went up shook the spheres, and when he had regained our camp limits, the General was seen clambering again to clutch the valve-rope. This time he was successful, and the balloon fell like a stone. So that all hearts were once more leaped up, and the cheers were hushed. Cavalry rode pell-mell from several directions, to reach the place of descent, and the General's personal staff galloped past me like the wind, to be the first at his debarkation. I followed the throng of soldiery with due haste, and came up to the horsemen in a few minutes. The balloon had struck a canvas tent with great violence, felling it as if by a bolt, and the General, unharmed, had disentangled himself from innumerable folds of oiled canvas, and was now the cynosure of an immense group of people. While the officers shook his hands, the rabble bawled their satisfaction in hurrahs, and a band of music marching up directly, the throng on foot and horse gave him a vociferous escort to his quarters. (Townsend, pages 115-118)

On April 12, General Joseph E. Johnson, C.S.A., reached Richmond from northern Virginia and, after conferring with President Jefferson Davis and General Robert E. Lee, took charge of the Department of Norfolk and of the Peninsula. Prince John Magruder would have reinforcements. McClellan would face a larger army than he had faced the day before. On April 14, General Johnston reported from

WILLIAM WILLETT (1769-1844)

Yorktown, "Magruder had done well with the small number of men at his command, and he had bluffed superbly the superior force that threatened him, but his position was indefensible against such artillery and such a host as McClellan had." (Douglas Southall Freeman, Vol. 1, page 148)

Miss Mary Yates had married Gordon Arthur Willett on January 2, 1862, in Ionia, Michigan. On April 20, 1862, while staying with relatives in Utica, Mrs. Mary Yates Willett wrote to her husband, Gordon:

Utica, New York
April 20, 1862

On the J. R. Spaudling
Care of the Sanitary Commission
498 Broadway, New York

... Your letter of the 14th was just read. I am still at Aunt Libbie's ... Many prayers for your happiness and our speedy reunion,

Your Loving Wife,
M. E. Willett

In another letter, she wrote:

Utica, New York
April 27, (1862)

Dear Gordon,

... Heard ... there was a report of fighting at Yorktown yesterday. Where are you?... Is Jim going to stay here? You said in one letter he had offered his resignation.

Your Loving Wife,
Mary

On April 29, Confederate General Johnston wrote to Lee at Richmond, "The fight for Yorktown, as I said in Richmond, must be one of artillery, in which we cannot win. The result is certain; the time only doubtful. Should the attack upon Yorktown be made earnestly, we cannot prevent its fall; nor can we hold out more than a few hours. We must abandon the Peninsula soon." (Freeman, Vol. 1, page 154)

McClellan's siege was proceeding. The Sharpshooters lost a few wounded and an occasional man killed. On May 2, the Rebels commenced a cannonade at 9:00 AM and continued until 3:00 PM. On Saturday May 3, Federal Battery No. 1 opened a bombardment of Yorktown. The whole of the federal army artillery was expected to join the cannonade on the next day. On the night of May 3, there was another Confederate cannonade; however, this one proved to be the covering fire for the retrograde movement of the Confederates. McClellan had finally completed all his preparations to attack Yorktown on Sunday morning, May 5.

Confederate General Joseph E. Johnston was aware of the strength of his opponent and knew that Yorktown was no place for troops during a concentrated artillery, mortar, and naval bombardment. At midnight the Confederate cannons ceased fire after 56,300 Confederate soldiers had filed out of the Yorktown-Warwick line. Just at 3:00 AM Sunday morning, an explosion occurred within the Yorktown earthworks and was heard by the Union pickets. A few Rebel deserters came forward to announce that Yorktown had been evacuated! The pickets of the Sharpshooters were the first to enter the earthworks. A few more Confederate soldiers surrendered and informed the Union troops of torpedoes buried within the earthworks.

Captain Milan Willett had suffered greatly at the siege of Yorktown. Fellow Sharpshooter Matthew G. Callahan later wrote:

> Our command were exposed a great deal in cold rains during the siege of York Town Va., in the spring of 1862 and Captain Willett, the claimant, was on duty with us and owing to the exposures he endured, he contracted General Rheumatism and Rheumatic Lumbago, and also a difficulty which appeared to cause him a great deal of pain in his left side and in the region of his heart and which I support to be the Plurisa. ("Proof of Disability", dated June 1, 1892, and signed by Matthew G. Callahan; part of Civil War Pension File of A. Milan Willett)
>
> [Concerning Captain A. Milan Willett:]
> About the time of the surrender of York Town, or very soon thereafter, the Claimant suffered so much from his aforesaid difficulties that he was unfit for duty and went home on furlough and these troubles continued to disable him until he was obliged to leave the service. ("Proof of Disability", dated June 1, 1892, and signed by Matthew G. Callahan; part of Civil War Pension File of A. Milan Willett)

Another fellow soldier, Simon Danner added:

> I remember that during the siege of Yorktown, Va., in the spring of 1862, we were exposed to cold storms and Captain Willett who was on duty with us took a hard cold and was sick with the rheumatism in his back, limbs and shoulders and he complained of severe pains in his left side in the region of his heart which I suppose to be the Pleurasy. ("Proof of Disability" submitted by Simon Danner, dated July 13, 1892; in the Civil War Pension File of A. Milan Willett)

On May 4, 1862, Gordon A. Willett wrote from near Yorktown to his wife, Mary Willett:

PRINTED HEADING
Headquarters
First Regt. Berdan's Sharpshooters
Camp (the next part written out)
Winfield Scott, Near Y[orktow]n, VA.
Lord's Day May 4, 1862

Dear Wife,
Your letter of 30th ult was rec'd last evening, bringing, as do all messages from you, much to assure me of the steady and rapid growth of that peculiar and invaluable element of human nature which is the base of all happiness, the chief corner stone of the religion we profess, and try to practice, the nectar which flows from the purest and holiest fountain of celestial worlds.

God grant that nothing may interfere to impede the progress, but through his grace and favor, let it continue from day to day and year to year so to increase, as to render us the recipients of the greatest amount of happiness, which we are capacitated to enjoy.

Notwithstanding it is the Lord's day, we know or realize very little about it here, - is a day of much excitement and national interest, - My heart now thrills as I think of it; - O! if I could speak with you a while, and tell you what I have neither time, nor space, or ability to write, - Aye, I should be very happy, - but I must not think of it yet, but soon with the permission of our "Dear Father" I hope to be this privileged. - till then, I look to Jesus for all sweet communion, praying zealously for love to fill your heart and the hearts of those whom you are to be surrounded, that you may be contented and happy even during my absence, which at present I think will hardly be protracted.

The resignation of Q(uarter) Master Beebee was returned and in consequence there is no certainty that he will leave the Position - will probably know ere long. - he is still acting and perhaps will remain.

Well, there is so much in my mind about what has occurred within the last 24 hours that I will pen some of it, before writing else. At about ___ o'clock this morning two or three deserters came into our lines, and gave intelligence that Yorktown was evacuated upon which Sergeant Major with 4 men, accompanying Gen'l ___ who were on Picket went on double quick up to the Rebel Works - mounted the Parapet etc., soon after them followed Lieut ___ Co I USSS with 20 men, who also were on Picket. Soon after other troops (Mass) went up and news came back of same when the Regt was ordered to pack everything but tents, preparatory to receiving marching orders which were constantly expected - but it is after 4 PM and we are yet and will undoubtedly stay tonight. A company of the Picket have just returned from Yorktown - brought as trophies a large Secesh Flag (11 stars) Tobacco, Candles, Shirts, Havelocks, etc, - say the tents and huts they occupied were the filthiest holes imaginable and from the Boxes etc which contained their stores etc, there arose such a stench as was almost unendurable. - deserters report that they have fallen back to Richmond, - that there was mutiny, several Regts throwing down their arms and declaring it was no use, they could do nothing. I am feeling very much disappointed, having expected to accompany Col. B(erdan), Lt. Col. Ripley and Adjutant to Yorktown, where they are now gone. The cause of my disappointment was that the horse I was to ride was being shod and could not be ready in time - but I live in hopes of going there tomorrow, or soon at all events. They left in such haste that a large number of Guns and Mortars, Tents, Equipage, Clothing, Baggage, Commissary Stores etc were left behind, which of course our troops will have the kindness to care for. Some of the Guns were Spiked.

Our Gunboats have gone up the River in pursuit of them and judging from the heavy cannonading in that direction they have overhauled them and are giving them Hail Columbia. - This morning after our SS had entered the Rebel Fortifications a young man, (sergeant in Rebel Artillery) came and gave himself up and showed them where the enemy had buried shells with torpedoes attached so as to ignite when stepped upon, thus blowing up everything near them - several of a Mass Regt were killed and wounded by them, after which a guard was stationed to prevent a recurrence of the casualty. - Same Sergeant reports that the USSS had done them more injury that all the rest of McClellan's Army, which I presume may be true and certainly so saying nothing about the Artillery execution, which without a doubt had been quite effective, as the boys say the effects are quite visible all about the Fortifications and works and fields adjacent.

[unsigned - perhaps a page is missing]

YORKTOWN

The Sharpshooters remained in camp before Yorktown until May 7th when they moved forward four miles and into the deserted redoubts and earthworks of Yorktown.

Yorktown immediately became the Union point of disembarkation as wounded troops were sent back to Washington and new troops and supplies were forwarded to the Army of the Potomac. York River was a sea of sails. Steamers came and went. Gunboats cruised past and continued up the York River to the junction of the Pamunkey and Matapони Rivers, at West Point, Virginia. Already, McClellan was jumping forward to create a supply depot at Cumberland Landing and a Headquarters at the White House on the Pamunkey River.

On May 8, 1862, the Sharpshooters finally received the long awaited Sharps rifle.

CUMBERLAND LANDING

On May 9, the Sharpshooters and Colonel Berdan were on board the steamer *The State of Maine* when someone stole his personal Colt pistols. The steamship carried Berdan's Regiment up the York River to West Point, the new forward landing point for McClellan's Army.

As Norfolk was falling to the Federal Army, the CSS *Virginia* could not move up the James River to Richmond and safety; she drew too much water to navigate on that river; furthermore, on advice of some James River pilots, the CSS *Virginia* had been stripped of as much weight a possible in an attempt to move her upriver towards Richmond. The stripping of weight had left her wooden hull exposed above the waterline. And still the *CSS Virginia* drew too much water to cross the Newport News Bar. So, on May 10, neither able to move upriver to safety or to come out fighting the Confederates blew up the *CSS Virginia* and sent her to the bottom of the Elizabeth River. McClellan and the Federal navy could breathe a sigh of relief, as the enemy ironclad was defeated, not in naval battle with a worthy opponent, but by the depth of water that she drew.

On May 11, 1862, Gordon Willett wrote to his wife Mary:

Steamer Wilson Small
Yorktown Harbor, Va.
Sunday, May 11, 1862

Dearest Wife,

More than a week has passed since I have been favored with any tidings of you, and you may be assured that a message would be very gratefully received, and be a source of much satisfaction especially if it brought tidings of health and happiness on your part, - I don't allow myself to think anything is out of the way, that I don't hear from you, - the cause being in the fact of my changing locations - shall probably get your letters soon, as Adj't promises to send them as soon as possible - expect to receive one at least today or tomorrow, - hardly know what to write or how to write it, as I don't know exactly where you are, or how you are situated just at present. I really wish you were here with me today, - think it would afford each of us more happiness than we can well imagine - but as you are not, I content myself with the thought that you may be in the course of a few days, or if not, I shall be with you somewhere, without any doubt in my mind - if I stay here, you must be with me, - else I shall probably make a limited stay.

What think you about coming to help take care of the wounded and sick, a part of the time - several ladies, young, old, married, and single are here.

Steamer Elm City
Tuesday P. M. May 13th

Well, Dearest, I will now attempt to finish this which I was obliged to leave Sunday and have had no opportunity to attend to since and now don't know when I may get a chance to mail it. - Sunday I was called from writing this to take charge of stores etc. for fitting up the *Steamer Elm City* which together with Fred L. Olmstead and Mr. Napper, (representatives of the Sanitary Commission) and some ladies I went on board taking general charge fitting up for hospital to transport the sick and wounded Soldiers to Washington, N. York and any where else, as per order - have been on the go, so much that I think some of sending for an insurance policy for the insurance of my feet and limbs, - one not experienced knows little of the labor, responsibility and consequent fatigue, yet I get along well with only inconvenience and weariness as drawbacks on my part. I have shouldered a very considerable responsibility but have no fears of the outcome, so long as my health is good - doubtless you will be better pleased, than to have had me take the position of the Q[uarter] Master in the U.S.S.S.

Well as I said we came down on the *Elm City* Sunday and commenced our operations by taking Supplies of 400 mattresses, 400 sheets, 400 Quilts, 500 Blankets, 600 Pillows and cases, Bread, crackers, Oranges, Lemons, Liquors, Socks, Shirts, Drawers, Jellies, Condensed Milk, Brooms, Pails, Tin Cups, Tin Plates, Bandages, Rags, Lint, Towels, Camp Stools, Bathing Tub, Farinaceous Food, Farina, Eggs, Butter, Beef Soup (in cans) medicines etc. etc. Commenced operations, I said, by which I mean we went to work and that too without a lack of earnestness notwithstanding it was the Lord's Day, for all around us were waiting many poor sufferers whose relief depended somewhat upon our exertions - all hands on board helped us and thus we were enabled to call ourselves in readiness to receive the sick and wounded, last night. We run up York River, yesterday PM to Queens Creek and today have been receiving from small crafts, sick and wounded from Williamsburg who were brought pr. Ambulance to the dock and thence by the above named tugs. We are to take on board 400 more or less, as pr. Order and sail for Washington, return and get another load for New York - we have now 200 aboard and may not receive the bal. Till tomorrow - may leave tonight and be off in morning - Will take 12 to 16 hours to run to Washington - have found no sick or wounded as yet with whom I was acquainted - have seen many severe wounded - have some on board - they are a most uncouth, filthy, meager looking lot as a man ever beheld - several from our boat, the Capt. Mate, Stewart, Engineer etc went to the Battle Field of Monday Week today - they give interesting accounts of the general appearance - the stench is almost unendurable - Secesh dead are hardly covered or buried in the trenches etc.

Mr. Knapp has gone to Yorktown and may bring me a letter from you - hope so really. Have rec'd none yet since a week last Sat. Have heard nothing from Capt. [Milan], Adj't. [Floyd], [or] Jim since they embarked for West Point.

At 3:00 AM, on May 13, Berdan's regiment moved out on foot towards Richmond. The day was hot. The march was fatiguing and slow. Only a soldier who experienced it first hand can know of the halting, creaking movement of an enormous army on the move. The Sharpshooters left Cumberland Landing. But also leaving on the same road were cannons, infantry, wagon trains, teamsters, couriers and officers flying first through the troops on the march and then back down through the troops again on the only narrow road. Stop, go, halt, open file, rest - a seemingly endless incremental staggering movement of 12 miles. And at the end of the day, troops were fatigued and exhausted by the hot Virginia sun.

May 14, 1862 was a day of parade and review. Secretary Seward had come down from Washington and with Gen. McClellan reviewed the Union troops. For pomp and circumstance, parades and reviews are newsworthy; but for the soldier in the ranks standing in the hot Virginia sun – well the average soldier probably had a different view of that day.

On May 15, 1862, Gordon Willett wrote to his wife, Mary:

> Washington Harbor
> *Steamer Elm City*
> Thursday, May 15, 1862

Dear Wife,
I have no time to write but will take enough to finish this and send it this P. M. - left Yorktown yesterday A. M. with 428 sick and wounded in charge - have been here long enough to go uptown and call on the Sect. Sanitary Commission (Dr. Jenkins) the Surgeon General and Medical Director, which took most of the little strength I had left as it was a 3 mile walk or more - met in carriage with Dr. Jenkins - got

some dinner and am now in my stateroom writing to one of whom I have heard nothing in so long a time - O how I wish you were here - if I knew you would reach me before we leave for Yorktown I should Telegraph for you to come - I expect to go to N. York next week and then will manage to have you meet me and stay with me - you don't know how much I want to see you expect you are able to estimate by your own feelings - May God protect and help you daily and bring us together very soon.

I called to see Chas. Bennett a few days since - he was on Drill - so he must have been well - have heard nothing from the S. S. yet,

If you leave Utica, I think you had better go to New York and so come when I send for you, if I don't go to N. York myself.

(Letter sent to Utica
c/o S. Bennett)

I don't know what I have written nor when I wrote it, neither have I time to look it over to see but will send it as it is, knowing that it will be quite acceptable in any shape - yes I know it will be, for I know your heart and the circumstances - I hope I shall not again see the necessity of foregoing so much - so very much. I am now waiting orders from the Medical Director about unloading the Soldiers - Expect to unload today - then clean the Steamer (an awful job as she is large, 300 feet long). Then procure stores and etc. for a trip of 7 days for 500 - expect to make the trip to New York - perhaps to Albany and maybe back to Washington - Don't know till ordered and then don't know till the trip is made as there are so many very rapid changes in the course of events - war makes everything uncertain with us in this work. However things may be I want you with me. If I don't go to New York I must send for you to come with some one - you must be ready to start at an hour's notice, or perhaps even less - you had better put your things that you don't need, in a box and bring your Trunk - bring nothing that you don't want to use - I may remain on this Boat or may be transferred to take charge of some other or something else - may go to Richmond, Port Royal, or elsewhere - makes little difference where, if you are with me - Don't know how long I may be in the employ of the Commission, but will tell you something of the prospects although I would like to say it to no one but myself or a part thereof, for you know I don't like flattery, nor to praise myself - Well, I went into the Employ of the Commission under quite unfavorable circumstances, on trial, with Mr. Knapp - after a day or two, I was put above those who had been my superiors and who had been in the Commission several months. Mr. Knapp said to me, several times, that he found me much more efficient than he expected and that I had relieved him [of] a great deal of care and responsibility - the position which I occupy is by no mean an easy one, nevertheless I have no difficulty in attending to the duties thereof, of which I have not time to speak. You will write often till you come if that is not immediately, and direct for present to Yorktown, Va., care Sanitary Commission.

G. A. Willett

If Herbert [Yates, Mary's brother] is East or is to be soon he had better come down with you - it will cost him nothing from N. York and will do him good.

On May 15, the regiment was ordered to fall in with 60 rounds of ammunition, and prepare to march immediately to meet the enemy. It was raining furiously. Colonel Berdan was sick with a bout of typhoid fever and a congestion of the liver; he remained in the house of a Mr. Toler and did not rejoin the regiment until May 23. The Sharpshooters moved only five miles from 6:30 AM until 4:00 PM when they finally arrived at White House, the plantation where George Washington and Martha Custis had been married. The present owner was Mrs. Lee, wife of General Robert E. Lee. Unfortunately, Gen. Lee had removed his family from Arlington Plantation overlooking Washington on the Potomac River to White House Plantation on the Pamkuney River, his wife's plantation, for their greater safety. Here it was that the Army of the Potomac came. Mrs. Lee and her family had to flee again, this time to a friend's house outside Richmond. The wheat fields around White House Plantation were full and had the promise of a good year's crops, until Gen. McClellan made White House his headquarters, and 100,000 Union troops marched through the plantation enroute to the front. The road between Cumberland Landing and White House quickly became another quagmire, and eight to ten horses were required to move each cannon. The heat and rain were breaking down the soldiers faster than enemy action. It is a simple fact that many more soldiers died or became unfit for service due to campaigning under such harsh conditions than were killed or injured by the enemy.

The Sharpshooters encamped in a clover field on White House plantation. Steamers and sailing craft came up to the plantation wharf. The Sharpshooters were just 20 miles east of Richmond! Intentionally or otherwise, the Union soldiers destroyed the crops as they encamped around and marched over White House plantation. On May 19, tents were struck and the Sharpshooters proceeded to pass Tunstall Station and Barker's Mill, enroute to the forward Union lines on the Chickahominy River and Swamp. From May 22 to May 26 the Sharpshooters encamped at Barker's Mill. Farmers sold fresh provisions to the Union soldiers, gladly taking silver and gold coin in return for potatoes, sweet potatoes, corn, eggs, and chickens, albeit at inflated wartime prices. In many instances change was made in Confederate scrip, which the Union soldiers often accepted. Confederate scrip was in reality nothing more than a souvenir of their stay in Virginia, as the Union soldiers well knew that the same farmers would not take the Southern script in exchange for later purchases. Even this early in the war, economics was a more powerful motivator than sentiment. In the afternoon of the twenty-sixth, the Sharpshooters encamped on Gaines Hill from which they had a clear view of Richmond

HANOVER COURT HOUSE

The Confederate cavalry demonstrated on the right of the Union line and threatened to make a dash at the supply lines and the supply bases at White House and Cumberland Landing. On May 27, 1862, at the at the Battle of Hanover Courthouse, the 1st Regiment was aroused at 3:00 AM as part of Gen. Porter's 5th Corps,

> in the midst of a furious rain storm. Sixty rounds of ammunition were given out, and at daylight the regiment marched to attack Richmond. Colonel Berdan remained behind, sick again, as did Adjutant Willett. The regiment marched 17 miles and fought the first half of the battle ... All supposed the battle had ended ... Soon after, firing was heard in the rear, and the regiment ordered to back double quick ... (Stevens, page 83)

The weather rapidly turned from a morning of rain and mud to an afternoon scorcher. Soldiers perspired in their woolen uniforms and the fatigue from constant marching set in. Again, the Sharpshooters were ordered ahead as skirmishers, with the 25th New York Infantry in support. They crossed Kinney's Farm, and ran into a shower of minnie balls and canister shot. Company I (Milan Willett's) was held in reserve to the rear; the rest of the Sharpshooters advanced, taking hits, and one sharpshooter was killed.

As the Sharpshooters advanced, the Confederates withdrew a distance of over two miles, leaving behind their wounded and some surgeons attending the wounded. The Sharpshooters' losses were one man killed and nine wounded. However, the main force of the Confederates under Gen. Branch of North Carolina were to the left and rear; this led to the Sharpshooters and other skirmishers being sent back at the double quick to face the new threat. Again there was an assault in the heat of the day with heavier casualties among the 5th, 25th and 44th New York, 2d Maine, 9th (Irish) Massachusetts, and the 1st USSS. The Sharpshooters slept the sleep of exhaustion in place and under arms that night. Total loss by the 1st USSS in killed and wounded for this one day of action was twenty. Gen. Porter's 5th Corps had faced 8,000 Georgia, North Carolina, and Virginia units. The next day the Sharpshooters remained on the field in case the battle was renewed.

On the morning of May 29, rations were bought up and in the afternoon the Sharpshooters started their return to their encampment on Gaines Hill. However, muddy roads slowed their progress and it was late at night when they finally arrived. They then had a few days respite on Gaines Hill camp, with a memorable and terrible thunderstorm that hurled bolts of lightning and rain in torrents (Stevens, page 93).

On May 29, Gordon Willett telegraphed his wife:

> New York, Albany, and Buffalo Telegraph Company
> To: Mrs. Mary E. Willett By telegraph from New York
> 58 Charlotte St., Utica, May 29th, 1862, Rec'd 2:30 P. M.
>
> Come immediately Stop at Astor House. Leave New York Saturday morning.
>
> G. A. Willett

Mrs. Mary (Yates) Willett began a diary on May 29, picking up exactly as she received the above telegram. Her diary entry is as follows:

Recd telegram from New York at 3 P.M., and at 4:10 was on way there from Utica. Went to Albany in cars and from there by boat.

Friday, May 30
As soon as it was light we went on deck and admired the scenery along the Hudson – Arrived at N. Y. at 7:30. Went to the Astor House, washed and dressed then lay down and slept till 9:30. Was just going to have some breakfast when Gor sent his card to our room and soon after came himself. We came to the Steamer *Spaulding*.

Saturday, May 31
Left N. Y. at 8 A.M. ... We stopped at Fort Lafayette and took on 90 Rebel regulars and 30 men as guard ... have been homesick. (Mrs. Mary Willett diary, per date)

FAIR OAKS

On May 31 the fighting erupted at Fair Oaks, and the sound of battle was clearly heard at Gaines Hill. Several times the Sharpshooter regiment stood to arms, but nothing more was required of their outfit that day. One of the most momentous single events of the war occurred on the night of May 31. Gen. Joseph E. Johnston was personally commanding troops at Fair Oaks when he was seriously wounded by a fragment of an artillery shell. This wounding led to the appointment, on June 3, of Gen. Robert E. Lee as commander of the Confederate armies before Richmond. On June 1, the Sharpshooters moved out as pickets on the south side of the Chickahominy River. Union Artillery was preparing their positions on Gaines Hill. Professor Lowe had two hot air balloons in the air overlooking the battlefield. On the afternoon of June 2, the sharpshooter regiment returned to camp. (Stevens, page 94, 95)

Returning to Gordon and Mary Willett on the *SS Spaulding*:

Sunday, June 1
... We arrived Fortress Monroe at 4 and went ashore, stayed till dark – saw the tide come in. The Fortress is well worth a visit.

Monday, June 2
We arrived at White House at noon ... Saw

Yorktown and West Point at a distance. We anchored in the river below the house. Milan came here today.

Tuesday, June 3
Came up to the W. H. Landing before noon to unload Government stores. Captain and wife, Stewart's wife, and a young man, Milan and myself, visited the plantation and house. Found in the yard under a tree the grave of Sidney. Poor boy, he was killed accidentally on the 13th of May. Then we went to the R. R. station and saw the wounded from Fair Oaks – bought in, dreadful it is to see them.

Wednesday, June 4th
Finished loading the ship and about commenced taking the wounded. Miss Whetten and I have been busy all eve in the pantry. Some terrible sights I have seen. (Mrs. Mary Willett diary, per date)

On June 4, 1862, a Leave of Absence was granted to Lieutenant F. A. Willett for two weeks "for the benefit of his health," signed by Command of Major General McClellan. During his absence Lt. Floyd Willett had "a severe attack of typhoid fever." He wrote to Col. Berdan requesting a two or three week extension of his leave due to his present illness. If his request was not granted, Lt. Willett stated that he would be "forced to resign for in my present state of health I can not perform the duties of my office." (personal letter from Lt. Willett to Col. Berdan, dated June 11, 1862)

[Mary Willett on the *SS Spaulding* continues her diary] Thursday, June 5th
Finished taking on wounded and left White House at noon. Came to Fortress Monroe where we are to stay all night.

Friday, June 6
Left the Fortress at 7. Went to Portsmouth, left the 30 worst cases and took 61 from there. Had a fine view of Norfolk across the river. Gor went over, it was raining quite hard. Miss W[hetten] and myself have been very busy all day taking care of the Soldiers. I carried around some oranges for which they seem very thankful ... as well as for my attention. Came back to Fortress Monroe. I have taken off hoops.

On June 6, on duty before Richmond, the Sharpshooter

regiment was broken up and each company was sent as pickets and skirmishers to a different division. Company I (Willett's) was assigned to Gen. "Baldy" Smith's division on the right wing on the south side of the Chickahominy. The Sharpshooters occupied a redoubt called Fort Davidson, and provided twelve forward pickets a day. The Confederates were at times less than 150 yards away. (Stevens, page 98)

Fighting in, around, and over a swamp was breaking men down faster than hostile action. More than one-third of the men were on the sick list. One day the pickets were caught in the swamp by advancing Rebels. They were knee deep in water, and only the rapid repeating action of their Sharps rifle permitted them to extricate themselves without loss.

> Saturday, June 7
> ... Left F. M. at 1 P. M. and are now on our way to Philadelphia. Have been at work in the pantry nearly all of the day. After dinner I took some little tracts and books to the men. They were very glad of them ... One man died just before noon and [an]other just after ...two are just alive. (Mrs. Mary Willett diary, per date)

The *SS Spaulding* hospital ship arrived in Philadelphia on June 8, and the wounded were removed from the ship. Three more soldiers had died during the night and morning. For the next two days they stayed in Philadelphia and did some sight seeing and shopping while the ship was cleaned and restocked.

> Monday, June 9
> ... Have the leisure of wearing hoops again. Miss W, Gor and I went to the San[itary] Com[mission] rooms ...

> Wednesday, June 11
> Gor is not well ... After [3] we sailed for F. M.

> Thursday, June 12
> Gor and I have both been sick .. before tea we arrived at Fortress Monroe ... We sailed for W[hite] H[ouse] ...

> Friday, June 13
> We came to Yorktown last night and anchored. This morning we left there for White House where we arrived about 11 ... Gor and I and Mrs. Neading went

to W, House Landing this eve. We found the wounded being brought on the *Elm City* and were told that a Guerilla band of rebels had fired into the train of cars coming from the front, about 6 miles distant. One was killed and several wounded, some seriously. We had gone on shore and were immediately ordered back on the boats, and the boats to go down river.

We came back to this ship ... 12 o'clock a company of 25 had been sent for to remove the sick from the hospital tents. Other boats steam past but the *Spaulding* remains were she has been anchored. Milan came on the train, is here. (Mrs. Mary Willett diary, per date)

Such were Mrs. Mary Willett's comments on what would become known as Stuart's ride around McClellan. On June 12, Gen. Stuart had left Richmond on with the announced intention of re-inforcing Gen. Jackson in the Shenandoah Valley. Instead he called a halt at and bivouacked in some pinewoods at Hanover Court House. On the morning of June 13, his men were summoned without to their duty in utmost quietude. When mounted Jeb Stuart turned his cavalcade of mounted troopers to the east. It was not until that moment that his troopers knew the true direction that Friday, June 13 would take them. They rode down two Union cavalry units, crossed and burned the York River Railroad; it was at Tunstall Station that the event which Mary wrote of occurred. Jeb Stuart had gained the information he was sent out to discover (the location of Gen. McClellan's right wing), and now Stuart had a decision to make. Should he return the way he had came? But the Union army now was alert to his force and gathering infantry forces to oppose or annihilate him. Or should he continue across the Chickahominy into the swamps, and hope that McClellan's left wing did not reach all the way to the James River? Gen. Stuart made his decision, completed his circuit of McClellan's army, and made history at the while only losing one man killed during the entire raid.

Saturday, June 14
... Miss W. and Mr. Grenville, Gor and I visit the White House. While they looked at the house, Gor and I visited the grave of Sidney. Poor boy, if he could only be carried home. He was 22 years, 4 months and 7 days old ... (Perhaps Sidney was Mary's cousin Sidney Sessions, of Ionia, Michigan).

Sunday, June 15
... This morning Dr. Gilbert and daughter, Milan and a lieutenant left for home ... (Mrs. Mary Willett diary, per date)

On June 17, 1862, General Thomas J. Jackson left the Shenandoah Valley and raced across the Virginia Piedmont with his own army to make a juncture of his army and "Bobby" Lee's army before Richmond. The Southern defensive campaign as carried out under General Joseph E. Johnston leadership was at an end. And even though the Confederate Army did not know it, "Bobby" Lee, the King of Spades, was going on the offensive. All the fighting and marching which had already occurred was only preliminary to that which would follow. Suddenly, the Confederates were in front of McClellan's Army in force and a hornet's nest was about to be let loose on the over-confident Union army. The opposing cannons continued their relentless duels. But every common soldier on the front line knew that something was going to happen - soon.

On June 17, 1862, Charles Bennett, a cousin of Mary E. Willett, tried to get a pass to see Mary and Gordon Willett who were only 16 miles away at White House Supply Depot and Landing, but no one was allowed to leave camp. A letter was carried to the Willetts by Lieutenant Landon, of the 44th Regiment, New York State Volunteers, who had been injured in the battle at Hanover. He was still convalescing and was going north soon.

Tuesday, June 18
... We are worried about Jim [Willett] have not seen him for a long time.

Wednesday, June 18
Waiting as usual for orders .. This P. M. we visited the Gunboat *Savage* ... Jim has come, is better ...

Friday, June 20
... At about 11 someone came on board and brought me a letter and told us to prepare to receive wounded. 31 were brought on board and we left for Yorktown. (Mrs. Mary Willett diary, per date)

Saturday, June 21
At Yorktown, Gor and I went ashore this morning visited the rebel fortifications there are really wonderful. We took on board about 360 wounded and

left for Fortress Monroe about 3, arrived a ½ [past] 6 and left about 9 ... [going] to N. Y.

News of the casualties and hospital ships was making the northern newspapers: Mary's aunt Mrs. Sila Bennett wrote to Mary on June 22:

Utica
June 22, 1862

... I saw in the paper this morning the *Spaulding* had to run from her moorings at the White House for fear of falling into the hands of the Rebels. Was you there and did you get frightened? ...

Aunt Sila

The *Spaulding* arrived in New York on June 23. Gordon and Mary had both been sick on board. In New York, Mary's cousins Mary and Norman Caulkins met them and Mary Willett stayed with her cousins for a few days. They took her sightseeing to Central Park, and also shopping. Gordon was busy on the ship, but came in the evenings. On Thursday, they sailed out of New York harbor into the Atlantic Ocean and began their run down the New Jersey coast.

Thursday, June 26
... Cousins Norman and Mary came to the ship with me. They like it very much. At 6 we sailed and are now on our way to Fortress Monroe.

Friday, June 27
Very pleasant indeed. I do not think anyone has been sea sick. Saw porpoises this P. M. for the first time, and a great many of them ... (Mrs. Mary Willett diary, per date)

SEVEN DAYS IN JUNE

On June 25, McClellan attacked the defensive forces of the Confederate forces at Oak Grove outside Richmond, beginning what soon would be known as the Seven Days Battles. At the same time, Gen. Jackson was moving into position to attack the right flank of McClellan's army.

DAY ONE, JUNE 26: MECHANICSVILLE

On June 26, 1862, the Sharpshooters regiment was at the Battle of Mechanicsville. Private William C. Kent of the 1st USSS Regiment wrote to his father concerning the events of June 27. "On Thursday, June 26, all the forenoon, there was heavy fighting in direction of Mechanicsville, but not more so than we were accustomed to every day. Toward noon, it grew heavier, and while we were eating dinner, the orders came to fall in light marching order. In a few minutes we had started toward the scene of action under Lieutenant Colonel Ripley." (Marcot, page 54) The Sharpshooters were lucky that first day - they suffered no casualties.

DAY TWO, JUNE 27: GAINES' MILL

Soon after the infantry commenced firing, gunsmoke lay so thick over the landscape that it obscured the view just a few feet in front of a soldier. His only recourse: fire and keep firing at the sound and noise of battle to his front. The troops slept under arms that night, and a new horror was added to their war-time experience: too many wounded, just a few yards away grievously, piteously crying for assistance when no aid could be given.

Before dawn, the Sharpshooters were out in front in their rifle pits. On June 27, the Sharpshooters were at Gaines Mill and in the ensuing battle lost five men killed, three wounded, and three missing in action. (Marcot, page 50) Gen. Porter's 5th Corps was given the assignment of holding Lee's left wing from flanking the Army of the Potomac. Early in the morning the Sharpshooters were well forward in their rifle pits when Gen. John F. Reynolds personally came all the way forward to the rifle pits and ordered them to quietly withdraw as the Rebels were successfully flanking the Army of the Potomac. At daylight, the advance elements of the 1st USSS, finding themselves alone, quietly began to withdraw, keeping particular notice not to make any noise which would have been answered by the Rebels with a concentrated volley of fire.

Private William C. Kent's letter of July 28, to his father related the events of June 27:

> A brisk firing commenced on our right [the Battle of Gaines Mill], and scattered along until it came opposite to me. Tremendous volleys of small arms and the peal of heavy guns were the last things I heard before I went in. We fought pretty much on our own

hook, the officers being far to the right, and the human voice was of no account. The Rebels rushed down the hill in line of battle, but it wasn't quite so easy rushing across a swamp, waist deep in thick mud. And as they tried it, we fired Sharps rifles at eight rods, firing as fast as we could put in cartridges, the distance being so short that aim was unnecessary. We couldn't help hitting them, and our vigorous fire held them in check for some minutes. (Marcot, page 54)

Maj. Roy Stone, commanding the 1st Pennsylvania Rifles ("Bucktails"), reported on two companies of the US Sharpshooters, those of Capt. Drew and Capt. Gioux:

At daybreak of the 27th I was informed that the army would retire at once to a new line on Gaines Hill, and I was directed to hold with my regiment and the battery the position I then held until that movement could be effected. I extended the Sharpshooters up to my right and left, to keep up the appearance of still occupying the whole line, and as soon as it was fairly light opened fire upon the enemy, who had advanced under cover of the night and planted new batteries with grape-shot range. Their infantry came down with apparent undiminished force, filling the roads towards the ford with a solid column ... A little after 6 o'clock A. M. we were ordered to retire as best we might to the main body three miles distant. After leaving the entrenchments we were still obliged to go more than half a mile before escaping the range of the same batteries which had annoyed us all the morning. (Stevens, page 109)

General Lee had attacked, and although severe fighting had ensued, Major General McClellan began his retrograde movement towards the James River. Harrison Landing was to be his new supply base and had the added protection of naval covering fire from deep draft gunboats. However, the movement away from Mechanicsville and towards the James River by McClellan left General Lee in possession of the field and gave all the appearance of the Rebel army having been successful on the field of battle at Gaines Mill. Another night was spent by the soldiers lying in the field under arms, amidst the carnage of war.

But the day had just begun. Now the 1st USSS were back at Gaines Mill, having fallen back on the main body of Gen. Porter's 5th Corps. Union cannon were massed and fired at the long range of two and a half miles until the Confederates found a more covered way of approaching the 5th Corps in its blocking position. Gen. Porter had been ordered to hold back the Rebel army while the rest of the Army of the Potomac continued its movement to the James. At ten o'clock, Gen. Porter's line was formed. About noon the first assault began on Porter's right and was repulsed. At three o'clock the attack became general and continued unabated until after dark. About seven or eight o'clock, the Rebels broke the lines of Morell's division - but after a full day of assault, the Confederate attacking force was disorganized, its energy spent and not of sufficient strength to press the advantage the day's fighting had created. [Editor's note: Regardless of what was said later by Union apologists.] At that moment, there was a great deal of demoralization and an awful confusion caused by the breaking of Morell's division and the repulse of the Union cavalry which had disastrously charged the river bottom at sunset. Riderless cavalry horses were everywhere. Here occurred Col. Berdan's rallying of fleeing Union soldiers.

The day had been hotly contested, and only the absence of Confederate Gen. Jackson prevented the Confederates from being more successful. Gen. Jackson's reluctance to engage his troops on that fateful day has been often misunderstood, and his seeming inaction seldom defended. Gen. Lee had no intimation of Gen. McClellan's change of base, and had instructed Gen. Jackson to attack the Union army as it was being pushed back towards its base of supply - - White House and Cumberland Landing. When McClellan did not retire in that direction, Gen. Jackson had no orders to do other than what he did - wait until he could make a flank attack on a Union army. Unfortunately for his orders and Gen. Lee's battle plan, McClellan's army was not going to be moving towards White House and its previous base of supply.

The chaos and confusion of war was never more evident than that day. Gen. Lee had not foreseen Gen. McClellan's change of base; all of Lee's plans hinged on driving McClellan back on his White House line of supply. That Gen. Jackson never had the opportunity to attack McClellan's flank is an indication of the genius that McClellan possessed. Long after the war had ended, Lee was asked who was the most able commander he had been up against. The questioner evidently thought that Gen. Grant would be the answer. Lee replied that Gen. McClellan was the best Union commander. And that he, Gen. Lee, was relieved when Gen. McClellan was eventually replaced with less able commanders. Grant's final winning tactic after four years of terrible war was to do what

Gen. McClellan had proposed to do in the spring of 1862 - sever Richmond's supply line to the interior of the Confederacy by attacking Petersburg and the rail lines which ran into the capital city. Such siege tactics had at the same time the added benefit of tying down the Rebel army to a static defense thus eliminating the element of maneuver which had been so crucial to Confederate victories.

Early in the morning of June 28, 1862, the Union troops were across the Chickahominy River, destroying the four bridges, to keep them from being used by the Rebel forces in pursuit. McClellan thus reunited the two wings of his Army of the Potomac that had been separated by the swamp. The Sharpshooters Companies A and I remained in the abandoned Fort Davidson until everything of use to the Rebels was destroyed. Confusion reigned as cattle were being driven to the south towards the James River; the camp had been struck and desolation was everywhere as the quartermasters were firing whatever stores could not be removed in the hasty movement south. About ten o'clock the Rebels make a great rush on Fort Davidson, supposing that it was undermanned, but they were mistaken. The Sharpshooters had laid an ambush and so disrupted the charge that afterwards the Confederates requested a truce to bury their dead. Pursuant to the orders of Gen. William Smith, Commander IX Corps, the 1st USSS abandoned Fort Davidson and retired towards the main body of the Union army.

From a distance, Mary and Gordon witnessed some of the confusion after the battle:

> Saturday, June 28
> Were going up the Pamunkey and met steamers, schooners, tugs and everything coming down. White House is burned and everything near that could not be taken away. We went to Cumberland [Landing], took tow, and came back to West Point. (Mrs. Mary Willett diary, per date)

The York River Railroad Bridge across the Pamunkey River was destroyed by the vacating Union forces. The bridge was nothing more than a smoking ruin. Railway cars full of ammunition were lying in the river. They had been purposely plunged headlong by the Union in to the Pamunkey River, McClellan's method for ensuring they did not fall in the hands of the Rebels.

On June 28, 1862, when Mary and Gordon arrived at West Point, they were at the head of the York River.

Sunday, June 29
At West Point this morning rec'd letters from home and from Utica. Took 14 schooners in tow and came to Fortress Monroe ... Jim [Willett] is here and most sick. (Mrs. Mary Willett diary, per date)

Mrs. Mary Elizabeth Willett was with her husband on the *S. R. Spaulding.* The following is a letter Mrs. Willett wrote to her sister Sarah Yates in Ionia County, Michigan, evidently she began the letter one day, wrote as she had time, and completed it at a day removed from the beginning of her missive:

S. R. Spaulding
York River, June 28th, 1862

Dear Sister Sarah,
I wrote to Mother and mailed the letter last Thursday and today have thought I would write to you. We left New York at 6 Thursday eve and yesterday (Sat) were going up the Pummukey [sic] where we met the shipping coming down.

We were of course surprised and on asking the cause were told the Rebels were in possession of White House and everything burned. We were ordered up 15 miles for "tow" and went to Cumberland and took 2 Schooners in tow that is tied up there on behind and came down a little way then anchored for the night.

We came to West Point this morning and took 14 schooners in tow and are now going to Fortress Monroe and from there are to go up the James River. Jim Willett came here today from White House he says he came with the last Steamer from there and, tells us that all was removed that could be and the rest set on fire. The White House is burned, the Negroes all brought down here on canal boats towed by others. One old [Negro] man refused to come.

It is said to be a stratagem of McClellan and if it works well our troops are probably in Richmond, and the Rebels can have White House which can be of no earthly benefit to them.

We hope to know the truth of it ere long. Yesterday we heard that the Rebels were in possession there but we know it was not true. Jim is quite sick today says he has not been well since we saw him before.

I have written to Aunt Sila and Mary today and

expect to mail these at Fortress Monroe. Last week I visited Yorktown and fortifications. I wish you could be here and see the sights as I can see them. I had a very pleasant time in New York. Cousin Mary [Caulkins] took me to the Central Park Thurs along where we saw everything to make it beautiful and all artificial too. A beautiful lake where we counted about 30 large white swan and several little ones. Also chicks and geese - There were boats to take visitors out on the lake but we had not time. There were 5 or 6 deer in a space enclosed by a wire fence and two large Eagles -

There were bridges across the lake which is narrow and very singular in shape and has many little fish. The ground was very rocky and marshy but is now a most beautiful place. There is a cave which we visited and I walked over the bridge that the Prince of Wales crossed. There are many bridges and no two alike and all beautiful. I wish you could see it.

Monday Morning

Last night after tea I went on deck and a few spoke at evening service. We had no chaplain, but had a prayer meeting which I enjoyed very much. We were only a short time as it commenced to storm, and we were obliged to come down. It lightened beautifully all the eve but did not thunder any. I have just been to breakfast would you like to know what we had? Well we had tea and coffee, baked potatoes, fish, potatoes hashed, beef steak, Johnny cake, bread, toast and crackers and boiled eggs - O That is a specimen of our breakfasts, sometimes we have ham and fried eggs. For dinner yesterday we had Roast beef and mackerel, for meats, soup, potatoes, cabbage boiled, beets, onions, green peas and turnips and tomatoes and pudding almonds and raisins and oranges for desert also, bread and butter which I left out of in the proper place and pickles, and wine for those who chose, I did not. For tea we had toasted buttered, bread, cold ham, beef and tongue and sardines, preserved peaches, cheese, crackers and two kinds of cake.

We are now at Fortress Monroe and there this is to be mailed soon so you will get it as soon as possible. Do you go too school and how does Jane do as a teacher. Has Mother a girl yet if not she must have? Ask her how she would like me to bring her a black girl to work for her. We have two. Write to me very soon

WILLIAM WILLETT (1769-1844)   67

and tell me all that is going on. I have not had a letter from home since Herbert wrote just after he was sick. I am hoping for one today. Tell Gilbert he may look for a letter in a few days When we can visit the "Wilson Small" where our Post Office is. Direct as before till I tell you different. Or to Headquarters of Sanitary Commission Va. Care of Fred L. Omlstead.
How does Herbert get along? I hope he is much better.

On June 29, Companies A and I of the Sharpshooters were sent to Bottom's Bridge on the Chickahominy River as skirmishers. During the afternoon, they destroyed Bottom's Bridge by sitting on fire an Union ammunition train and sending it out on the trestle. The resulting explosion was a climactic throwing of train and bridge fragments thousands of feet into the air. The Sharpshooters kept the Confederates from repairing the bridge; all the while the Union supports were moving further away. Once called off of duty at Bottom's Bridge, the companies passed a deserted Savage Station as they moved towards White Oak swamp.

SAVAGE'S STATION

The Battle of Savage's Station commenced on June 29, at 4:00 PM. The Union wagon trains were there. The station was a depot for supplies and a collecting point for sick and wounded Union soldiers. The Rebels under Gen. Magruder attacked down the Williamsburg road, but were repulsed. The Rebels charged a second and a third time, and nearly broke the center of Gen. Burns' position. However, the Union infantry held firm, and the immediate threat to McClellan's wagon trains and supplies was ended. General Burns was ordered on June 30 to abandon the position; also abandoned that day were twenty-five hundred Union sick and wounded with their attendant medical officers of the Second and Sixth Corps. Thus war is made.

FRAZIER'S FARM

On June 30, Companies A and I again were out as skirmishers protecting Gen. Smith's division as it moved away from White Oak swamp. More than thirty Rebel cannon opened fire in the forenoon and continued to cause confusion and disruption of the Union troops until the Rebel batteries were silenced. It was in the heat of the day and the forward skirmishers were doing their duty, trying to silence as many

Rebel cannon as possible. This fight was only the opening battle of that day. It seems strange, in light of the huge contest of arms which was occurring around them, but Berdan's Sharpshooters stopped fighting and were mustered to receive their pay.

Both sharpshooter companies were down to about 50 men each. About 4:00 PM the two companies moved into a woods before an open field; then they were ordered to the exposed slope of the field. Suddenly an outlying regiment of Union infantry broke and tried to run over the Sharpshooter's position to the relative safety of the woods beyond. It was obvious that the Rebels were preparing to charge. It was here that the greatest losses of the day occurred as the Sharpshooters poured shot into the forming Rebel attacking force. None too soon, the Sharpshooters were ordered to fall back to the woods and in doing so lost more wounded. The Rebels made their charge, but were repulsed from the fire coming from the cover of the woods. All of the Sharpshooter fallen, dead and wounded, were left on the open field. (Stevens, page 138) On June 30, at Glendale (also called Frazier's Farm), the 1st Regiment lost six men killed, five wounded, and one missing in action. (Marcot, page 50) General Lee had tried to cut off McClellan's retreat towards the James River and the protection that could be given by the long range cannon of the Union gun boats. General Lee failed in this attempt. Union generals Reynolds and McCall were captured. Opposing units were mixed together in the darkness in the woods and it was the unlucky Rebel or Unionist who laid his weary body down on the ground to sleep that night but woke up amongst his foes!

Back on the *Spaulding*, Mary and Gordon Willett were being sent to the new supply base at Harrison's Landing:

>Monday, June 30
>Left F. M. [Fortress Monroe] at 4 PM came up to Harrison's bar arrived at midnight. Saw the [USS] *Cumberland* which was sunk [off Newport News point by the *CSS Virginia*].

DAY SEVEN, JULY 1: MALVERN HILL

On July 1, the Battle of Malvern Hill was fought, ending what would become known as the Seven Days Battle. From midnight until noon of July 1, the tired and battle-weary Union troops poured into position at Malvern Hill, where McClellan was determined to turn again upon the Rebels. For all seven days, McClellan had been slowly, methodically moving from the northeast to the southwest. He had given up his exposed position with a right wing of his army unsupported by the left wing due to the intervening Chickahominy River and associated swamps. Now his army was united and needed only to move to Harrison's Landing to be under the protection of his naval guns. However, it was obvious that another rear guard action would have to be fought and that the only relief would come at nightfall, when the fighting would cease.

McClellan chose Malvern Hill because it commanded the fields to the north and east. It had the added advantage of forcing his opponent to charge uphill, if the Confederates chose to attack his army. Malvern Hill was the last natural defensive position before the Union troops reached Harrison's Landing and the safety the naval guns afforded. Maj. Trepp's command, Companies A and I, were on the right of Malvern Hill with Gen. Smith where they occupied an advanced position. The battle began about ten o'clock in the morning when the Rebels opened with artillery and skirmishing. The artillery battle did not cease throughout the day ending only after dark, about 9:00 PM. The heat was intense that day and water was at a premium. Late in the day, about four o'clock the Confederates tried to assault Malvern Hill with the heaviest charges. The Confederates desperately attempted to charge across an open field and up Malvern Hill, only to be repulsed with severe losses. The most severe fighting was on the Union left, and Gen. Porter's Corps took the brunt of it. Each of the seven days of fighting had seemed like the worst that the soldiers had ever encountered up to that time. But the final day, July 1, was truly the worst.

The Sharpshooters on the right stayed forward as skirmishers until their ammunition was expended; late in the day, because of their forward position, they were withdrawn by a circuitous route to the rear. (Stevens, page 147) The worst fighting was on the left, and the Sharpshooters there took serious casualties that day. The Rebel cannonade finally ceased. Then the troops lying on the field knew the infantry attack would be coming soon. Strangely, there would be silence just before such an assault - a moment between when the cannon ceased and when the opposing infantry was moved into position, readied, and ordered to charge. Then with a shout the Rebels would burst out of the woods into the open and a continuous roar of musket fire would announce that the battle had begun. And then the killing would begin in earnest.

No Rebel infantry assaults reached the top of Malvern Hill; all assaults were stopped by massed double-shotted cannon fire, by infantry musket fire, and by continuous heavy cannonading from the gunboats on the James River. And yet, the Rebels came again and again until they could come no more. The 1st Regiment lost four men killed, and nine wounded, (Marcot, page 50) with all the casualties from companies E, F, and K. From a defensive point of view, Malvern Hill was a perfect Union position, a hill heavily crowned with artillery and soldiers in depth. Even Gen. Lee had seen the futility of attacking such a position, but was unable to recall in time the orders he had issued to attack. These orders had been issued earlier in the day in preparation for overwhelming the Union Army, before Lee had personally reconnoitered the Union position. The Federal soldiers pulled out of Malvern Hill late during the night and fell back on Harrison's Landing and the safety of the gunboats.

The *Spaulding* was already at Harrison's Landing awaiting it next cargo wounded soldiers. Mary's diary entries continue:

> Tuesday, July 1
> At Harrison bar, and it looks like war. The northern shore is covered with men and horses, army wagons and mules. At 11 recd ordered to go up above City Point [now the city of Hopewell]. We passed the "Monitor" were told on passing City Point that the passengers must go below. Mattresses were piled up to the wheel house, Gor went on deck and I went for him. We came to Carter's landing and in P.M. Gor and I and Miss W. went ashore and carried tea, lemonade and crackers, we worked till ½ - 6. Terrible – came back tired. At 11 the stores are being put back on the ship. What for we don't know. The shore looks beautiful. We have seen the shells bursting and heard canon, and seen the flash from the sarise [?] we do not know where it is but supposed at Fort Darling. Jim is with us yet and not well.

THE BATTLE IS OVER

McClellan had one last crisis to be met. As his army filed off Malvern Hill during the night, McClellan left Gen. A. W. Averell and the Third Pennsylvania Cavalry to hold back the Confederates from attacking his forces while they were being withdrawn to Harrison's Landing. On the morning of July 2, a dense morning fog obscured the fact that the Union cannon no longer crowned Malvern Hill. Gen. Averell kept up a show of cavalry horses moving to and fro, giving the appearance that fresh artillery was being bought up to the hilltop. And only with a great show of reluctance did Averell agree to a two-hour truce so the Confederates could bury their dead; and to an additional two hour extension. Just as the truce expired, Frank's Battery arrived to support Averell and also brought the news that the Army of the Potomac was safe at Harrison's Landing. Averell rejoined the main body. Averell had not lost a man that momentous day!

More wounded Union soldiers were left on the field to the mercies of the Confederates. In the weighing of claims after a battle as to: Who won the battle? And who lost? A simple test determines the winner. The test is, <u>Who holds the ground on which the battle was fought</u>? By this measure, since the Union Army vacated the battlefield after dark, the Union Army lost the Battle of Malvern Hill. But after seven days of continuous fighting, Gen. Lee and the Confederate Army were in no position to attack again; his own troops were worn out from the same seven days of fighting, and as the attacking force, his soldiers had sustained heavier losses than those sustained by the Army of the Potomac. This was the first truly great battle of the Civil War. It was the longest battle to date, fought continuously for over seven days. A greater number of soldiers were involved than had been in any previous battle to date. And a greater number of casualties occurred as a result of this prolonged battle. Richmond became one huge hospital, for wounded Confederates as well as for the captured wounded Union soldiers.

Wednesday, July 2
Found ourselves this morning at the same place we were yesterday morn. News are that the men we were with yesterday are in the hands of the enemy and our forces have fallen back near here. We hope it is not true, but fear. The report says also that the rebels have batteries planted below us during the night. Well! Have we not the Monitor and several good gun boats. We have 10 wounded on board ... (Mrs. Mary Willett diary, per date)

On shore at Harrison's Landing with the 1st USSS,

On the afternoon of July 2nd, a heavy rain fell lasting all night, making the ground very wet and muddy, causing the greatest discomfort to the weary troops who were mostly without shelter, tents, or blankets, with little or nothing to eat; who in consequence were anxious to get into comfortable camps so as to obtain the rest so greatly needed, also to provide for the sick and disabled ...

On July 3rd, the troops were brought hurriedly into line, crowding the entire plain, and kept standing for hours half-way to their knees in deep mud - - virtually stuck fast - - exposed for a time to the rapid shelling of a Rebel battery that had run up a hill behind us ... " (Stevens, page 156) [This was Jeb Stuart and his cavalry].

Thursday, July 3
At Harrison's Bar. This morning we attended to the men and went on the Hurricane deck. Miss W. was with the men till noon. We heard cannon firing and saw shell burst, Four gun boats have been up the river, where we were Tuesday, and the Monitor and another are down the river shelling the bank. The whole army is said to be near us and the boats and unloading army stores. We have one very sick man here he cannot live – Shot in the neck and his whole body paralyzed. We now have 12. Mrs. B. and myself have been with the men this P. M. and all of us this eve ... We have come to another wharf – Gor brought me a little Secesh Chicken. (Mrs. Mary Willett diary, per date)

On July 4, 1862, Lt. Floyd Abram Willett, Adjutant, Berdan's Sharp Shooters, letter of resignation was accepted and he was forwarded $280.44 in pay for May 1, 1862, until July 4, 1862 (Special Orders 196, Headquarters, Army of the Potomac, Camp near Morrison's Landing, Virginia). According to a deposition signed by Lt. Col. Ripley, on August 15, 1863, at Rutland, Vermont, 1st Lt. Willett was "a gallant and in all respects capable officer - he was mustered out for disability." (Letter dated August 15, 1863, signed Lt. Col. Ripley)

Friday, July 4
Independence Day but we do not have the privilege of spending it in Richmond as we talked, or with friends at home which would be far better ... At 10 Gor came for me to go ashore ... we went to visit the plantation of Mr. Selden. He took us about the garden and grounds which are very fine. We brought back a few flowers to press saw a very old monument in the garden, The place is called Westover.

Saturday, July 5
We arrived at Fortress at 7 this morn where we took on 50 men which makes 420 some quite sick. [Sailed for New York]. (Mrs. Mary Willett diary, per date)

On July 7, 1862, Floyd Abram Willett was discharged from the army because of illness.

By July 7, 1862, it became obvious that the Army of the Potomac's encampment at Harrison's Landing on the James River was a poor choice of location for such a huge and concentrated force. The ground was low, the heat oppressive, and there were hosts of flies swarming, causing great discomfort to Northern troops unused to the weltering Southern climate. Eight Sharpshooters died from either their wounds or disease while encamped at Harrison's Landing. "They were buried low in the shade of the deep wood by their remaining comrades. Parting salutes were fired over their graves. Gray blankets were their only shroud, with a network of branches below and above them, then covered with earth." (Marcot, page 52)

On July 8, President Lincoln came from Washington by steamer and reviewed Major General McClellan's Army of the Potomac at Harrison's Landing by moonlight. President Lincoln was appalled by the large numbers of dead and wounded.

The *Spaulding* had arrived in New York on July 7. A woman who had boarded in Virginia with her husband, gave birth to a daughter on July 7. "Miss Whetten and I did not of course know what to do." A doctor was found to assist with the delivery. Jim Willett was with them. On July 8, Gordon, Mary and Jim visited Barnum's Museum. On July 10, Mary wrote, "Jim is quite sick. Wrote to Nettie." That day they also learned that Mary's cousin Charlie Bennett had been wounded and was in a hospital in Baltimore.

Gordon and Mary sailed from New York at 9 on July 11.

Saturday, July 12
Arrived at Fortress Monroe at noon and about 4 left to come up the river about 9 were ordered by the gun boats to anchor and wait till morning. (Mrs. Mary Willett diary, per date)

They had cruised to Newport News Point and began to run up the James River when they were stopped by the Union gun boats on station below Jamestown.

Sunday, July 13
Started about 4 accompanied by gun boats. Gor and I stayed in the pilot house till 6. Expected a salute at Ft. Powhatan but heard nothing. At 7 arrived at Westover. (Mrs. Mary Willett diary, per date)

HEADQUARTERS, WESTOVER, HARRISON'S LANDING, 1862
"The Photographic History of the Civil War", 10 volumes
Vol. One, page 335

On July 14, 1862, General Halleck ordered a retrograde movement of General McClellan's Army of the Potomac to support General Pope's activities in northern Virginia.

Monday, July 14
[We] were kindly recd by the cap – shown over the boat all the parts were explained –- Jim went to the reg't tonight with Guard – we called at the *Wilson Small*.

Tuesday, Jul 15
... Gor has gone nearly all day and Jim came

back with him. (Mrs. Mary Willett diary, per date)

Mrs. Mary Willett took on an additional task, that of teaching some of the contrabands to read.

Wednesday, July 16
... heard the contrabands read down on the lower deck which is the coolest place on other ship. McClellan's tent is in sight of us just on shore. We had another storm this eve ... There is a report that 6,000 rebels are on the south side of the river. Have heard we are to go to White House for our wounded prisoners, in rebel hands.

Thursday, July 17
Colonel Berdan took dinner with us today also Dr. Winslow, Chaplain of the 44th N. Y. .... Tonight Moses asked me to read to him from the testament. (Mrs. Mary Willett diary, per date)

On July 18, Sila Bennett of Utica wrote to her niece, Mrs. Mary Willett, speaking of her concern for her son, Charlie Bennett:

Utica, July 18th, 1862

Dear Mary,
Your last letter from NY came safely with Mary's and Allie's. You need never hesitate to tell me what you hear of poor Charlie [Bennett]. The reality can not be worse that the suspense. We looked for poor Charlie till my heart was ready to give up still he did not come home and all we come hear was that he was wounded in the foot. I feared the Rebels had him and I cannot tell you what I didn't fear till Sunday we received a letter dated Harrison's Landing July 5th telling us how he was. You may imagine how thankful I was. I must tell you how we come to think Charlie was in Baltimore. Dr. Landon was hurt you probably know at the battle of Hanover C. H. well somehow he got away by the way of the White House and wrote from Newport News to Mary that he saw Charlie on Friday June 29 going with his regiment to battle he had not been very well, of course I was glad to get any news. We heard nothing more till 4th of July in the New York Herald Charlie's name was among the wounded. I took one long breath, every day we saw the

papers the wounded sent away but one name was always left out, so it was Tuesday afternoon July 8th Mary received a telegraph from Dr. Landon dated Baltimore Hospital saying Charlie was wounded in the foot, direct letters to Baltimore. Well, I was goose enough to think it was on Charlie's account the Telegraph was sent, and looked for a letter, and looked. Then I was sure he was sick and so I stewed till I was sick. Mary and Will began to think by Thurs Charlie was not there. The Dr had Tel on his own account but did not tell me Mary wrote to Bal to find out and Will wrote to Charlie to Fortress Monroe. Sat Mary got a letter from the Dr. Saying he knew nothing of Charlie but what he had seen in the papers. I was vexed enough, what did I care where the dr. was, he might be in Jericho for all we (cared). Mary kept saying, Mother the Tel was sent to me, not to you, well suppose it was what do you care where the Dr is if Charlie is not with him but Sunday morning Charlie's letter came and I left abusing the Dr. I had one comfort out of it that my boy was so near home and probably well cared for. Mary thought I had no reason to complain.

 I think it is too bad McClellan could not have taken Richmond, it would seem some compensation for all our losses to have that contemptible City put where she could do no more mischief, but I do not despair God rules, the right we must have, and our cause is surely a great one, but when is the end, and how much more must we suffer God only knows ...

[Here follows news from Mary's home]

 We want to hear from you much again. I begin to fear for you going up James River. The Rebels have got so mad there is no knowing what they may do if they could.

 Mary I am heart sick for the suffering through our whole land it is all in mourning. Have we not suffered enough, are we not humbled enough, will not God accept the sacrifice and heal this broken people. I feel to cry day and night that he would spare us more bloodshed and save our country remember me to your husband and may God bless and keep you is the prayer of your ever affectionate

Aunt S. Bennett

 Mary Willett was continuing her instruction of the recently freed slaves who where on board the ship.

Friday, July 18
... On going to give the contrabands their lessons I found Mr. Norris there to assist me. I promised to go down again tomorrow. Had two new scholars and a very great interest is manifested. Jim is here. Expects to go to the Regt. Tomorrow.

Saturday, July 19
... went down at 4 to "my school" as the boys call it. Miss Whetten went, also Mr. Winslow and three others, so I have plenty of help. Col. Berdan dined with us again today.

Sunday, July 20
... Have not been well today but attended to school and went on deck, and am some better tonight. Gor has been quite anxious about Jim. (Mrs. Mary Willett diary, per date)

Here the Mrs. Mary (Yates) Willett dairy ended. How much longer they stayed with the Sanitary Commission is not clear.

At some point in July, 1862, the Sharpshooters sent four officers who had been wounded in battle but were considered fit enough to travel, to recruiting duty in the north. Captain A. M. Willett was one of these officers. After several weeks these officers wrote to their commander that they had not recruited one man owing to their own continued ill health. (Marcot, page 55)

On August 10, the elusive General Thomas J. Jackson slipped behind Pope's Union lines and wreaked havoc on the rear supply depot of General Pope.

On August 14, 1862, the 1st USSS turned in their knapsacks and everything else possible to decrease what they would have to carry on their backs during the forced march. The Sharpshooters began the seventy-mile land route march from Harrison's Landing to Newport News. They marched to Charles City Courthouse, through the woods and fields and across the Chickahominy River, to reach Williamsburg, Virginia, past Warwick County Courthouse, and then to the encampment at Newport News, arriving there on August 19. The farther they moved away from Harrison's Landing the more their physical condition improved. On the march they had access to fresh vegetables, and fresh air. Eventually they reached their destination of Camp Butler, at Newport News point. Camp Butler had become a huge Union depot and transit point that had been built on the open farm land when overcrowding became a problem at Fortress Monroe. At Newport News point the 1st USSS embarked on board transports on August 21. The steam propelled transports moved through Hampton Roads, past Fortress Monroe and the rip-raps, continuing northward into the Chesapeake Bay, turned northwestward up the Potomac River. On the very next morning, they arrived at Aquia Creek, Virginia, and the rail head which terminated there.

The steamships drew too much water at Aquia Creek, so everyone was transferred to small boats for the trip ashore. Once ashore, they took rail cars to Falmouth, twelve miles further south, and then began their westward march towards Barnett's Ford and the sound of cannon and battle off in the distance. On the twenty-fourth they were on the Warrenton Pike; on the twenty-fifth they were near the river; on the twenty-sixth they passed Barnett's Ford, and on the twenty-seventh, after a hard march of 20 miles, they arrived at Warrenton Junction where they camped in an open field. (Stevens, page 175)

In the dark of the evening of the twenty-eighth, at 9:30 PM they drew rations for three days, and received orders to march at 1:00 AM. Promptly at one, Col. Berdan began to march but there were sleeping soldiers everywhere. There was much grumbling and cursing as the Sharpshooters woke the sleeping units spread across their path. Unfortunately for Col. Berdan, the 1st USSS, and for the previously sleeping troops, the order to begin the march had actually been countermanded but, as so often happens in the fog of war, Berdan had not been notified of the change. The order to march was now changed to 3:00 AM, and at that hour there was a perfect traffic jam of units on the move - all heading to Bristoe Station. The Sharpshooters arrived at Bristoe Station sometime between 10:00 and 12:00 AM on August 28.

SECOND BULL RUN AND DAWKINS' BRANCH

On August 29, both the 1st and 2nd Regiments of the Sharpshooters were united and saw action at Dawkin's Branch, suffering two dead and two wounded. This action was on the extreme left of the Union line of battle and the 1st USSS were part of Gen. Fitz-John Porter's Corps. However, the worst fighting of the Second Battle of Bull Run was (fortunately for the Sharpshooters) some distance away where Gen. Jackson's II Corps had attacked Gen. Gibbon's Division while it was strung out on the march. Gen. Pope refused to believe that a Confederate Army was so close and in such strength and discounted reports of the Sharpshooters that the

Confederates were indeed in force. Most of the day, the Sharpshooters were with Gen. Butterfield's brigade on the extreme left of Gen. Porter's V Corps. Gen. Pope's disbelief of the strength and position of the Confederate forces under Gen. Jackson and later under Gen. Longstreet, led Gen. Pope to court martial Gen. Porter and end the career of a capable and dedicated Federal officer.

BATTLE OF GROVETON

On August 30, at the Battle of Groveton, General Porter's V Corps was outflanked by General Longstreet's artillery and suffered heavy casualties. Berdan's 1st Regiment of Sharpshooters deployed forward as skirmishers and in front of Gen. Butterfield's brigade. Thus began a desperate day for the Union forces. The Union brigades making frontal assaults on the waiting Confederates were terribly shot up by the defending lines of Rebel forces. Yet more and more Federal assaults were made on Gen. Jackson's position. To the credit of Union soldiers and in the face of an insurmountable Confederate defensive position, the attacking Union forces nearly reached the Rebel flags. It was a desperate fight on both sides. The Confederates deployed the last of their reserves to repel the Union attack. Both armies were spent, and although the Union forces fell back from the field of battle, the Rebels were too weak from the battle to press their advantage. The 1st USSS felt the full brunt of Gen. Longstreet's flank attack that day. Col. Berdan's two regiments were out in front as skirmishers just ahead of Col. Roberts' Brigade of infantry. About noon, they were ordered to advance through the woods to their front and engage the Confederate forces that they were to find to their front. Instead of enemy forces in the open, as they emerged from the woods, a railway cut provided defensive protection to the much larger Confederate forces.

Col. Berdan went to Col. Roberts and told him that it was impossible to advance further without more support. (Stevens, page 185) In the afternoon, the skirmishers were ordered forward; they moved to within three hundred yards of the railway cut, where the superior fire of the Confederates pinned them down in a shallow ditch. (Stevens, page 187) The Union infantry began a charge, and as they reached the skirmishers, the Sharpshooters raised up and joined the charge, only to have the charge broken up by massed Rebel volleys, and the order to fall back was given. The 2nd Sharpshooters lost forty-two men at Bull Run, including those captured. To give an idea of the hazardous service that the

Sharpshooters were called upon to perform, on August 10, 1862, at Falmouth, there were between 600 and 700 in the 2nd Regiment. At the first roll call after the battle at Bull Run, taken near Alexandria, Virginia, on September 2, 1862, only 127 sharpshooters answered when their names were called. (Stevens, page 188) The 1st Sharpshooters lost sixty-five men including nine killed, out of 290 present. (Stevens, page 189)

On September 1, they were ordered back to their original starting point of five months previous at Fort Corcoran, near Washington.

The following is a fragment written by Floyd Abram Willett, presumably to Gordon Willett, about this time:

No date

... Heard from Jimmy yesterday. He was in the hospital in Annapolis, Md. Sick with ague and fever, He was detailed to help the wounded from Manassas and has been there since. Milan saw the governor, but can do nothing as there are no vacancies. Milan is in the south part of the State at work, but fears of the draft have passed. He finds it hard recruiting. Julia [Milan's wife] and the children are at Jane's [Gordon's sister, Jane Smith Cummings, in Kalamazoo, Michigan] yet but will start for home on Monday ... Anna is about as usual. Consider is 1st Sergt in New York State Normal School Company composed mostly of students in the School.

Yours truly,
F. A. Willett

At this time, most likely, two of the Willett brothers were in Michigan recruiting, and Jim was in the hospital.

"On September 12, what was left of the 1st Regiment of Sharpshooters, 14 officers and 411 men, departed Washington for the field under the command of Captain John Isler." (Marcot, page 57) They marched through Washington, D. C., and onto the Frederick Pike winding their way into western Maryland, towards the range of low Catoctin Mountains which are part of the Allegheny Mountains.

On September 14, General McClellan broke through Crampton's Gap at the Battle of South Mountain. The 1st USSS caught up with the main body of the Army on the sixteenth.

SHARPSBURG

On September 16, 1862, the 1st Regiment of Sharpshooters occupied the center line of battle, and Captain Willett's Company was at the battle of Antietam (Sharpsburg) where the 1st Regiment surprisingly only lost one man being held in reserve most of the day. "At Antietam the First Regiment of Sharpshooters were held in reserve with other troops of their corps, being at times under heavy artillery fire, holding a perilous position during the entire engagement in protecting the center and supporting the batteries" (Stevens, page 202). Berdan's 2nd Regiment of Sharpshooters did not fare as well, and saw much action in the notorious cornfield, losing 66 men killed and wounded. It is not clear from the official record whether or not Captain Milan Willett was with his company at Antietam.

On September 17, Gen. Lee and the whole Confederate Army waited upon Gen. McClellan to renew the contest. But the infantry divisions of the Army of the Potomac had been fought out in the worst single day loss of dead and wounded of the entire Civil War. Union units were scattered, and the various Union Corps were not "in proper condition" to renew the attack so soon (Stevens, page 200). During the night of the eighteenth, and morning of the nineteenth, Bobby Lee and the Army of Northern Virginia crossed the Potomac River, and thus ended the Confederate invasion of the North.

BOTELER'S (BLACKFORD) FORD

"On September 19 and 20, the 1st Regiment of Sharpshooters ... were involved in heavy forays and skirmishes around Sharpsburg" (Marcot, page 58). Gen. Porter had ordered the First Sharpshooters to cross into Virginia at Blackford's Ford, where during heavy skirmishing they crossed the ford under fire and captured four cannon (Stevens, page 207). Company I 1st USSS pushed ahead and followed the retreating Confederates until were met by a superior force from Gen. Lawton's Brigade, C.S.A. As the Confederates charged the Sharpshooters fell back and soon the Confederates had retaken their lost guns. Gen. Jackson, was not about to leave his cannon on this or any other field.

On the twentieth, the 118th Pennsylvania Regiment ("Corn Exchange") was pushed back from their forward position on the Virginia side to a high bluff where murderous Confederate fire kept them from crossing. The 1st US Sharpshooters moved towards the sound of the fighting and from their position on the Maryland side of the Potomac River, they laid down a protecting fire.

On October 2, Lieutenant Colonel Caspar Trepp of the Sharpshooters noted that Company I, had been organized in Michigan with 93 enlisted men, which had only 51 remaining, and that Captain A. M. Willett and all officers were absent sick (Marcot, page 61). Based upon the soon to be issued medical discharge of Private James W. Willett, also of I Company, Private Willett was most likely still in the hospital in Annapolis. And Adjutant Floyd A. Willett had also departed (or been replaced) by George Marden as Adjutant in October, 1862.

On October 3, President Lincoln visited the camp of the 1st USSS. It would have been a pleasant diversion, except the men were kept out in a hot sun for three hours (Stevens, page 211).

Gen. McClellan may have rightly criticized Gen. Halleck for the lack of any congratulations due the Army of the Potomac for stopping the Confederate invasion. But Lincoln thought Gen. McClellan too slow to pursue and not aggressive enough in the attack. So on November 7, 1862, Major General McClellan was relieved as Commander of the Army of the Potomac and replaced with Gen. Ambrose Burnside.

Either Gordon Willett's health, or a re-organization within the Sanitary Commission caused his departure. For whatever reason, by October 1862, Gordon was back in Michigan, where he was able to rest and recovery. His brother Abram, who was in Kalamazoo, Michigan, wrote the following fragment:

Kalamazoo
October 9th, 1862

If you're coming this way, bring mother. Lydia is worse ...

F. A. Willett

On October 10, Gen. Stuart began his justly famous cavalry raid into Maryland. The futile pursuit of Jeb Stuart delayed any movement of the Union forces into Virginia.

On October 19, James W. Willett wrote to Gordon A. Willett the following, urging him to return to Washington to join him in the business of sutlering:

Armory Square Hospital
October 19th 1862

Gor, I would not advise you to stay in Mich one more week after you become strong enough to come this way. You wished to know how a furnishing business would pay and all I have to say is that as far as I have knowledge and I have been around a good deal, that it is the best business in this city. Everything in the line of Military is in good demand and brings extravagant prices. With a capital not very much extensive the business would warrant one or two hundred dollars per month and that is much better than anything in Mich can or will afford. There is a pretty good sight here for most any kind of business paying around 40 to 100 dollars pr month if one is right sharp. Every time I read about the *S. R. Spaulding* I think of Cheese wish we had a few more such chances.

I saw Mr. Knap on the walk the other day but was with the Col and did not stop to talk to him. They are carrying on quite a sanitary business in the city. The Col seems to be as good to me as a little dog after he has been kicked a few times and brought to know how and where etc. I guess he is going to help me all he can if so I am hopeful I will come out fifty cents above par. I shall not hold a commission a great while I'll bet you and will be ready to go into business with you and if I should have a little more good luck financially speaking I will be able to put in half a thousand. Not a very big pile but does pretty well for Him to Commence on especially in these times when there is such a chance to make as well as to spend a few dimes. I have never seen Brownald yet but I saw his clerk who told me he had often spoke about me and sayed he was owing me and would pay it when he saw me. I went and got some goods of his brother the same day we left Harrisons for Mager [the Major?] and made five dollars just to pay expenses on the road while we were coming to this place and it just lasted me though have spent considerable since coming here and guess I must make about ten this week to pay back expenses for it wont answer to run behind when on light pay although I suppose I am getting 24 per month excluding clothing. I suppose I shall see Abram ere long. I had a letter from Mrs. Burdick and friend mailed the same time as yours. They were both first rate and all the news I got this day pretty good save the health of Miss Germain which I hope will be better the next I hear from her as I have not heard in about two months and

I don't know as I shall in two to come. I have written twice and think I will hold up for a year or two and see if she will find time to ans the ones already written if she don't I'm sure I will not have to hear such news from Edie. It is really bad that he should use Jose for a Breeder although it may be a mistake but one that has been to Cal ought to know how to travel and not get on a bust. But if it has got to be so be it. I'm glad It naut my case and I'm sorry its Josies. My best respects to all and love too Mary My much loved sister in whom I'm well pleased.

                                                As Ever Your Jim

G. A. Willett
Muir Mich

    Miss Germain was Mary Annette Germain, called Nettie, whom James Willett would later marry.
    On October 21, 1862, F. A. Willett wrote to his brother, Gordon asking for his help in securing a recommendation for a position in Washington:

                                      Detroit 21st Oct 62

Gordon
    Enclosed you will find a "recommendation etc" already signed by Chas. S. ___ of Kal[amazoo], Republican Candidate for Lieut. Gov. which I wish endorsed by Zach Chandler as he is to speak at Ionia on Friday this week. I would like you to get him to sign it in some form. You can get Tower or Albert Williams or Alonzo Sessions to present the matter to him if you can not. He is out of town today or I would see him myself. I expect to leave here tonight for Washington and I want it there as soon as you can get it there.
    Milan is here. Came this morning. He has been recalled but will send on his resignation again and certificate. I shall take it on for him and press matters to a close for him. Now be sure and see that this paper is presented to Chandler for his Signature if nothing more.
    I do not know whether Milan will go out home before his resignation is accepted or not. He did not know. Send your letters to me at Washington D. C. Milan says Jimmy is there yet. I shall try and see him the first thing.

In Haste
Your etc
F. A. Willett

On October 30, the depleted 1st USSS broke camp near Sharpsburg; on November 2, they were at Snicker's Gap in the Blue Ridge Mountains. Thus ends the Willett participation in the story of the 1st US Sharpshooters.

From the pension records, it appears that Floyd Abram Willett received the commission as Major, but never raised a company. The next two years he was in Washington working for the Treasury Department. He was referred to in family correspondence as "Colonel". (It was not just the Southerners who had such informal promotions to Colonel.)

The following was written by F. A. Willett to his brother Gordon Willett on (November) 3, 1862:

[Piece of letter missing]
Washington, (November) 3rd, 1862

I re[a]d your letter with recommend Enclosed on Saturday, it having been mislaid in the P. O. and advertised before I got it although I called twice every day. Jimmy has written to you all the news that I can think of. He says there are some very good openings here for business. If you come I would not bring Mary till you get settled here. Board is $25.00 per month at least. $6.00 per week. Jimmy is trying to get loose. I don't know whether he will make it or not. News of no special importance. If you come you will find Jimmy at Armory Square Hospital. I am stopping at Mr. Moore's yet. My compliments to all my friends.

Write soon and oblige
Yours
F. A. Willett

Captain A. Milan Willett's resignation of his commission was accepted on November 8, 1862, due to his ill health. (*Michigan Volunteers, 1861-1865*, page 134)

Private James W. Willett was honorably discharged on November 22, 1862. He was issued a "Certificate of Disability for Discharge" by reason of chronic diarrhea. (Certificate dated November 15, 1862, signed by Surgeon, Dr. Moss, Armory Square Hospital, Washington, D. C.)

Between campaigning and the severe extremes of Virginia weather which attacked a Northern soldier's body with various maladies, all three Willett brothers were physically unfit for continued military service. The brothers each left the service and returned home to Michigan or went into business in Washington. Collectively, they had participated in some of the worst battles of 1862 (Seven Days, Second Bull Run, Groveton).

By December, 1862, James Willett had become a sutler to a New York regiment. On December 15, 1862, he wrote to his brother Gordon about Fredericksburg:

> Falmouth, Dec 15th 1862
>
> Bro Gor,
> This is the first opportunity I have had since leaving Washington. We had an awful rough time getting through. Was six days on the road and I got one of the colds not very conducive to good health in general. We had a severe snub in this fight. Our loss was very heavy. Saw most of the fight. If there be any letters for me send them by Mr. Brownald. Have you got the money for the watches yet. I have sold three watches.
> We have sold nearly all our goods. It is mighty rough this time out. No good sight at present. although there may be if the Army go into winter quarters here part of them have been paid. They have lots of tobacco in Fredericksburg I have not heard from Consider yet.
> Has Abram got his position and is Herbert in Washington yet. Write all the news. My best wishes to all.
>
> As ever yours
> Bro J. W. Willett

At the time of this letter, James and Gordon were in partnership in the sutler business, and Herbert Lockwood Yates, Mary's brother, was on his way from Michigan to clerk for them. Herbert Yates would die of illness at home in Ionia, Michigan, in March, 1863.

By 1863, the draft was in effect. Mary joined Gordon in Washington. On May 19, 1863, Gordon Willett wrote the following to Gilbert Yates, Mary's younger brother in Ionia, Michigan urging him to join them in Washington:

> No. 448 6th Bet E & F
> Washington D. C.
> May 19th, 1863

Gilbert,
I have not time just now to write you a letter, although I would like to do so.
We are very much in need of one or two clerks. I have just written John Sessions and offered him $26 pr month and expenses to commence and to come immediately if possible. If you wish to, and can come I will give you the same, or $5. More pr month and pay your fare if you stay a few months. This will give you a chance to come here and see the sights as well as the country and Army, although you might get a chance to see all these otherwise, in the course of a few weeks, for instance, as traveling agent for Uncle Sam with full furnishing, knapsack, Haversack, Canteen, Blankets, Musket, etc - at $13 and expenses all pd.

Now Gilbert I want you to come if you feel disposed, immediately after you have consulted with your father and mother and obtained their full consent. I have no doubt you would like the business and we will do well by you if you come and do well, which I have no doubt you would if you would come. Please don't make any delay whatever if you conclude to come, as time is money just now. If you can possibly Telegraph me next Saturday, or at least next Monday, whether you can come or not and when you will start, do so, or even Tuesday or Wednesday if this letter should be delayed.

If you come, don't wait for clothes, as time is worth much more than clothes just now. If you don't come write me, after you Telegraph, to me at 448 6th St, Between E and F.

Yours etc
G. A. Willett

G. S. Yates
Ionia, Mich

P.S. Mary is well and will write tomorrow.

(Back Page)
Dear Brother,
If you come, bring my trunk, that you had, with my spreads, bed quilts 1 pair of white blankets, and my picture, Woman and Child and the frame that had Mr. and Mrs. Liptrott's picture in, and rose that Mary

B. gave me. put your clothes in the same trunk. If they are not ready I will attend to them when you come, and while you stay.

Your affectionate
Sister Mary

P.S.

And also if you can get my large Dictionary, Glee Book and Family Testament at Milan's in my trunk of books - it is locked but they can open it some way i.e. if you can send for them without detaining you – don't delay on that acct.

(The picture mentioned in the above letter had been painted by Mary and had been much admired by family and friends).

Gilbert Yates followed up on this request and joined the Willett brothers and his sister in Washington.

On August 26, 1863, Julia and Alfred Milan Willett wrote from Ionia County, Michigan to Gordon and Mary Willett in Washington, D. C:

August 26, 1863

Dear Friends Mary and Gordon,

Your last epistles were received and read by us all with pleasure ... Jimmy made us an unexpected visit for which we were very thankful that is for the small part we enjoyed of it for some way or other there was a strong attraction for him towards the North Pole in consequence of which we could not keep him here very long at a time. Isn't strange how these young chaps will act ... I have not seen the Yates people since we were there with Jimmy have heard your mother was going east. I hope to see her before she goes.

Cases folks are well. Mother is well. She has not gone east to work in the County house yet. Thinks two dollars a week small pay. Jimmy has probably told you of the offer made her by Mrs. Mann. Cummings folks have met with quite a loss in the burning of their barns. Have they moved I am sorry for them ...

Milan ... is just full of mischief as need be and plagues me or tries to all he can but then I rather think I can stand it. Eva and Carrie are very healthy and have been to school already. Carrie reads in the first reader and Eva in the third.

Eva has written you a short letter and will send it in this. How is Abram and Annie? I am looking for a letter from her she had best to set herself to writing or she may hear from me. Give her a bit of my love and tell them the Sunday Chronicle is duly received and read every bit of it. We take the Detroit Tri-Weekly paper Tribune and Advertiser it is called and very good for us. The free press we despise as we do anything of the copperhead stamp. I wish they might all get their just deserts but I am afraid they will not. Some recruiting is going on at Muir and Lyons. Charlie Soule is going in the 10 cavalry today he wore a 1st lieutenant's uniform. Ambrose is recruiting for cavalry
...
Mother sends her love to all accept my love and believe me as ever

Your Sister Julia Willett

P. S. My better half is going to write some Ma says you must write her just as much as though she wrote.

Sunday Evening (continued)
Gordon,
As Julia has left one page for me to write I improve the opportunity. Where is Jim we have heard nothing from him since his departure. We have been somewhat uneasy of late concerning you as we hear of many Sutlers being captured by Mosby gang but we conclude you are all right or we should have heard from you some of you ... I am very busy at present preparing for seeding and Julia has told you all the news .. please write often and let us know how you get along tell Abram to write our love to them and my best respects to Mrs. Rolfe.

Yours A. M. Willett

At this time James ("Jimmy") Willett was engaged in a long-distance courtship of Nettie Germaine who was back in Ionia County, Michigan. James, Abram, Annie, Gordon and Mary were all in Washington, D.C.

On October 11, 1863, Mary E. Willett wrote to her husband Gordon A. Willett who was probably away on sutler business with the Union army:

[Washington, D. C.]
Sunday Oct 11th 1863

My Dear Husband,
I have looked each day for a letter from you but none has as yet been rec'd. I was nearly sick yesterday, but a little better today. We went to church this morning, and I came home and prepared dinner for 10, C. H. [Consider Heath Willett, first cousin to Gordon Willett] is here, and Albert makes no effort to leave, that I can see. Mr. White is sick and will probably be there tomorrow. Mrs. King is able to go down to her meals.

Mother is improving and we "did" the patent office last week.

Jim [Willett] and Gilbert [Yates] came Friday night. I was so disappointed not to have a letter from you, and of course got no consolation from them. You did not care to write you were here so lately, and would be well enough they had sent you for a load of corn. Of course I need not care but could not help it and so had to ___. I wont say what, because it would not sound well to you. Mrs. C. O. Thompson came here and gave Mrs. King, and Perry's wife some information concerning me. Think she had better look at home. It is lonely here without you, when will you come back.

I sleep with Mrs. King now and but for the door bell and people coming in at all times of the night I should sleep very well. Miss Kate Stoddard called here yesterday, and took Mary with her to lunch. Did not ask her to dinner. She tells some large stories. Will tell you when you come, all about it.

We want to get up a party to go down to Mount Vernon while Mother is here, and before Mrs. King leaves if we can. Consider will go if he can know when we go. Dr. Landon has been here stayed till 12 last night and took dinner Thursday. He will go too when we do. Now dearest when will you come so we can go. Mother and Mary think So much of it, and I seeing you. Mary Hayes wants to know how much a Photograph album will cost She wants one Cant you buy one for her if she wishes and send it by Mother. I will write and ask if she wants you to, if you think best. Do come as soon as you can. I want to see you so much. I do hope to get a letter from you in the morning. I have been so tired and nearly sick I could not write for two evening past I wanted to but could not.

I don't know whether Jim will go back in the morning or not, but will direct this as usual. Mother and Mary [Bennett] seem to enjoy themselves very well. Albert bought a very fine Album last eve for 11.50 to send to Hoboken I imagine but I must go and find Mother so good by dearest.

> May God bless and keep you
> and your loving wife
> Mary E. Willett

Mary was Mary Willett's cousin, Mary Bennett of Utica, and Mary Willett's mother was Jane Yates of Ionia, Michigan. They had came together by train from Utica, New York, for a visit and to see the sights.

On February 14, 1864, James Willett wrote to his brother Gordon using the writing paper with the imprint of Lovejoy's Hotel, corner of Park Row and Beekman Street, New York City. James spoke of the 59th New York regiment being uncertain of when they were returning to the field. James had been home to Muir, Michigan, and had attended the funerals of Carley Soule, Mrs. Perrine and Judge Robinson, and said that it was "A Hard blow for Muir". He also speaks of intending to be vaccinated against small pox.

On Sunday June 26, 1864, F. Abram Willett wrote to his wife from Washington, D. C. Evidently, she had returned to either to her home in New York, or to Michigan with her new baby [which she had been born in Washington, D. C.]. Abram complained of the heat, staying in the 90s, and at one point at 100 degrees, and wished for rain. He added, "I must acknowledge to you that I'm not really very well, although not sick - am quite bilious, yet with plenty of lemons and care I hope to keep above board. Had an attack of diarrhea yesterday morn, but have made liberal use of $15.00, Brandy and sugar which seems to have done good service".

On August 1, 1864, F. Abram Willett wrote to his brother Gordon A. using Treasury Department stationery. Gordon and Mary were back in Michigan; Herbert Lockwood Willett had been born there in May.

Washington, August 1, 1864
Bro. G. A.,
Enclosed find a letter I found at the Office on Saturday.
I am in usual health and sweating away like a porpoise. Weather 98 degrees in the shade. Gal-low-vi-us- (sic).

No news from any one. Have not heard from Jim since he left here except by way of others. Had either of you been here you might have got a good chance to operate in the army sutlering. The sutlers are all dipping in largely. Anna and the baby [Jane, born April 12] are getting on finely. Have you been to see the Grape Land yet or do they Keep you tending baby [Herbert, born May 5] most of the time. In haste.

Yours F A. W.

Gordon Willett returned to Washington, D.C., where he wrote on March 12, 1865,

Washington D. C., Sunday, P. M. 12/3/65 [March 12]
Dear Mary,
... Jim, Nettie and Jennie are going to have photographs taken on Jim's 26th birthday - goodbye, God Bless and Keep You. G.

Undated letter from Gordon Willett to his wife, Mary written about this time from Washington, D. C:

Eve 7 O'clock
Have not attended church today as I anticipated - weather is very fine and quite mild - large flocks of wild Geese were flying north last eve, so we look for spring weather - all well here - Jim came up this morning - don't know how long to stay - am progressing in all matters satisfactorily - shall probably leave here sometime this week for Pa, - Ohio. Perry and his wife were here Friday Eve, had good visit of course - all wished you and baby were here - all send love and kisses. Oscar and family are well. Attended meeting of Mich. Soldier's Relief Ass. Last Eve at Patent Office, - it had pretty much died for want of breath, until a remittance of some over $6,000.00 was rec'd from the good people of Ontonagon Co. Mich. Which had the good effect to resuscitate as well as to astound them, coming as it did from an extreme northern Co. where no one was supposed to have lived.

Well dearest Col. [Abram] Has just brought from the office No. 3 [Mary's letter] of Tuesday Eve 7th inst. For which I will try to repay you by promptness ... Mary E. Willett, Muir, Ionia Co. Mich, In Christ I remain your husband. G. A. Willett.

On April 6, 1865, Gordon wrote to Mary:

>Washington D. C.
>Thursday 8 ½ P. M. 6/4/65
>
>Dear Mary,
>Yours 28th Ult. (No. 9) was rec'd last eve having been detained somewhere on the route as it came after one (No. 10) written Friday 3rd Ult ... God be praised for his great mercy in dealing with poor mortals like us, together with thousands of other great blessings, companions, in whom we can and do put our whole confidence and trust and have no fear of faithlessness in any degree, believing implicitly that each possesses virtue, integrity and love, sufficient to withstand any and all temptations or combinations which may attack us, and are so liable to be thrown in our paths to lure us to deeds of wrong and change for the paltry and meager enjoyments of a moment, the unlimited bliss and happiness of time and perhaps Eternity. Oh! How great exertion we can and will afford to make in the culture of our Christian virtues, in view of the grand results attainable thereby. May God help us ... Nettie heard from Jim yesterday - he is at City Point and hopes to get to Petersburg or Richmond with his goods. Nettie thinks of starting for Mich. Next week and will probably go if she don't change her mind. Have not consummated that for which I have been waiting for a week or two past, yet hope to this week and so be ready to take my leave of the Capitol this coming week. The excitement created here by the capture of Richmond has somewhat subsided, although not entirely. Monday morn I went to the P. O. about 10 o'clock and found a large crowd in front of the Patent Office on F Street and being addressed by Judge Usher and others and a noisy set they were too - soon after they adjourned and formed procession and marched to the state department and got a short ... (remainder of letter missing).

Gordon wrote to Mary on Thursday, April 13, 1865:

>Washington D. C.
>Thursday 5 P. M. Apl 13th, 65
>
>We were to have started last night but could not

get baggage checked in time - also went down this morning but were too late - overslept and saw Jim Kennedy last eve at the Depot was going to N. Y. Jim is still at City Point - has cleared off and is pleasant and mild ... Your aff[ectiona]t[e] husband in Christ.

Mrs. Mary E. Willett   G. A. Willett

Below is City Point as Jim Willett saw it in 1864.

CITY POINT, 1864
"The Photographic History of the Civil War", 10 volumes
Vol. One, page 133

WILLIAM WILLETT (1769-1844)

Unidentified Regiment QM
1st or 2nd Regiment USSS
(William Styple Collection at
USA Military History Institute)

Pvt. Charles E. Mead
Co F, 1st Regiment USSS
(William Styple Collection at
USA Military History Institute

Col. And Surgeon, A. C. Williams
2nd Regiment USSS
(Div. of Military and Naval Affairs, NYS Adjt. Gen. Office,
Albany, NY at
USA Military History Institute

1888 SHARPSHOOTER REUNION AT GETTYSBURG

The Twenty-fifth Anniversary of the Civil War commenced in April, 1886. "Thousands of members of the grand Army of the Republic and thousands of Confederate Veterans, met at sites of the battles in which they had fought twenty-five years earlier" (Marcot, page 320). July 1, 1888, saw another encampment of the veterans of the Grand Army of Republic (G. A. R.) at Gettysburg, Pennsylvania.

1890 BOSTON ENCAMPMENT

In 1890, the Grand Army of the Republic held its encampment at Boston. It was here that 200 charter members of Berdan Sharpshooters formed the Association of Berdan's Sharpshooters. General Berdan was elected the first president.

CHAPTER SEVEN

ALFRED MILAN WILLETT (1829-1906)

OF IONIA COUNTY, MICHIGAN

I.1.1.7.1a
MILAN WILLETT SMITH (ALFRED MILAN WILLETT)
And **JULIA YAGER**
Of Ionia County, Michigan

Milan Willett Smith (later changed to Alfred Milan Willett) was born April 18, 1829, on a farm at Volney, Oswego County, New York. When he was about 6 months old, his parents moved to Vesper, Onondaga County, New York.

Milan Smith received a common school education in Onondaga County. His father, Alfred Floyd Smith, died in 1844, when Milan was 15, and Milan was apprenticed out to learn the joiners trade in Skaneateles. Eventually, he was able to teach during winters to supplement his income.

In 1850, he made his way to Minnesota and spent a summer at St. Anthony's Falls, now East Minneapolis. In November of the same year, he returned to New York, where he remained until the fall of 1853. His next change of residence was to this state (Michigan), and from his arrival in Ionia County until 1860 he worked at his trade in Muir. In the latter part of that year he bought a farm and abandoned his trade for the life of a farmer (*Portrait and Biographical Album*, 1891, page 772).

Milan Willett Smith married first on September 8, 1852, Julia Yager (b 1832, New York), the daughter of Wendel Yager. The marriage took place at the bride's home.

1859 NAME AND SURNAME CHANGE
MILAN WILLETT SMITH BECOMES
ALFRED MILAN WILLETT

In 1859, Milan Willett Smith, by an Act of the Michigan Legislature, changed his name to Alfred Milan Willett, as did his wife, who became Julia Willett, and their daughters became Eva Willett and Carrie Willett.

In 1860, Alfred M. Willet and family are listed in the Lyons, Ionia County, Michigan census, as follows:

Willet	Alfred M.	head	31	NY	carpenter
	Julia	wife	29	NY	
	Eva M.	daughter	6	NY	
	Carrie	daughter	2	MI	
	Gordon A.	brother	25	NY	clerk
	Hannah	mother	50	NY	

(sic age 50: Hannah was actually 55)

The war broke in upon Mr. Willett's dreams of quiet, rural life, and in 1861 he recruited a company which, in the early months of its career was popularly known as "Willett's Fifth Company of Sharp-Shooters." It was mustered into Colonel Berdan's famous regiment and did a great deal of duty on outposts and as skirmishers. It was one of the six companies of sharpshooters organized in Michigan and of its one hundred and eleven members Ionia County contributed forty-eight, Montcalm thirty, Washtenaw eleven, Eaton seven, Clinton four, St. Joseph three, and Ingham, Wayne, Monroe, and St. Clair each one. The company rendezvoused at Detroit and was mustered into service March 4, 1862. (*Portrait and Biographical Album*, 1891, page 772)

Colonel Hiram Berdan's Regiments "were to be armed with the most reliable rifle then made and to be employed as sharpshooters and skirmishers ...Each Applicant had to pass a shooting test, no men were enlisted who could not put ten bullets in succession within a ten-inch circle at 200 yards at rest and 100 yards off hand." ("Berdan Sharpshooters" undated newsletter)

A. Milan Willett, age 33, enlisted in October, 1861. He entered service as Captain of Company I, 1st U. S. Sharpshooters, on February 5, 1862, at its organization, for three years service. He mustered in on March 4, 1862. Albert Richardson wrote the following: "Indeed Albert Ariel Richardson was my grandfather. He served in Company I starting in November, 1861, The Company received their basic training in Muir, Michigan, at Capt. Willett's home. It was mustered in to the Army of the Potomac in Detroit in February, 1862. They left for Washington, D. C., shortly afterward."

They remained in Camp Instruction until Gen. McClellan began his ill-fated Peninsula Campaign (letter signed Albert Richardson, to Arthur [surname not mentioned], undated letter, courtesy Arthur Ruitberg). Captain Milan Willett suffered greatly at the siege of Yorktown. Matthew G. Callahan wrote, "Our command were exposed a great deal in cold rains during the siege of York Town Va., in the spring of 1862 and Captain Willett, the claimant, was on duty with us and owing to the exposures he endured, he contracted General Rheumatism and Rheumatic Lumbago, and also a difficulty which appeared to cause him a great deal of pain in his left side and in the region of his heart and which I support to be the Plurisa." ("Proof of Disability", dated June 1, 1892, and signed by Matthew G. Callahan; part of Civil War Pension File of A. Milan Willett)

It is uncertain whether or not Captain Willett was at the battle of Antietam (Sharpsburg) where Berdan's Sharpshooters saw much action in the notorious cornfield.

Captain A. Milan Willett resigned his commission on November 8, 1862, due to ill health. (*Michigan Volunteers, 1861-1865*, page 134)

> Captain Willett was in active service thirteen months, when he resigned on account of disability.
>
> After his return from Southern battlefields, Captain Willett made his farm one of the best in the vicinity, rendering it popular by his great success in breeding fine sheep. (*Portrait and Biographical Album*, 1891, page 772)

In 1870, Milan Willett and family are listed in the Township of North Plains, Ionia County, Michigan census, page 10, dwelling 73-75, as follows:

Willett	Milan	head	40	NY	farmer, 16,000
	Julia	wife	37	NY	house keeping
	Eva	daughter	16	NY	at home
	Carrie	daughter	13	MI	at home
	Allia	daughter	3	MI	at home
Coledge	Chas.	NR	12	MI	apprenticed
Willett	Hannah	mother	65	NY	mother at son house

In the 1880 North Plains Township, Ionia County, Michigan census, 10-88-31-7, is listed A. M. Willett and family, as follows:

| Willett | A. M. | | 57 | m | | NY |

Julia	48	f	NY	
Carry	23	f	MI	daughter
Alla	13	f	MI	daughter
Bamborough, J.	28	m	NY	son-in-law
Eva	26	f	NY	daughter
Julia	12	f	MI	d. – l.
Stoddard, Willard	21	m	MI	SI (sic)
Bigelow Alverett	17	m	NY	SI (sic)

(Photograph Courtesy
Of Mr. and Mrs. Robert Willett, Florida)

Julia Willett
Taken in the 1860s

Mr. Willett makes a specialty of breeding American merino sheep, and is more extensively engaged in that business than any other person in the county. (*History of Ionia and Montcalm Counties*, Michigan, John S. Schenck, Philadelphia, D. W. Ensign

and Company, 1881, page 276)

Alfred Milan Willett was Supervisor several terms and president of the agricultural society. In 1881-1882, and 1883-1884, he was a state representative from Ionia County, Michigan.

(Photograph Courtesy
Of Mr. and Mrs. Robert Willett, Florida)

A. Milan Willett
Taken in the 1860s

In 1888, A. Milan Willett was elected a Probate Judge for Ionia County, Michigan; he moved to the county seat, Ionia, and resided there the remainder of his life.

Mrs. Julia (Yager) Willett, age 60 years, 6 months, 16 days, died on January 16, 1894, in Ionia, Ionia County, Michigan of Typhoid and Pneumonia. (State of Michigan, Death Certificate Record Number 2008, of Julia Y. Willett)

PICTURE FROM:
HISTORY OF IONIA COUNTY, MICHIGAN, PAGE 276

A. M. WILLETT.

1. **Eva M. SMITH** (changed in 1859 to **Eva WILLETT**): b September 10, 1853, New York; m in Ionia County, Michigan, on December 20, 1877, James C. Baumborough of Ionia Township, Michigan; d December 6, 1936.

2. **Carrie H. SMITH** (changed in 1859 to **Carrie WILLETT**): b August, 1859, Michigan; m in Ionia County, Michigan, on May 6, 1885, John D. Strachan (b August 10, 1859) of Muir, Ionia County, Michigan.

3. **Alice** ("Allie", "Allia") **J. WILLETT**: b December 1, 1869, Michigan.

I.1.1.7.1b
ALFRED MILAN WILLETT and HARRIET J. NORTHRUP
Of Ionia County, Michigan

Alfred Milan (Smith) Willett, age 62, married second in Saginaw, Saginaw County, Michigan, March 30, 1893, Harriet J. Northrup, age 51, widow of Ruel L. Northrup, the daughter of Evan and Sarah Thomas. Harriet Thomas married Ruel L. Northrup June 14, 1860. Ruel L. Northrop died of consumption September 26, 1875, at Ionia City, Ionia County, Michigan

In 1900, Albert (sic) M. Willett and family are listed at 156 E. Washington Street, Ionia City, Ionia County, Michigan census (31-12-7-8), as follows:

Willett Albert M.	head	Apr 1828	72 NY
Harriett	wife	N/R 1842	58 NY

Alfred Milan Willett, age 76 years, 10 months, 26 days, died in Ionia City, Ionia County, Michigan, March 14, 1906, of heart disease. (State of Michigan, Death Certificate Record Number 7095) At his death, A. Milan Willett was described as a "man of leisure".

Mrs. Harriet Willett filed a Civil War Widow Pension Claim (No. 8455827). She must have become increasingly senile with age, as she had trouble remembering when she was married, and other vital record dates. This inability to recall actual dates caused her much trouble with the Civil War Claims Commission who caught the discrepancies and continually required her to file amended statements in support of her claim to a widow's pension.

(Bookstaver, 1906, page 70; *The Willett Families*, 1985, pages 167-168; *History of Ionia and Montcalm Counties, Michigan*, John S. Schenck, Philadelphia, 1881, page 276; *Michigan Biography*, Volume II, page 449; *Legislative Manual of the State of Michigan for the Year 1883*, Conant, page 522; *Portrait and Biographical Album of Ionia and Montcalm Counties, Michigan*, 1891, pages 771-772; *The Corridor of Years*, Herbert Lockwood Willett, 1967, privately printed, page 3; Civil War Pension File No. 816531, of A. Milan Willett).

NOTE: It is interesting to note that there is a Willett Northrup (born 1802; d October 15, 1869, buried Hindsdale cemetery, Hindsdale, Cattaraugus County, New York) who resided in Dearfield, New York.. Willett Northrup's relationship to the Willett family is unknown.

CHAPTER EIGHT

FLOYD ABRAM WILLETT (1833-1868)

OF STEUBEN COUNTY, NEW YORK

I.1.1.7.3
ABRAM WILLETT SMITH (FLOYD ABRAM WILLETT)
And ANNA HOWELL MINER
Of Wayne, Steuben County, New York

Abram Willett Smith was born November 29, 1833, in Onondaga County, New York. He received a common school education in Onondaga County. His father, Alfred Floyd Smith, died in 1844 when Abram was 11, and Abram was apprenticed out to learn the printer's trade in Virgil, Cortland County, New York. Abram made his home with his uncle Abraham Willett at Blodgetts Mill five miles out of town.

Abram Willett Smith married in Tully, Onondaga County, New York, August 31, 1861, Anna Howell Miner (b March 30, 1836, at New York City, New York; d August 13, 1918, Buffalo, Erie County, New York, at the home of her daughter, Mary. Cremated and buried at Syracuse, New York). When his mother and the rest of his family went to Michigan, Abram Willett Smith remained in New York State and practiced dentistry at Tully and Auburn, Cayuga County, New York.

After a time, Abram Willett Smith came to Muir, Ionia County, Michigan, and opened a dentist office in the home of his brother, Milan Willett. (*The Corridor of Years*, page 4)

1859 NAME AND SURNAME CHANGE
ABRAHAM WILLETT SMITH BECOMES
FLOYD ABRAHAM WILLETT

Between 1859 and 1861, Abram Smith changed his name to Floyd Abram Willett. At the time of his name change, he was living in New York State.

Floyd Abram (Smith) Willett, age 27, of Kalamazoo County, Michigan, answered President Lincoln's call for volunteers, and was commissioned on August 21, 1861, as a First Lieutenant with Company C, 1st U. S. Sharpshooters (Berdan's Sharpshooters). He mustered on August 26, 1861, and was promoted to Adjutant on October 18, 1861. He resigned on June 7, 1862 (*Michigan Volunteers, 1861-1865*, page 120). At the time of enlisting, he was a "sound healthy man ... And that exposure and hardship said Floyd A. Willett in or about the Spring ... contracted in the Service of the United States, Bronchitis and Pulmonary disease." (Deposition signed by A. M. Willett, on January 30, 1872)

(Photograph Courtesy of Mr. And Mrs. Robert Willett of Florida Brady photograph taken in Washington, D.C., 1864)

According to the volume *Michigan in the War*, by John Robertson, Floyd A. Willett was promoted to Major to recruit another regiment. Colonel Berdan gave hime permission to return to Micihgan and recruit another regiment f sharpshooters. The regiment was never completed, but thereafter Abram was always called "Colonel" in family letters of the period (1863-1865).

Due to ill health, Floyd resided his commission. During most of the period after his resignation Floyd Abram Willett worked in Washington, D. C. at the Treasury Department, which was in charge of the sutlers. His specific assignment at the US Treasury Department is unknown.

On January 19, 1866, Floyd A. and Anna Willett were staying with Gordon and Mary Willett, at North Plains, Ionia County, Michigan, when their second child, Mary was born.

Abram returned to Steuben County, New York. However, his health was broken, most likely by campaigning in 1862, and he never truly recovered his health.

Abram Willett's last letter was written on April 13, 1868, and sent to his brother Gordon Willett. It appears that his mother, Hannah, was with him:

> Wayne Steuben Co. N.Y.
> Apr. 13, 1868
>
> Dear Friends,
> I will write you a few lines to let you know of our condition. Anna is quite well and works hard, Both children have hard colds and a good deal of (e)arache, first one then the other. Mother continues as usual. We got Mary's letter a day or two ago. So far as I am concerned, <u>I think</u> I am failing constantly and gradually. Our folks at the other house and I guess Anna have given me up as past help. I do not think that mother has, still she says nothing. But I may linger along a good while and I may go more suddenly, but when I go I have a kind "Heavenly Father" to be my support and help. Should I not be able to write you again, let me assure you of my attachment to all my family and (tha)t my daily prayer is that we may (al)l meet in that celestial Kingdom (whe)re sorrow pain and affliction cometh (no)t but where joy and bliss reign forever. (An)d may we all meet there.
> Should my departure be sudden or otherwise, you will be duly informed (by) telegraph.
> Our kindest and greatest love for you and yours. I remain your Brother in the Lord.

F. A. Willett

(Get this letter to Milan and James if you can. Put in envelope and send to either at Muir and they should do the same for I cannot write much).

Postmarked Penn Yan, N.Y.

Floyd Abram Willett died on June 6, 1868, at Wayne, Steuben County, New York, from bronchitis leading to consumption which had been contracted during his military service. One source, the family Bible, says Floyd died at Keuka, Steuben County. Abram's last letter to Gordon had a heading "Wayne, Steuben County"

Wayne County adjoins Cayuga County, New York, and both have their northern borders on Lake Ontario, and their southern boundaries in the Five Finger Lake District of western New York State.

In 1870, [Mrs.] A[nna]. H. Willett [widow] and family are listed in the Wayne Township, Steuben County, New York census, dwelling 52-52, as follows:

Willett	A. H.	head	33	NY	keeping house
	J. F.	daughter	6	Washington D. C.	
	M. A.	daughter	4	MI	

On November 16, 1873, the Pension Bureau certified Anna H. Willett's claim to a $17.00 per month pension beginning June 6, 18688, and an additional $2.00 per month for each of her children under the age of 16 years. (No. 138,407, Pension Bureau, document)

Mrs. Anna H. Willett, widow, died on August 13, 1918. Her daughter, Jane F. Willett, collected $250.50 Reimbursement from the US Government for her mother's funeral. The following bills were itemized:

32.00	physician
24.00	undertaker's bill
194.50	undertaker's bill

An additional $33.33 was paid for accrued pension due decedent.

(Bookstaver, 1907, page 70; *The Willett Families*, 1985, page 169).

1. **Jane** ("Jennie") **F. WILLETT**: b April 12, 1864, Washington, D. C. Unmarried on July 4, 1918, when she

filed for Reimbursement for her mother's funeral expenses. Residing (1918) at 23 The Westgate, 746 Seventh Street, Buffalo, New York.

2. **Mary** ("Mollie") **A. WILLETT**: b January 19, 1866, North Plains, Ionia County, Michigan.

CHAPTER NINE

GORDON ARTHUR WILLETT (1835-1898)

OF IONIA COUNTY, MICHIGAN

I.1.1.7.4
GORDON ARTHUR SMITH
[GORDON ARTHUR WILLETT]
And MARY ELIZABETH YATES
Of Ionia, Ionia County, Michigan

Gordon Arthur Smith was born August 23, 1835, in Onondaga County, New York. His father, Alfred Floyd Smith, died in 1844 when Gordon was nine.

Gordon Smith received a common school education in Onondaga County. Times were hard for a family of five children without a father, and Gordon was apprenticed out to live with Robert Earl, a dealer in produce, sheep and cattle hides, meat, eggs, and shipper in Vesper, New York. He stayed there seven years, slept in the store, went to school summers, and also worked on the farm and in the store. There was little compensation besides room and board and the chance to learn a trade. He had been promised that he would be set up in business, but nothing came of the promise and he had little more than the clothes furnished by his mother, shoes from Mr. Earl, and an education.

> He left home after the death of his father, and lived with Robert Fields Earl, the senior member of the firm of Earl, Clark, and Company, of Vesper, Onondaga County, New York. He remained with them for seven years and while there was allowed to attend school about half the time, alternating this with work in the store. Later he spent a year with Henry A. Shaw, a merchant in Otisco, New York, serving him as clerk
> ...
> The young man came to Michigan in 1855 and first settled at Ionia, where he spent a year with the firm of Lake, Wilson, and Kennedy. After that he wrote for some time in the Register's office. In 1857, he purchased a half interest in the Gothic mills at Lyons,

which he sold out in 1858. He engaged as agent for Soule, Robinson, and Company in the sale of real estate. (*Portrait and Biographical Album*, pages 819-820)

In December, 1858, Gordon A. Smith wrote to his brother, Abram Smith in New York. "We are going to change our name. Do you wish to do the same? We are bound to do it."

In his diary Gordon wrote on January 18, 1859, "Had petition drawn by A. F. Bell to change our names from Smith to Willett and gave it to Tower." The next day, he wrote, "Mr. Drudgeon announced he would later introduce the petition to change the names of Hannah, Milan, Gordon, Julia, Eva, and Carrie Smith to Willett."

1859 NAME AND SURNAME CHANGE
GORDON ARTHUR SMITH BECOMES
GORDON ARTHUR WILLETT

On January 29, 1859, a bill was signed by the Michigan Governor's office, and Gordon Arthur Smith assumed the surname of Willett, becoming Gordon Arthur Willett.

In 1860, Gordon Willet is listed in the household of his brother, Alfred M. Willett in the Lyons, Ionia County, Michigan census, as follows:

Willet	Alfred M.	head	31	NY	carpenter
	Julia	wife	29	NY	
	Eva M.	daughter	6	NY	
	Carrie	daughter	2	MI	
	Gordon A.	brother	25	NY	clerk
	Hannah	mother	50	NY	

Gordon Willett kept a diary from August, 1860, until April, 1861. His handwriting is difficult to read, and he speaks of the mundane things of life, such as on August 16, 1860, "Exc[hanged] Oxen with L B for Gold Watch and am to have $7.50 in money". Mainly noted are his comings and goings around Ionia, Lyons, and Muir, accounts of payments and purchases, and his interest in the preaching of Elder Errett. Also mentioned are a Melon Festival and the Michigan State Fair, Ratification Meeting (November 8), Bonfires, [political] speeches, and Bell Ringers. On November 6, 1860, Gordon "Went to Lyons and voted straight Republican ticket." At this time, Gordon must have been in business with his brother A. Milan manufacturing and shingles; the quantity of shingles and method of payment are noted frequently in his diary.

Gordon Arthur Willett became interested in the preaching of Minister Isaac Errett who was connected with the young religious body known as the Christian Church or Reformers, and later as the Disciples of Christ.

Among the adherents of the movement were the various members of the Yates family, the Willetts of North Plains, and Muir, and others of the neighboring localities. These were all received upon confession of their faith in Christ, and baptism by immersion, after the custom of the primitive Christian Community. The baptisms were usually held in Prairie Creek, and as the meetings generally took place in the winter season, the ice in the stream had to be cut to afford opportunity for the rite ...

As was natural, the young people of this widening circle of church members were drawn together by opportunities offered by their common religious interests, and social gatherings, sleighing parties, spelling bees and singing societies were the order of the day. This inevitably led to more permanent attachments and to marriages, several of which were consummated in the ensuing years. Among them was that of Gordon Arthur Willett and Mary Elizabeth Yates, which took place in the Yates home on the farm everyone knew by that name, and at this event "Elder Errett" was the officiating Minister. The date was January 16, 1862. (*The Corridor of Years*, Herbert Lockwood Willett, 1967, page 5)

Mary Elizabeth Yates (b January 23, 1839, Ionia, Ionia County, Michigan), was the daughter of Job Lockwood and Jane (Sessions) Yates. The Yates were early settlers of Ionia County, having arrived at Ionia from Onondaga County, New York, on September 4, 1835.

After marriage, Mr. Willett aided in the recruiting service and in April, 1862, he went to Washington, in expectation of being appointed Quartermaster of Berdan's Sharp Shooters. He was, however, disappointed in this plan ... (*Portrait and Biographical Album*, page 820)

GORDON WILLETT
Matthew Brady Photographs, 1863
(Photographs Courtesy of
Mr. and Mrs. Robert Willett Of Florida)

Meantime, the War Between the States had broken out, and at its beginnings, with the attack of Fort Sumter and President Lincoln's call for volunteers, the four Willett brothers, Milan, Abram, Gordon, and James, registered for service. They had to undergo examination as to physical fitness, and while Milan, Abram, and James were accepted, Gordon was not approved, owing to defective vision. This was a source of deep disappointment, particularly as Milan was commissioned to raise a volunteer company in the North Plains area, of which he was made captain, Abram soon reached the rank of Colonel, and James Willett and Herbert Yates, Gordon's brother-in-law, were in the ranks. (*The Corridor of Years*, Herbert Lockwood Willett, 1967, page 5)

MARY YATES WILLETT
Washington, D. C., about 1863

NOTE: Abram Willett was actually breveted as a Major, but later he was referred to in family correspondence as "Colonel."

He was however engaged in the employ of the Sanitary Commission as Executive or Administrative Agent. For a time he was in charge of their supplies on the store ship, and afterward on the ship *Elm City*, which was engaged in carrying sick and wounded soldiers from the battlefields and camp hospitals to hospitals in the cities. He was subsequently transferred to the ocean steamer *S. R. Spaulding* and continued thus until the demands for ships in the transportation of troops was so great as to necessitate the employment of every one in that service, thus crippling the Sanitary Commission. In 1863 and 1864, Mr. Willett resided in Washington City. (*Portrait and Biographical Album*, page 820)

An incident from this time period is of interest in defining the character of the young bride, Mary Willett.

On entering the service, he had left his wife, a bride of a few months, at her father's home, the Yates farm in Ionia County. But after a time of separation, she insisted on joining him and undertaking the work of a nurse on the hospital ship. Much against his judgment, he at last acceded to her wishes, and she left for Washington. There, after spending some days in the home of a relative [her aunt, Sila Bennett] in Utica, New York, she was met by her husband in New York City and then joined him on the next arrival of the *Spaulding* with its cargo of sick and wounded from the South.

It was a trying ordeal to which she was now introduced. ... She had no training as a nurse, save such as family illnesses might demand. She had now only the brief period of preparation while the ship went down to Pittsburgh Landing for its next consignment of war victims. She often told of the deadly sickness that would come over her as she tried to be of some help in the gruesome work of assisting the doctors in their operative tasks. The sight and odors of a hospital ship were vastly trying to her, and many times her husband urged her to give up the service and return home, or at least to accept the urgent invitations of the friends in Washington and to stay with them. But she felt that her experience was not worse than that of most of the other volunteer nurses, and she wanted to do her part in the war and to be near her husband. ...

At length, her health showed signs of breaking, and as there was another and primary reason for her leaving the ship, her husband insisted on her return to Michigan. Early in April, 1864*, she arrived at the family home on the Yates farm and her son, Herbert Lockwood Willett was born there on May 5, 1864. (*The Corridor of Years*, Herbert Lockwood Willett, 1967, pages 6-7)

NOTE: The above quote is slightly in error: Mrs. Mary Willett left for Michigan in the fall of 1862. And actually, it was Gordon Willett who asked Mary to join him and to serve as a nurse on board the ship.

GORDON WILLETT
(Photograph Courtesy of Mr. And Mrs. Robert Willett Of Florida)

In 1865, our subject went to the oil fields of Ohio and leased oil lands from which he has never had any income, but still (in 1891) holds his leases on this unproductive property. After becoming discouraged there, he returned to Michigan where he indulged in stock speculation. In 1867, he formed a partnership with his father-in-law, J. Yates, and bought a stock of farming implements, hardware, field seeds, etc., and engaged in this line of trade, continuing in it for ten years, after which Mr. Willett took the business alone and carried it on until a paralytic stroke in 1885 compelled cessation of business. This paralysis was the result of an injury as Mr. Willett had been thrown from his buggy upon the railroad track and severely injured upon the head. *(Portrait and Biographical Album*, page 820)

The result of his accident was that he was a partial invalid for the remainder of his life.

The Disciples of Christ grew in Muir, and Mr. Errett was often in Ionia to hold meetings. The Willett family were founding members of this group, and their children grew in the faith. Mr. Willett served as an Elder and teacher in the church. Mr. Willett was a Republican who supported Ulysses S. Grant and James A. Garfield. Garfield was of the Disciples of Christ faith and had visited in Ionia with Pastor Errett on several occasions.

In the 1880, Ionia, Ionia County, Michigan census, 10-95-30-42, is listed Gordon A. Willett and family, living on West Main Street.

Willett	Gordon A	44	m	NY	
	Mary E	41	f	MI	
	Herbert L	16	m	MI	son
	Arthur J	9	m	MI	son
	Leslie J	5	m	MI	son

In the spring of 1895, he went to Chicago, to assist his son Herbert in the pastoral work of the Hyde Park Church. In the fall, while living with his son, he was ordained as a minister in the Church of Christ (Disciples). He assisted Herbert in the Hyde Park church for about two years, until his health failed.

Gordon A. Willett's obituary spoke of him thus:

> For many years he was an elder of this church (North Plains) and I think gave more time and attention to its duties than any one before or since. He greatly excelled in one of the conditions prescribed as a qualification for the position, he was given to hospitality. His home was the home of nearly every visiting minister or lay member of the Churches of Christ ... His knowledge of the Scriptures far excelled that of any other member of the Ionia Church. He studied the Scripture, not merely read it, and to all of us, he was authority on Bible history, prophecy and facts, and as Bible class teacher he was always prepared and was always instructive. (G. K. Berry)

WILLIAM WILLETT (1769-1844) 119

Gordon Arthur Smith Willett died July 18, 1898, at Petosky, Emmett County, Michigan, and his body was returned to and is buried at North Plains Township, Ionia County, Michigan, alongside his wife, Mary Yates Willett, and infant son, Enos Hale Willett.
(Bookstaver, 1907, page 70; *The Corridor of Years*, Herbert Lockwood Willett, 1967; *Portrait and Biographical Album*, 1891, pages 819-820; *The Willett Families*, 1985, pages 168-170; Obituary, [Gordon A.] Willett, July 18, 1898).

1. **Herbert Lockwood WILLETT**: b May 5, 1864, Ionia County, Michigan; graduate of Bethany College, and University of Chicago; m at Kenton, Hardin County, Ohio, January 4, 1888, Emma Augusta Price (b April 27, 1865, Kenton, Hardin County, Ohio; d August 26, 1949, Evanston, Cook County, Illinois); Professor, University of Chicago in Semitic studies; d March 28, 1944, Winter Park, Orange County, Florida, buried family plot Kenton, Hardin County, Ohio. See next I.1.1.7.4.1.

2. **Arthur Floyd WILLETT**: b September 20, 1870, Ionia, Ionia County, Michigan; 1898, graduate Bethany College; m at Dowagiac, Cass County, Michigan, October 1, 1896, Miss Sylvia Day (b October, 1870) of Dowagiac; Disciples of Christ pastor at Petosky, Michigan; d at Dowagiac, on December 4, 1899, after a rapid decline in his health over a period of several months. See next I.1.1.7.4.2.

3. **Leslie Gordon WILLETT**: b February 14, 1875, Ionia, Ionia County, Michigan; June, 1896, graduate Bethany College; m at Dowagiac, Cass County, Michigan, October 1, 1896, Miss Pearl Groves, the daughter of Rev. R. S. Groves, in a double wedding which included his brother Arthur; pastor of Christian Church, Elgin; Leslie had tuberculosis and removed on February 5, 1898, to Denver, Denver County, Colorado, for health reasons; d in Denver, Denver County, Colorado, March 1, 1898. See next I.1.1.7.4.3.

4. **Enos Hale WILLETT**: b 1883; d October 10, 1884, Ionia, Ionia County, Michigan, in infancy. Buried with his parents in North Plains Township, Ionia County, Michigan. Herbert Willett never saw his brother as he was away at Bethany College at that time. Enos only survived a very short time.

I.1.1.7.4.1
HERBERT LOCKWOOD WILLETT
And EMMA AUGUSTA PRICE
Of Chicago, Illinois

Herbert Lockwood Willett (I) was born on May 5, 1864, at the Yates farm in Ionia, Ionia County, Michigan. His father did not believe in public education, so Herbert was educated at home by his mother.

At the age of 17, Herbert Willett passed the examination for certification as a teacher. For two years he taught in the local school system of Ionia County.

In September, 1883, at age 19, he entered Bethany College, West Virginia, the Disciples of Christ Collegiate Institution founded by Alexander Campbell. He received an A. B. degree in 1886, and was graduated with an M. A. degree in 1887.

Herbert Lockwood Willett married in Kenton, Hardin County, Ohio, on January 4, 1888, Emma Augusta ("Gussie") Price (b April 27, 1865, Kenton, Hardin County, Ohio; d August 26, 1949, Evanston, Cook County, Illinois), the daughter of Henry Price and Margaret Fink.

In the spring of 1886, Herbert Willett accepted the pastorate at North Eaton, Ohio, a small rural community. He arrived in July, 1886, and remained for one year during which time he completed by correspondence work on his Master's Degree in Theology. Then, Herbert Lockwood was offered (1887) and accepted the pastorate of the Central Church, Disciples of Christ at Dayton, Ohio. He was ordained to the ministry of the Church of Disciples of Christ in 1890.

He requested and was granted a leave of absence to pursue his theological studies. In September, 1890, Herbert Willett, Gussie and their young son moved to New Haven, Connecticut, where Herbert entered Yale Divinity School as a graduate student. He chose Semitic Studies as his specialty on the advice of Dr. William Rainey Harper, the head of the Department of Semitic Languages and Literature, who supported the new Higher Criticism (i.e., historical method and critical research into the study of the Bible.)

On July 14, 1892, Herbert Willett sailed on the *State of Nebraska* for Glasgow, enroute to Edinburgh and London for a series of Bible lectures. The trip lasted a few weeks.

In 1893, after studying for a time at Yale University, he resigned from his Dayton, Ohio, pastorate, and entered postgraduate studies at the newly founded University of Chicago which was headed by his Yale mentor, William Rainey Harper. (In the summer of 1893, the World's

Columbian Exposition was held in Chicago and the huge Ferris wheel dominated and overshadowed the University of Chicago's grounds.)

From 1894 to 1897 he was pastor of the Hyde Park Church Disciples of Christ, in Chicago, Illinois, and was concurrently the acting Dean and head of the Disciples Divinity House at the University of Chicago (1894-1896). In 1895, Dr. Willett resided at 5716 Kimbark Avenue, Chicago, Cook County, Illinois.

In the spring of 1896, Herbert Lockwood Willett took his Ph. D degree from the University of Chicago.

In autumn of 1897, the Willett family moved to 329 East Fifty-seventh Street, Chicago, Illinois.

THE FAMILY CIRCA 1893

On October 18, 1898, Herbert Willett and family, including sister-in-law, Flora Price, sailed on the *Southwark* to Antwerp, thence Brussels, Rotterdam, and The Hague, enroute for post-doctorate study at the University of Berlin. Completing his studies there, they returned to America leisurely by way of Leipzig, Potsdam, Frankfort, Limburg,

Cologne, Paris, Versailles, and London, returning to America in early May, 1899.

THE FAMILY CIRCA 1900

This brief recital of travel and academic achievements does not do justice to the intellectual growth and wide respect that Dr. Willett had obtained as a lecturer and Biblical scholar. One indication of his stature in the academic world is that on July 1, 1899, President Harper of the University of Chicago offered Dr. Herbert Willett the deanship of a graduate school for Christian Workers as part of the University of Chicago. This was followed on April 10, 1900, with the promotion to Assistant Professor in the Department of Semitics. On December 27, 1928, Dr. Willett was promoted to the status of Professor Emeritus.

On April 4, 1900, Dr. and Mrs. Willett and their three sons sailed on the *Germanic* to Liverpool for ten weeks of Bible lectures in ten English cities, under the direction of the Christian Association of the Free Church Councils.

On October 4, 1902, Mrs. Willett and Mrs. Muckley and their children sailed on the *Neerdam* for Rotterdam enroute to Dresden.. They resided in Dresden for most of the time. Gussie took china-painting lessons, and painted a dinner service for 12 of Dresden China. They had a German housekeeper. The boys learned to speak German. Dr. Willett and Mr. Muckley joined them the following spring and on May 20, 1903, the whole group departed Liverpool on the *Haverford*.

In 1910, Herbert L. Willett and family are listed at 120 56th Street, Chicago, Ward 7 (Tract G), Cook County, Illinois census, ED 396, Sheet 5A, Supplement, as follows:

Willett	Herbert L.	head	46 m-22	MI NY MI
			Professor University	
	Gussie P.	wife	45 m-22	OH OH OH
	Floyd P.	son	21	IL MI OH
	Robert L.	son	14	IL MI OH
	Paul Yates	son	12	IL MI OH
Muir	Alice	servant	23 s	CANENG

Dr. Willett was pastor of the First Christian Church, Chicago, from 1907 to 1910, and the Memorial Church of Christ, Chicago, from 1910 to 1920. While in Chicago, he was a leader in expanding the then narrow social activity of the Baptist churches. Herbert took a lead in extending the church into social activities that benefited the community at large, which also offered an opportunity to evangelize those who would not otherwise be reached. For his day, Herbert was very progressive, and while his church doctrine forbade "jiggling", his church made an exception in 1909-1911, to this otherwise forbidden ritual. The term "Jiggling" today raises perhaps an eyebrow of wonderment. "Jiggling" was an euphemism for dancing, and Herbert saw that by permitting dancing in a Christian environment sponsored by the church, the church was reaching out to youth. Other groundbreaking social programs were social clubs, gymnasium classes, girl's organizations, sewing classes, domestic science classes, and music. Herbert helped to change the church from a Sunday-only preaching experience to a Christian community center. (The Chicago Evening Post, article "Union of Churches Unique in Religion, Exists in Chicago", February 26, 1913)

> Mr. Willett is one of the most democratic of university men, and of engaging personality. He is always a pleasing and persuasive preacher. It has been said that no honest man can hear him publicly present the proofs of the Scriptures and then say that he does not believe the Bible without a feeling of shame. He is a prolific writer, and for some things that he has thus said he has subjected himself to the criticism of his fellow Disciples.

A Church Federation Council meeting was held in February, 1910. After the session of the day there was an informal dinner at the Great Northern Hotel, followed by brief speeches by different men. Next to the last to speak was a minister noted for his denominational proclivities. He said that it was puerile to array the scriptures against denominational Christianity when there were Jewish Christians, Gentile Christians, etc. Then he remarked that the people who had the most to say about unity were the most sectarian of all, and even little. He was once in a Western town where the people were holding a revival, and they advertised as the one true apostolic church of Christ, that there was only one people who had the presumption and littleness to do that, etc.

When Mr. Willett rose and began in his most gracious manner, attention was riveted upon him. After a word of introduction, he took up the address just heard by saying, "In regard to our people whom Dr. has done us the honor to mention." Then followed a skillful, polished and thorough-going answer. It was clear, full and unanswerable defense of the Disciples. And there was an eloquent silence that followed it. (Haynes, Nathaniel S., *History of the Disciples of Christ in Illinois 1819-1914*, 1915, biographical sketch, Herbert L. Willett, pages 633-644)

Dr. Willett made numerous tours to Palestine for the Dunning and Company of Boston. Originally, course credit was provided through the University of Chicago, but after 1912-1913 the connection with the University disappeared. Trips varied from ten weeks to ten months of around the world travel. Dr. Willett conducted tours for Dunning in 1904, 1907, 1912-1913, 1919, 1924-1925, 1930, 1935, and a final trip to Oxford, England, to attend the Conference of Universal Christian Council for Life and Work. Dr. Willett always arranged his travels so he could be back at the University to teach during summer semesters. He felt those times attracted the most dedicated and serious students and he particularly enjoyed teaching them.

In 1920, Herbert Willett and family are listed at 6119 Woodlawn Avenue, in the Chicago City, Cook County, Illinois census, SD 1, ED 388, Ward 7, Sheet No. 2 A, taken on January 2 or 3, 1920, as follows:

Willett Herbert   head   54 MI NY NY
                      Professor University

Gussie P.   wife   53 OH OH OH
Robert L.   son   24 IL MI OH
             Solicitor American Legion
Paul Y.   son   21 IL MI OH
             Attends School

Dr. Willett was pastor of the Kenilworth Union Church from 1926 until 1944, and resided at 319 Richmond Road, Kenilworth, Illinois, a suburb of Chicago.
Dr. Willett was associated with the University of Chicago throughout its earliest years and until his death. He was a noted Biblical scholar, authority on the Talmud, pastor and visiting pastor to numerous Churches of Christ, experienced public speaker, and a noted Bible lecturer on the Lyceum and Chautauqua circuit. For many years he was associated with the *Christian Century* Magazine as co-editor and contributing editor.

Dr. Herbert L. Willett was the editor of:
A Guide to Bible Study, by J. W. McGarvey, President College of the Bible in Kentucky, 1897

Dr. Herbert L. Lockwood was the author of:
Alexander Campbell, 1897
Life and Teachings of Jesus, 1898
Prophets of Israel, 1899
Our Plea for Union and the Present Crisis, 1901
Basic Truths of the Christian Faith, 1903
Popular and Critical Bible Encyclopedia and Scriptural Dictionary, 1908
The Moral Leaders of Israel, 1911
Our Bible, its origins, Character and Value, 1917
The Daily Altar, 1918
The Bible Through the Centuries, 1932
The Jew Through the Centuries, 1932
The Ruling Quality
Teachings of the Books
The First Book of Samuel
The Call of Christ

Dr. Herbert Lockwood Willett died at Winter Park, Orange County, Florida, on March 28, 1944, of a heart attack, at the age of 79. He is buried in the family plot in Kenton, Hardin County, Ohio.
Mrs. Emma Augusta (Price) Willett died on August 26, 1949, in Evanston, Cook County, Illinois, and is buried in the family plot in Kenton, Hardin County, Ohio.

(*The Corridor of Years*, Herbert Lockwood Willett, 1967; Herbert Willett obituary, "Dr. H. L. Willett, Scholar, Church Leader, is Dead", Chicago Daily Tribune, March 29, 1944, page 27; Haynes, Nathaniel S., *History of the Disciples of Christ in Illinois 1819-1914*, 1915, biographical sketch, Herbert L. Willett, pages 633-644; Moore, W. T., editor, *The New Living Pulpit of the Christian Church: A Series of Discourse, Doctrinal and Practical, by Representative Men among the Disciples of Christ*, 1918).

1. **Herbert Lockwood WILLETT, Jr.** (a.k.a. Floyd Price WILLETT): b March 13, 1889, at Dayton, Montgomery County, Ohio; of Washington, D. C. (1944); m first in Princeton, Mercer County, New Jersey, on March 27, 1917, Clara Bradley Hoskins (b November 1, 1892, in Zahleh, then in Syria now Lebanon; d October 1, 1962, Washington, D. C., and is buried in the family plot in Kenton, Hardin County, Ohio, with her husband); m 2d in Williamsburg, Virginia, on January 5, 1966, Margaret ("Peggy") Long Stanley (b November 2, 1897, Kansas City, Jackson County, Kansas; d June 22, 1975, Wichita, Sedgewick County, Kansas); d January 11, 1972, Wichita, Sedgewick County, Kansas, and is buried with his first wife in the family plot in Kenton, Hardin County, Ohio. See next I.1.1.7.4.1.1.

2. **Robert Leslie** (originally Lockwood) **WILLETT**: b October 27, 1895, at 5716 Kimbark Avenue, Chicago, Cook County, Illinois; m in Chicago, Cook County, Illinois, on May 3, 1924, Katherine Bliss Mehlhop (b September 20, 1898, Chicago, Cook County, Illinois; d April 26, 1982, Rockledge, Brevard County, Florida); business manager of the *Christian Century*; d August 4, 1973, Toledo, Lucas County, Ohio, and is buried with his wife in Pentwater, Oceana County, Michigan. See next I.1.1.7.4.1.2.

3. **Paul Yates WILLETT**: b June 1, 1898, at 329 East Fifty-Seventh Street, Chicago, Cook County, Illinois; m on April 28, 1923, Edith Doan (b March 28, 1896, Danville, Vermilion County, Illinois; d October 22, 1985, Freeport, Stephenson County, Illinois. Her ashes were scattered in the Gulf of Mexico. There is a memorial grave marker in the family plot in Kenton, Hardin County, Ohio); co-owner of advertising agency associated with the International Harvester Company; d February 16, 1976, in Sarasota, Sarasota County, Florida, and his ashes were scattered in the Gulf of Mexico; there is a grave marker in the family plot in Kenton, Hardin County, Ohio. See next I.1.1.7.4.1.3.

I.1.1.7.4.1.1a
HERBERT LOCKWOOD WILLETT, JR.
And CLARA BRADLEY HOSKINS
Of Chicago, Illinois

Herbert Lockwood Willett, Jr., was born March 13, 1889, at Dayton, Montgomery County, Ohio. He was originally named Floyd Price Willett, and used that name until sometime after his college days at the University of Chicago, Class of 1911. His son (Herbert Willett III) believes that his father took the name Herbert Lockwood Willett, Jr., about the time that he went to Beirut to teach at the Syrian Protestant College (now American University).

1914 JUST ENGAGED
Courtesy of Herbert L. Willett, III

That three-year assignment had a most significant outcome. In Beirut, he was invited to the home of Dr. and Mrs. Hoskins, American missionaries, where he met their daughter, Clara. In accordance with the custom of American families of the region, children were always sent back to America at age thirteen for schooling. Clara had graduated from Mount Vernon Seminary in Washington, and returned to work in Beirut with her parents. A romance flourished, and during his first year as a "staffite" they became engaged.

During Herbert's second year in Beirut, The Great War (later known as World War I) broke out in Europe. Although

America was not yet involved, the Turks instituted strict censorship of textbooks and of mail. Working and teaching conditions worsened considerably. All unfavorable references to the Turks had to be razored out of all history books, or the teacher would have been held responsible. That meant calling in all textbooks and many nights of mutilating pages. Library volumes also had to conform to Turkish rules.

1914 JUST ENGAGED
Courtesy of Herbert L. Willett, III

Courtesy of Herbert L. Willett, III

Dr. Hoskins much earlier had written several books about the region, which were being used as textbooks by the

English. When Dr. Hoskins was summoned by the Turks to explain this, the family was seriously fearful that when he left, they would never see him again; fortunately, his explanation was accepted by the Turkish authorities.

By the summer of 1916, conditions had reached a very serious state. There were multitudes of Armenian refugees in the city, clean water was very scarce, cholera and typhus were killing many people, particularly the English who had been interned, and people literally dying of starvation in the streets was a common occurrence. Devaluation of the currency had taken place, banking and financial accounts had to be recalculated regularly and paper money was printed on one side only. At the College graduation, the playing of the "Star Spangled Banner" came to an abrupt halt because the censor didn't like the word *free* and had eliminated everything in the music after *the land of the* ...

There were rumors that the United States was about to declare war. Such a development would close the College and mean internment of Americans. So the decision was made to leave Beirut after the College year had ended and travel back to America. Easier said than done. Dr. and Mrs. Hoskins, their two daughters, and four staffites, including Clara's fiancée, Herbert Willett, applied to Djemal Pasha for military permission to leave the country and travel on the railroad, used primarily for military transport. His signature was obtained, but there was no assurance that his seal would be accepted beyond his territory when they reached the sphere of authority of Enver Pasha, Djemal's enemy. Then they would have to obtain country visas to cross Bulgaria, Hungary, Austria and Germany.

The trip was full of frustrations, uncertainties, and delays. The party were subjected to repeated searches of their luggage, clothing and bodies (36 searches by actual count). Great care was exercised not to have anything written down that could be incriminating or to say anything that could be overheard and reported by spies that traveled with them. Constant questioning to pick up any discrepancies in their stories was a daily occurrence. When three rolls of toilet paper were confiscated, Herbert chuckled over the thought of someone having to look at each of 3000 sheets to be sure there were no maps or other information on any of them.

Part of the trip was by the Orient Express, and then in German Army trucks over the Tarsus Mountains. The family was fortunate to obtain passage on the Balkanzug train. The staffites took an alternate route, and although both parties overlapped in Berlin neither knew at the time of the other being there. They were finally reunited in Copenhagen, where they sailed for the United States.

Clara later reconstructed the whole trip day by day from memory and it has been reproduced at length in Volume I of *Further Corridors*, on pages 103-119, Herbert's autobiography which was privately printed in 1968.

Herbert Lockwood Willett married first in Princeton, Mercer County, New Jersey, on March 27, 1917, Clara Bradley Hoskins (b November 1, 1892, in Zahleh, then in Syria now Lebanon; d October 1, 1962, Washington, D. C., and is buried in the family plot in Kenton, Hardin County, Ohio, with her husband).

1917 WEDDING PHOTOGRAPH
Courtesy of Herbert L. Willett, III

In the summer of 1923, when he took his family of four to the Near East for the summer, he had to have his father sign an affidavit that Floyd Price Willett and Herbert Lockwood Willett, Jr., were one and the same person.
Herbert Willett resided in Washington, D. C., where he was the head of the Washington, D. C. Community Chest for 20 years. In 1966, he relocated to Wichita, Kansas, at which time he dropped the "Junior" from his name.

1. **Herbert Lockwood WILLETT, III**: b April 6, 1919, Chicago, Cook County, Illinois; m in Falmouth, Barnstable County, Massachusetts, on September 13, 1947, Mary ("Moll") Haskell Jones (b December 21, 1922, Englewood, Bergen County, New Jersey; d December 1, 1992, Falmouth, Barnstable County, Massachusetts). See next I.1.1.7.4.1.1.1.

2. **Jeanne Libbey WILLETT**: b April 5, 1921, Cambridge, Middlesex County, Massachusetts; m in Washington, D.C., on December 19, 1942, Edward ("Ted") Sprague Cobb (b July 16, 1918, South Orange, Essex County, New Jersey). See next I.1.1.7.4.1.1.2.

3. **Carol Hoskins WILLETT**: b March 13, 1930, Washington, D.C; m in Washington, D. C., on October 10, 1953, David Blackwell Rodman (b November 6, 1917; d July 21, 1988, Pittsfield, Berkshire County, Massachusetts). See next I.1.1.7.4.1.1.3.

I.1.1.7.4.1.1b
HERBERT LOCKWOOD WILLETT, JR.
And **MARGARET LONG STANLEY**
Of Chicago, Illinois

Herbert Willett married second in Williamsburg, Virginia, on January 5, 1966, Margaret ("Peggy") Long Stanley (b November 2, 1897, Kansas City, Jackson County, Kansas; d June 22, 1975, Wichita, Sedgewick County, Kansas). She was the widow of a classmate, fraternity brother and close friend. After their marriage he relocated from Washington, D. C. to Wichita, Sedgewick County, Kansas.
Herbert Lockwood Willett died January 11, 1972, following a heart attack in Wichita, Sedgewick County, Kansas, and is buried with his first wife in the family plot in Kenton, Hardin County, Ohio.

I.1.1.7.4.1.1.1
HERBERT LOCKWOOD WILLETT, III
And MARY HASKELL JONES

Herbert Lockwood Willett III was born April 6, 1919, in Chicago, Cook County, Illinois.

In 1941, he was graduated from Princeton University. In 1942, he entered the Army Air Corps and was commissioned at Harvard Business School. He served in Italy and in Germany until 1946. In Germany, he met his future wife, who was a Women's Army Air Corps (WWAC) cryptographer.

Herbert Lockwood Willett married in Falmouth, Barnstable County, Massachusetts, on September 13, 1947, Mary ("Moll") Haskell Jones (b December 21, 1922, Englewood, Bergen County, New Jersey; d December 1, 1992, Falmouth, Barnstable County, Massachusetts).

In early 1947, Herbert joined Merck and Company. He retired after 25 years at Merck and moved to Falmouth in 1972, where he has been active as a volunteer in a number of organizations. Herbert's wife died on December 1, 1992, in Falmouth, and her ashes were scattered in Buzzards Bay. Herbert resides (1999) in Falmouth (Quissett), Massachusetts.

I.1.1.7.4.1.1.2
JEANNE LIBBEY WILLETT
And EDWARD SPRAGUE COBB

Jeanne Libbey Willett was born April 5, 1921, in Cambridge, Middlesex County, Massachusetts. She was graduated from Smith College in 1943.

Miss Jeanne L. Willett married in Washington, D. C., December 19, 1942, Edward ("Ted") Sprague Cobb (b July 16, 1918, South Orange, Essex County, New Jersey). He was graduated from Princeton University in 1941, and had been a classmate and roommate of her brother, Herbert L. Willett III.

1. **Harvey Dayton COBB**: b March 6, 1945, Orange, Essex County, New Jersey; m May 16, 1975, Judith Alice Hunt (b December 29, 1944, Bronxville, New York).

2. **Brian Willett COBB**: b February 19, 1947, Orange, Essex County, New Jersey; m November 30, 1968, Nancy Jeanne Bailey (b December 17, 1947, Boston, Suffolk County, Massachusetts).

    1. **Adam Brian COBB**: b November 7, 1979, Newton, Middlesex County, Massachusetts.

    2. **Heather Ashley COBB**: b November 4, 1982, Newton, Middlesex County, Massachusetts.

3. **Cathanne Condit COBB**: b March 25, 1949, Orange, Essex County, New Jersey; m in Framingham, Middlesex County, Massachusetts, on October 5, 1985, David Gerard Higgins (b July 19, 1952, Sanford, York County, Maine; d November 25, 1997, in Hookset, Merrimack County, New Hampshire, in an automobile accident); they lived in Chester, New Hampshire. Cathanne now (1999) resides in South Carolina.

4. **Janice Willett COBB**: b July 22, 1952, Orange, Essex County, New Jersey; m May 22, 1976, Mitchell Richard Ziemba (b December 1, 1951, Greenwich, Fairfield County, Connecticut).

    1. **Melissa Leigh ZIEMBA**: b September 4, 1981, Greenwich, Fairfield County, Connecticut.

I.1.1.7.4.1.1.3
CAROL HOSKINS WILLETT
And DAVID BLACKWELL RODMAN

Carol Hoskins Willett was born March 13, 1930, Washington, D.C. She was graduated from Mount Holyoke College in 1952.

Carol Willett married in Washington, D. C., October 10, 1953, David Blackwell Rodman (b November 6, 1917; d July 21, 1988, Pittsfield, Berkshire County, Massachusetts, and was buried there). He saw considerable action as a carrier pilot in the Pacific Theater during World War II. After retiring from the Navy, David joined General Electric, and they settled in Pittsfield, Massachusetts, where he was the liaison with the British on the Polaris submarine program.

1. **Cynthia** ("Cyndie") **Willett RODMAN**: b February 21, 1960, Norfolk, Virginia; was graduated from Mt. Holyoke College, 1982. Cyndie resides (1999) Salt Lake City, Utah.

2. **Scott Lockwood RODMAN**: b October 23, 1961, Pittsfield, Berkshire County, Massachusetts. Was graduated from Babson College, and received his M.B.A. from the Wharton Business School at the University of Pennsylvania. He resides (1999) in New York City, New York.

I.1.1.7.4.1.2
ROBERT LESLIE WILLETT and KATHERINE MEHLHOP

Robert Leslie (originally Lockwood) Willett was born October 27, 1895, at 5716 Kimbark Avenue, Chicago, Cook County, Illinois. He served in France during World War I with the American Expeditionary Force (A. E. F.).

Robert L. Willett married in Chicago, Cook County, Illinois, May 3, 1924, Katherine Mehlhop (b September 20, 1898, Chicago, Cook County, Illinois; d April 26, 1982, Rockledge, Brevard County, Florida). Robert Willett was business manager of the *Christian Century*. For about 20 years, he was co-owner and business manager of Willett, Clark Publishing Company, specializing in religion and current events. He was also an avid golfer and a sports enthusiast.

MRS. KATHERINE (MEHLHOP) WILLETT

ROBERT LESLIE WILLETT, SR.

Robert Willett died on August 4, 1973, Toledo, Lucas County, Ohio, and is buried with his wife in Pentwater, Oceana County, Michigan.

1. **Louise WILLETT**: b August 24, 1925, Chicago, Cook County, Illinois; m in Evanston, Cook County, Illinois, on September 2, 1947, Frank Moore Wright, Jr. (b June 16, 1920, New Rochelle, Westchester County, New York; d July 5, 1990, Edgewater, Volusia County, Florida) (divorced February 12, 1976). See next I.1.1.7.4.1.2.1.

2. **Robert Leslie WILLETT, Jr**: b October 28, 1926, Chicago, Cook County, Illinois; m in Marilla Township, Manistee County, Michigan, on August 24, 1957, Donna Jean Bahr (b July 27, 1930, Marilla Township, Manistee County, Michigan). See next I.1.1.7.4.1.2.2.

I.1.1.7.4.1.2.1
LOUISE WILLETT and FRANK MOORE WRIGHT, JR.

Louise Willett was born August 24, 1925, Chicago, Cook County, Illinois.

Louise Willett married in Evanston, Cook County, Illinois, September 2, 1947, Frank ("Bud") Moore Wright, Jr. (b June 16, 1920, New Rochelle, Westchester County. New York; d July 5, 1990, Edgewater, Volusia County, Florida). The Wrights were divorced on February 12, 1976. Louise Wright lives (1999) in Merritt Island, Florida.

1. **Linda Gilbert WRIGHT**: b October 7, 1948, Evanston, Cook County, Illinois; m 1st in Grand Haven, Ottawa County, Michigan, on June 12, 1970, Warren Jay Dykhouse (b July 1, 1949) (divorced 1973); m 2nd in San Diego, California, May 1, 1976 Robert Burnley (b August 14, 1945); resides (1999) in Bonita, California.

   1. **Erin Louise BURNLEY**: b January 11, 1978, Chula Vista, San Diego County, California.

   2. **Kristen Frances BURNLEY**: b September 5, 1979, Chula Vista, San Diego County, California.

2. **Wendy Harmon WRIGHT**: b March 29, 1950, Kendallville, Noble County, Indiana; m in Bryan, Williams County, Ohio, February 21, 1970, William Kent Beck (b June 11, 1950). See next I.1.1.7.4.1.2.1.2.

3. **Katherine Bliss WRIGHT**: b March 29, 1950, Kendallville, Noble County, Indiana; m in Toledo, Lucas County, Ohio, on September 18, 1982, Garry Wilbur Newbury (b November 13, 1948); resides (1999) in Temperance, Michigan.

4. **Robert ("Bob") Alexander WRIGHT**: b May 29, 1953, Kendallville, Noble County, Indiana; m first in Toledo, Lucas County, Illinois, on May 23, 1981, Kathryn Sue Neuberger (b September 12, 1954) (divorced April 15, 1986); m second in Merritt Island, Brevard County, Florida, on June 19, 1993, Billie Jo Montgomery (b September 7, 1966, Topeka, Shawnee County, Kansas); d August 18, 1999, Merritt Island, Brevard County, Florida.

5. **Donald Owen WRIGHT**: b November 1, 1959, Grand Haven, Ottawa County, Michigan; m 1st in Toledo, Lucas

County, Ohio, on March 28, 1980, Mary Janet Hartung (b February 25, 1960) (divorced on July 31, 1991); m 2nd in Rockledge, Brevard County, Florida, on May 20, 1992, Diane Biordi (b March 17, 1954, Cleveland, Cuyahoga County, Ohio); resides (1999) Stuart, Florida.

    1. **Melissa Lee WRIGHT:** b September 26, 1980, Cocoa Beach, Brevard County, Florida. Attending (1999) Brevard Community College, Cocoa, Florida.

    2. **Nicholas Robert WRIGHT:** b December 13, 1982, Cocoa Beach, Brevard County, Florida.

I.1.1.7.4.1.2.1.2
WENDY HARMON WRIGHT and WILLIAM KENT BECK

Wendy Harmon Wright was born on March 29, 1950, Kendallville, Noble County, Indiana.

Wendy Wright married in Bryan, Williams County, Ohio, on February 21, 1970, William Kent Beck (b June 11, 1950).

They reside (1999) Toledo, Lucas County, Ohio.

    1. **Bradley Steven BECK:** b June 12, 1970, Bryan, Williams County, Ohio; m in Toledo, Lucas County, Ohio, November 19, 1990, Michelle Ann Vaughan (b December 28, 1968) (divorced).

        1. **Alexander Steven BECK:** b March 14, 1991.

        2. **Damon Bradley BECK:** b June 4, 1999, the son of Bradley Beck and Kathleen Wright.

    2. **Andrew William BECK:** b December 5, 1973, Toledo, Lucas County, Ohio; December, 1997, graduated from Ohio State University.

    3. **Michelle Renee BECK:** b May 22, 1977, Toledo, Lucas County, Ohio; student (1999) at Ohio State University.

I.1.1.7.4.1.2.2
ROBERT LESLIE WILLETT, JR. and DONNA JEAN BAHR
Of Cocoa Beach, Florida

Robert Leslie Willett, Jr., was born October 28, 1926, Chicago, Cook County, Illinois. He served in the US Army during World War II and again in the Korean War.

Robert Leslie Willett married in Marilla Township, Manistee County, Michigan August 24, 1957, Donna Jean Bahr (b July 27, 1930, Marilla Township, Manistee County, Michigan). Robert is a graduate of Knox College and Western Michigan University; he was a banker, serving as Vice President and President of Banks in Michigan, Florida, and Saipan, Mariannas Islands, .South Pacific Ocean

Since retiring, Bob volunteers as a banking consultant. In March, 1996, he was in Khabarovk, Russia, and in June, 1996, at Yuzhno-Sakhalinsk, Russia. In August, he was at Kampala, Uganda, with a weekend at Safari Lodge and a visit to the headwaters of the Nile. In 1998, he and his wife spent the summer as volunteers in the Russian Far East. In 1999, he was a consultant in Moldavia and Vladivostok

In 1997, Robert L. Willett published a Civil War volume, *One Day of War, April 10, 1863*. A second book, *The Lightning Mule Brigade, The 1863 Raid of Abel Streight into Alabama*, about Union Colonel Streight's raid is was published in 1999 by the Guild Press of Indiana. He is currently researching his third book, about the American Intervention in Russia in World War I. The Willetts reside in Cocoa Beach, Florida.

1. **Leslie Jean WILLETT**: b September 23, 1958, Grand Haven, Ottawa County, Michigan; m in Merritt Island, Brevard County, Florida, March 19, 1988, Timothy David Mitchell (b January 17, 1960, Sanford, York County, Maine); he makes and designs Sea Ray boats. Leslie was graduated from Florida International University in Miami and is employed by an entertainment production company; resides (1999) Merritt Island, Brevard County, Florida.

   1. **Timothy David MITCHELL, Jr**: b March 4, 1989, in Merritt Island, Brevard County, Florida.

   2. **Forrest Robert MITCHELL**: b January 24, 1991, in Merritt Island, Brevard County, Florida.

   3. **Sheldon Leslie MITCHELL**: b September 14, 1993, in Merritt Island, Brevard County, Florida.

2. **Thomas** ("Tom") **Lockwood WILLETT**: b October 26, 1959, Grand Haven, Ottawa County, Michigan; m on July 1, 1995, to Nadene Anne Kintigh (b July 2, 1957, Pittsburgh, Allegheny County, Pennsylvania). He is a graduate of Eastern Michigan University. He is employed as Assistant Director, Management Information Systems, *Florida Today* newspaper. He is also a rock musician, playing frequently in local rock bands; resides (1999) in Satellite Beach, Florida.

  A. **Frank ARMESON** (stepson): b June 2. 1982.

  B. **David ARMESON** (stepson): b June 2, 1982.

  1. **Bethany Kaye WILLETT**: b November 16, 1995, Cocoa Beach, Brevard County, Florida.

  2. **Samuel Lockwood WILLETT**: b October 28, 1998, Cocoa Beach, Brevard County, Florida.

3. **Barbara Lynn WILLETT**: b January 10, 1962, Grand Haven, Ottawa County, Michigan. She is a graduate of the United States International University in San Diego, and Ohio University in Athens, Ohio. She was a Peace Corps volunteer in Thailand, and worked (1996-1997) for Catholic Relief Services in Israel where she lived in Bethlehem. Barbara is now (1999) back in the United States, living and working in Orlando, Florida, and working on a doctoral program at Central Florida University, Orlando.

I.1.1.7.4.1.3
PAUL YATES WILLETT and EDITH DOAN
Of Illinois and Florida

Paul Yates Willett was born on June 1, 1898, at 329 East Fifty-Seventh Street, Chicago, Cook County, Illinois. Paul Willett married on April 28, 1923, Edith Doan (b March 28, 1896, Danville, Vermilion County, Illinois; d October 22, 1985, Freeport, Stephenson County, Illinois, and her ashes were scattered in the Gulf of Mexico. There is a memorial grave marker for her and her husband in the family plot in Kenton, Hardin County, Ohio).

Paul was trained as a lawyer; however, he never practiced law. He was co-owner of an advertising agency which was associated with the International Harvester Company (1944).

Paul Willett died on February 16, 1976, Sarasota, Sarasota County, Florida, and his ashes were scattered in the Gulf of Mexico. There is a memorial grave marker (for Paul and his wife) in the family plot in Kenton, Hardin County, Ohio.

1. **Florence Woodford WILLETT**: b December 11, 1925, Chicago, Cook County, Illinois; m in Kenilworth, Cook County, Illinois, on July 15, 1950, Austin Keith Ethridge (b May 5, 1925, Lanark, Carroll County, Illinois).

   1. **Philip Austin ETHRIDGE**: b June 23, 1956, Freeport, Stephenson County, Illinois; m July 1, 1993, Marty Hernandez.

   2. **Paul James ETHRIDGE**: b July 8, 1958, Freeport, Stephenson County, Illinois; m on September 4, 1995, Dana Nicole Smock Readling.

      A. **Christopher Scott READLING** (stepdaughter): b June 9, 1986.

      B. **Cara Danielle READLING** (stepdaughter): b August 6, 1987.

      C. **Ashley Faye READLING** (stepdaughter): b August 16, 1989.

         1. **Abigail MacKenzie ETHRIDGE**: b November 4, 1997.

I.1.1.7.4.2
ARTHUR FLOYD WILLETT and SYLVIA DAY
Of Cass County, Michigan

Arthur Floyd Willett was born on September 20, 1870, Ionia, Ionia County, Michigan. He was a storekeeper at the asylum. In June, 1896, he was graduated from Bethany College.

Arthur Floyd Willett married at Dowagiac, Cass County, Michigan, on October 1, 1896, Miss Sylvia Day (b October, 1870) of Dowagiac. He entered the ministry and was appointed pastor of a congregation first in Wisconsin and later at Petosky, and Dowagiac, Michigan.

ARTHUR FLOYD WILLETT
CIRCA 1895

Arthur Floyd Willett died on December 4, 1899, after a rapid decline in his health over a period of several months. A few months later a posthumous son was born. The following obituary is from the *Ionia Sentinel*, December, 1899:

A Brain Affection Cause of His Death at Dowagiac

The news of the death of the Rev. Arthur F. Willett, at Dowagiac, Dec. 4, was received with sadness here. He was for six years pastor of the Church of Christ at that place and died at the home of his wife's aunt, Mrs. Judd, several strokes of paralysis having affected his brain.

From a Dowagiac paper we learn that deceased had not been of a robust constitution since leaving school in 1896, and that last spring, while pastor of the Christian church at Rutland Center, Wis., he was compelled to give up his work, going to Dowagiac, residing there with relatives until his death.

During his last days, Mr. Willett's condition was pitiful. Through apparently in good health, he had no control whatever of the power of speech. He was on the streets the Thursday before he died, but was again stricken with paralysis the next day, and failed rapidly. His mother, Mrs. G. A. Willett of this city, was at his bedside with his wife and other relatives when he passed away.

Deceased was born in this city Sept. 30, 1870, being the second child of a family of four sons, only one of them, Prof. H. L. Willett, of Chicago, now survives. Arthur entered Bethany College, West Virginia, in 1896 (sic) [1893] and after rigorous study and hard labor was graduated a minister of the Christian church. Following his graduation in October, 1896, he was married to Miss Sylvia Day, of Dowagiac, who survives him. The wedding was a double one, his brother Leslie, who died in 1897, being married at the same time and place. Both have passed away in the height of young manhood with a brilliant career before them, one brother and their mother being the only surviving members of this well known and estimable family.

After their marriage the two brothers entered Chicago University. Leslie died there, and then overwork began to tell upon Arthur, he acting as pastor of the Christian Church at West Pullman. He went to

Petoskey and became pastor of the first Christian Church of that city. A year later he went to Rutland Center, Wisconsin, resigning in February, 1899.

While at Bethany College Mr. Willett was engaged in preaching at all opportunities, in that way procuring his schooling. He had many warm friends wherever he was located, particularly at Dogawaic where he is highly spoken of by the papers.

A postmortem examination resulted in finding that death was caused by an effusion into the lateral ventricles of the brain. The pressure of the fluid caused his demise.

In 1900, (Mrs.) Sylvia Willett, age 29, born October, 1870, Michigan, and her son, Arthur F. Willett, age "4/12" (i.e., born January, 1900) were listed as a boarder in the household of Fannie Judd (1900 Dowagiac, W. Division, Cass County, Michigan, census).

1. **Arthur Floyd WILLETT, Jr**: b January, 1900, Michigan; d 1918, during the worldwide "Spanish Influenza" epidemic. See next I.1.1.7.4.2.1.

I.1.1.7.4.2.1
ARTHUR FLOYD WILLETT
Of Dowagiac, Cass County, Michigan

Arthur Floyd Willett, Jr., was born in January, 1900, Michigan.
Arthur Floyd Willett died in 1918, age 18, during the worldwide "Spanish Influenza" epidemic.

ARTHUR FLOYD WILLETT
AGE 18

I.1.1.7.4.3
LESLIE GORDON WILLETT and PEARL GROVES

Leslie Gordon Willett was born February 14, 1875, Ionia, Ionia County, Michigan. In June, 1896, he was graduated from Bethany College. Leslie Gordon Willett married at Dowagiac, Cass County, Michigan, on October 1, 1896, Miss Pearl Groves, the daughter of Rev. R. S. Groves, in a double wedding which included his brother Arthur. He was pastor of the Christian Church, Elgin, Illinois. Leslie had tuberculosis and removed on February 5, 1898, to Denver, Denver County, Colorado, for health reasons.

LESLIE GORDON WILLETT
CIRCA 1896

Leslie Gordon Willett died in Denver, Denver County, Colorado, March 1, 1898. The following obituary was in the March 7, 1897, newspaper:

> Last Thursday afternoon, March 2d, at the residence of Mrs. Miles, corner of Twenty second avenue and Champa street, the pastor conducted the funeral services at the burial of Bro. Leslie G. Willett, a minister of the Gospel, who had come to Colorado about three weeks before for his health. Bro. Willett was born in Ionia, Mich, March 12, 1875. He was baptized into Christ by his brother, Herbert L. Willett, while the latter was pastor of the Christian Church at Dayton, O. He entered Bethany College, W. Va., in 1892 and was graduated in 1896. He went immediately to Chicago University, where his brother is now the Dean of Disciples' Divinity House and at the same time accepted the pastorate of the Christian Church at Elgin, Ill. He was married October 1, '96 to Miss Pearl A. Groves, the accomplished daughter of Bro. R. S. Groves, for a long time pastor of the Christian Church at Hamilton, O. Sister Willett was also a graduate of Bethany College, and had entered heartily with her husband upon the noble work of the gospel of the ministry. Bro. Willett preached at Elgin until November, when he became so ill that he had to relinquish his work, and, upon the advice of physicians, came to Colorado the 10th of February, thinking that the sunshine of the mountain region would prolong his life. But here, on the first day of March, surrounded by his father and mother, Bro. And Sister G. A. Willett, and his devoted wife, his spirit took its flight to the realm of eternal day. Thus passed out of this life one of the most brilliant minds, lofty, Christian characters, beautiful, noble lives, ever adorning this world. He was needed. He will be missed, but heaven is richer for his going into it. To the father, mother, brothers, and wife our hearts go out in tender sympathy.

CHAPTER TEN

ABIGAIL JANE SMITH (1837-1864)

OF KALAMAZOO COUNTY, MICHIGAN

N.1.1.7.5
ABIGAIL JANE SMITH and **JAMES R. CUMMINGS**
Of Kalamazoo County, Michigan

Abigail Jane Smith was born on October 1, 1837 at Sterling, New York.

(Photographs courtesy of Mr. and Mrs. Robert Willett Of Florida)

JAMES CUMMINGS

Abigail Smith married in Syracuse, Syracuse County, New York, in March, 1856, James R. Cummings (b 1830), the son of Asher T. Cummings and Permelia Willett (see I.1.1.1.)

ABIGAIL JANE (SMITH) CUMMINGS

Mrs. Abigail Jane (Smith) Cummings died on December 9, 1864 at Augusta, Kalamazoo County, Michigan, of consumption, age 27 years, 2 months.

James R. Cummings married 2nd on April 16, 1867, Miss Harriet E. Christie, the daughter of James and Ann Christie. In 1881, they resided at Kalamazoo, Michigan.

CHAPTER ELEVEN

JAMES W. WILLETT (1839-1906)

OF MONTCALM COUNTY, MICHIGAN

I.1.1.7.6
JAMES WILLETT SMITH (JAMES W. WILLETT)
And MARY ANNETTE GERMAIN
Of Montcalm County, Michigan

James Willett Smith was born March 13, 1839, in Auburn, Cayuga County, New York (born Auburn according to Schenck's, *History of Ionia*; also reported as born Sterling in the family Bible).

James came to North Plains, Ionia County, Michigan, in 1856, at the age of 17, where his brother, Milan Willett Smith, had previously settled.

1859 NAME AND SURNAME CHANGE
JAMES WILLETT SMITH BECOMES JAMES W. WILLETT

On January 29, 1859, a bill was signed by the Michigan Governor's office, and James Willett Smith assumed the surname of Willett, becoming James W. Willett.

In 1860, James W. Willett, age 20, born New York, was enumerated with Benjamin Soule, age 50, with wife Rhoda, and several children in the Lyons Township, Ionia County, Michigan, census, page 635 (117), taken on July 5, 1860.

> Upon the breaking out of the War of the Rebellion, he enlisted in Berdan's Sharpshooter's, and went to the front. He remained in the service until 1864, when he returned to North Plains and engaged in farming. (*History of Ionia and Montcalm Counties, Michigan*, John S. Schenck, Philadelphia, D. W. Ensign and Company, 1881, page 492)

Actually the above biographical quotation is in error as James remained in military service for one year and then remained in and around Washington as a civilian sutler for the remainder of the war.

Private James W. Willett enrolled in Company I, Regiment of U.S.S. Sharpshooters Volunteers, on October 28, 1861. Private James W. Willett was honorably discharged on November 22, 1862, after having served 1 year and 24 days. Private James W. Willett was issued a "Certificate of Disability for Discharge" by reason of chronic diarrhea. (Certificate dated November 15, 1862, Washington, D. C., signed by Surgeon, Dr. Moss)

James Willett married at North Plains, Ionia, County, Michigan, on July 4, 1864, Mary Annette ("Nettie") Germain (b June 18, 1845, New York; living 1900), the daughter of the Hon. George W. and Abigail B. Germain of North Plains, Ionia County.

(Photographs courtesy of
Mr. and Mrs. Robert Willett of Florida)

JAMES WILLETT

In 1870, Jas. W. Willett and family are listed in the Township of North Plains, Ionia County, Michigan census, page 1, dwelling 5-6, as follows:

Willett	Jas. W.	head	31	NY	farmer, 7,000
	Annette	wife	24	NY	house keeping
	Edith	daughter	4	MI	at home
	(not yet named)	daughter	1/12	MI	at home

In 1872, in company with his brother, he engaged in the manufacture of sash, doors, and blinds in the village of Muir. Here he suffered the loss of his property by fire, and in 1876 removed to Stanton and built the mill he now operates. He is at present (1881) engaged in lumbering in connection with his planing-mill, and owns twelve hundred acres of farming and pinelands. (*History of Ionia and Montcalm Counties, Michigan*, John S. Schenck, Philadelphia, D. W. Ensign and Company, 1881, page 492)

NETTIE GERMAIN WILLETT

On October 8, 1875, "at the Planing Mill of Willett, Muir, Mich., while in the act of adjusting one of the planers, I lost the three front fingers of my right hand." (Hand written Deposition of James W. Willett, dated August 9, 1895; part of his Civil War Pension file)

Drawing from the
History of Ionia and Montcalm Counties, Michigan,
John S. Schenck, Philadelphia,
D. W. Ensign and Company, 1881

In his political and religious affiliations, Mr. Willett is a Republican and a member of the Church of the Disciples. He is a man of pronounced temperance principles, and the cause finds in him an earnest advocate and a strong supporter. (*History of Ionia and Montcalm Counties, Michigan*, John S. Schenck, Philadelphia, D. W. Ensign and Company, 1881, page 492)

In the 1880 Sidney Township, Stanton, Montcalm County, Michigan census, 19-245-12-1, is listed J. W. Willett and family, as follows:

Willett	J. W.	41	m	NY	
	Mary A	35	f	MI	
	Edith	14	f	MI	daughter
	Genevra	10	f	MI	daughter
	William	8	m	MI	son

George	7	m	MI	son
Grace	9/12	f	MI	daughter

In 1882, James Willett purchased a house in Stanton that had been built by a prosperous lumberman, Mr. Gilbert, in 1877. The home at 306 N. Camburn, has been restored by its present owner, Joseph Barnes (1990), and is on the Michigan Register of Historic Sites (No. L1159A, Michigan Historical Commission). Mr. Barnes believes that the woodwork, doors, and sashes came from the Willett's Mill. There is also an original brass door key, which bears the inscription, "Willett."

In 1884, James W. Willett and family are listed in the Stanton, Montcalm County, Michigan State census, page 554, as follows:

Willett	James W.	head	45	NY	manuf. of sash and doors
	Nellie	wife	38	MI	housewife
	Edith	daughter	18	MI	
	Genevra	daughter	13	MI	
	William	son	12	MI	
	George	son	10	MI	
	Grace	daughter	4	MI	
Germaine,	Hattie	boarder	24	MI	school teacher
	Florence	boarder	21	MI	bookkeeper
McMillen.	Mary	domestic	28	Canada	

On May 25, 1895, "at my mill at the city of Stanton, I lost my right eye by the bursting of cylinder belt. My left eye being of little use since over heat or partial sun stroke while in the Army." (Hand written Deposition of James W. Willett, dated August 9, 1895; part of his Civil War Pension file)

In the 1900 Camburn Street, Stanton, Montcalm County, Michigan census, 56-142-10-69, is listed James W. Willett and family, as follows:

Willett	James W.	61	m	Mar 1839	NY
	Mary A	54	f	Jun 1845	MI
	Geneva A	30	f	Jan 1870	MI
	George G	26	s	Aug 1873	MI
	Grace A	20	f	Aug 1879	MI
	Fern H	14	f	Nov 1885	MI

In 1900, they resided at Camburn Street, Stanton, Montcalm County, Michigan. This was where he had his sawmill, to which he added a door, sash, and blind factory, which he continued to operate as long as he lived. (*The Corridor of Years*, Herbert Lockwood Willett, 1967, page 3) He and his sons, William and George, jointly owned and operated a portable saw mill engaged in logging operations, and a tract of leased land upon which they cut and sawed some timber.

James W. Willett died on October 17, 1906, at Bruce Crossing, Haight Township, Ontonagon County, Michigan. The only real estate he owned at his death was the home in Stanton, Montcalm County, Michigan, which was held jointly and passed to his wife upon his death. Additionally, he owned (along with his sons and equally) a team of horses worth about $150, and a portable saw mill worth about $800. (Civil War Pension File, No. 859210, Deposition of Mrs. Mary A. Willett, widow, of James W. Willett)

On December 5, 1907, Mrs. Mary A. Willett, widow, of Bruce Crossing, Haight Township, Ontonagon County, Michigan, filed a Civil War Pension claim, No. 859210, which pension was approved.

In 1908 after James Willett's death, his house was sold to settle his estate.

(Bookstaver, 1907, page 70; *The Willett Families*, 1985, page 170; Civil War Pension File No. 1166878, Original claim dated December 21, 1897, James W. Willett; Civil War Pension File, Declaration for Widow's Pension of Mrs. Mary A. Willett, widow, of James W. Willett, dated November 22, 1906; Civil War Pension File No. 859210, Deposition of Mrs. Mary A. Willett, widow, of James W. Willett, dated December 5, 1907).

1. **Edith A. WILLETT**: b November 16, 1865, Michigan; m in November, 1886, Clay Summers/Sommers; resided (1907) at Sheridan, Montcalm County, Michigan. See next I.1.1.7.6.1.

2. **Genevra** ("Eva") **A. WILLETT**: b January 16, 1870, Michigan; living (1907) at home with her mother; m Drake. She was a bookkeeper for her father's business.

3. **William George WILLETT**: b December 2, 1871, Michigan; m abt 1892, Margaret Elizabeth ("Lizzie") Dasef (b October, 1873, Michigan); resided Stanton, Montcalm County, Michigan, evidently departing there about 1907 (after his father's death) for Oregon and residing at 1625 NE 53rd Avenue, Portland, Oregon. See next I.1.1.7.6.3.

4. **George Germaine WILLETT**: b August, 28 1873, Michigan; m in Stanton, Montcalm County, Michigan, November 20, 1902, to Lena May Bachman, the daughter of

Dr. and Mrs. Norma E. Bachman of Stanton; resided (1907) near Bruce Crossing, Ontonagon County, Michigan.

5. **Grace A. WILLETT**: b August 29, 1879, Michigan; m L. F. Ryan; residing (1907) Ontonagon County, Michigan.

6. **Fern H. WILLETT** (female): b November 25, 1885, Michigan; a teacher (1907); living (1907) at home with her mother; a teacher.

I.1.1.7.6.1
EDITH A. WILLETT and **CLAY SUMMERS**
Of Sheridan, Montcalm County, Michigan

Edith A. Willett was born November 16, 1865, Michigan.
Miss Edith A. Willett married in November, 1886, Clay Summers/Sommers. They resided (1907) at Sheridan, Montcalm County, Michigan.

1. **Esther SUMMERS**:

2. **Germain SUMMERS** (male):

3. **Helen SUMMERS**:

4. **Marion SUMMERS**:

I.1.1.7.6.3
WILLIAM GEORGE WILLETT
And MARGARET ELIZABETH DASEF
Of Montcalm County, Michigan
And Portland, Oregon

William George Willett was born on December 2, 1871, in Michigan.

William G. Willett married about 1892 Margaret Elizabeth ("Lizzie") Dasef (b October, 1873, Michigan).

In 1894, William G. Willett and family are listed in the Evergreen, Montcalm County, Michigan State census, page 11, dwelling 49-51, as follows:

| Willett | William G. | head | 22 MI | farmer |
| | Lizzie | wife | 20 MI | housewife |

They resided (1900) at Camburn Avenue, in Stanton, Montcalm County, Michigan, evidently at the home of his parents. His parents, James Willett and Mary A., also resided on Camburn (Avenue), Stanton, Montcalm County, Michigan, in 1900, along with his 4 brothers and sisters.

In 1900, William Willitts and family, are listed on Camburn Street, in the Stanton, Montcalm County, Michigan census, 86-145-9-51, as follows:

Willitts	William	head	28 m	Dec 1871	MI
	Lizzie	wife	26 f	Oct 1873	MI
	Errol	son	5 d (sic)	Sep 1894	MI

William Willett was a carpenter.

In 1904, the family moved to Ontonagon County, Michigan, where William and George were partners with their father in a lumbering operation. In 1907, they removed to Oregon where they took up residence at 1625 NE 53rd Avenue, Portland, Oregon.

1. **Errol William WILLETT**: b September 26, 1894, Stanton, Montcalm County, Michigan; m in Boston, Suffolk County, Massachusetts, on November 15, 1919, Margery MacPherson of Boston (d September 22, 1990, Rhode Island); d September 3, 1975, Tampa, Florida. See next I.1.1.7.6.3.1.

I.1.1.7.6.3.1
ERROL WILLIAM WILLETT
And MARGERY MACPHERSON

Errol William Willett was born September 26, 1894, at Stanton, Montcalm County, Michigan.

He matriculated at Oregon State College in 1913-1914 and was graduated D.M.D. from the North Pacific College of Dentistry. He was commissioned a Lieutenant (j. g.) in the Dental Corps by the U.S. Navy on June 27, 1917. Lieutenant Errol Willett served in World War I as a Staff Dental Officer on the *U.S.S. Florida* while that ship served as a unit of the Sixth Battle Squadron, British Fleet.

Errol W. Willett married at Boston, Suffolk County, Massachusetts, November 15, 1919, Margery ("Marge") MacPherson (d September 22, 1990, Rhode Island) of Boston.

In 1920, he was a Lieutenant, Dental Corps, *U.S.S. Florida* (1920 Oregon State Yearbook). They were stationed in China in the late 1920s. In 1927-1929, he was a Lieutenant Commander and Brigade Dental Officer, Third Brigade, U.S.M.C., Tientsin, China, and he later served on the *U.S.S. Blackhawk*, in Chefoo, China.

In 1932, he served on the *U.S.S. Altaire*, in San Diego, California. In 1937, he was on the *U.S.S. Pennsylvania*, in Bremerton, Washington. In 1946, he was Naval Captain and Senior Dental Officer at the U.S. Naval Station, Alameda, California.

Errol Willett and his family were stationed at Pearl Harbor, Hawaii on that fateful day of December 7, 1941, where he was assigned as a Dental Officer for the U.S. Naval Air Station. His twelve-year old son, Peter, was feeding rabbits as the first Japanese fighters swept into the bay on that Sunday morning.

Captain Errol Willett, retired from the Navy on July 1, 1952. He taught dentistry for twelve years at Emory University. He liked to duck hunt and fish, enjoyed his cocktail, pipe, and moustache. For a while he lived at Charleston, South Carolina.

Errol Willett died on September 3, 1975, in Tampa, Florida. He was cremated and his ashes spread at sea.

("Officer Biography Sheet," E. W. Willett, Capt, DC, USN, dated August 10, 1949; Peter Willett file).

1. **Edith WILLETT**: b December 26, 1920, San Francisco; B.A. Stanford University; m April 15, 1944, Hugh Samson; resides Adamsville, Newport County, Rhode Island (1990). See next I.1.1.7.6.3.1.1.

2. **Peter Stuart WILLETT**: b February 6, 1929, Shanghai, China; military service during the Korean War; m in Jackson, Mississippi, on September 2, 1955, Lucy Carolyn Kochtitzky (divorced); resides (1994) Oak Bluff, Massachusetts. See next I.1.1.7.6.3.1.2.

AUTUMN 1990
AT HOME OF HUGH AND EDITH SAMSON, ADAMSVILLE,
RHODE ISLAND
MEMORIAL SERVICE PHOTOGRAPH OF DESCENDANTS OF
MRS. MARGERY MACPHERSON WILLETT

FRONT ROW: LEFT TO RIGHT
Isaiah Samson (son of D. S.); Zoe Samson (daughter of D. S.)
unknown; Carolyn Kochtitzky Willett; Edith Willett Samson
Sue Sabin Pollard; Edith Samson (daughter of D. S.)
Peter Stuart Willett; Hugh Maxwell Willett, Peter Sabin Willett

BACK ROW:
David Samson; Maria Samson; Errol Stanley Willett
Claire Dulaney Willett (daughter of P. Sabin Willett)
Mary Kate Willett; Hugh Willett Samson; Margaret Anne
Brown Samson
Katherine Willett Samson (daughter of P. S.)
Peter Samson; Judith Clayton Samson; Charles Felix Samson
Blake Anthony Samson; Blake Sabine
Leonie Glen Willett; Hugh Samson

Pictured on this page are all then-living descendants of Errol W. Willett and Margery MacPherson Willett except Wade

Stuart Willett; Gurion Seal Willett (son of W. S.); Poiema Seeson Willett (daughter of W. S.); David Porter Samson (son of Peter); Brian McCawley Samson (son of Peter); Seth, Carleigh, Clayton, Chip Samson (children of Charles and Judith Samson).

I.1.1.7.6.3.1.1
EDITH WILLETT and HUGH SAMSON
Of Adamsville, Rhode Island

Edith Willett was born on December 26, 1920, at San Francisco, California. She received a B. A. Degree from Stanford University.

Miss Edith Willett married on April 15, 1944, Hugh Samson.

They reside (1990) at Adamsville, Newport County, Rhode Island.

1. **Blake Anthony SAMSON**: b February 28, 1947.

2. **Charles Felix SAMSON**: b April 18, 1948; m August 1, 1981, Judith Clayton.

3. **Hugh SAMSON**: b December 31, 1949; m August 6, 1983, Margaret Anne Brown.

4. **Peter SAMSON**: m December 22, 1973, Heath Bannard Porter.

5. **David SAMSON**: b June 16, 1953; m Maria.

I.1.1.7.6.3.1.2
PETER STUART WILLETT
And LUCY CAROLYN KOCHTITZKY
Of Oak Bluffs, Massachusetts

Peter Stuart Willett was born February 6, 1929, at Shanghai, China, where his father was serving as a U. S. Naval Officer. Peter had military service during the Korean War.

Peter Stuart Willett married in Jackson, Mississippi, on September 25, 1955, Lucy Carolyn Kochtitzky (divorced).

Peter S. Willett spent much of his career as a reporter and editor for the (now defunct) United Press International (UPI) in Raleigh, North Carolina, Georgia, Barrington, Illinois, and New York City.

As a "Unipresser", he covered the Olympic Games in Mexico City and Munich. When the Palestinian terrorists took the Israeli athletes hostage, he posed as a Hungarian athlete (a ruse whose success gave him great pride) and sneaked into an adjoining apartment in the Olympic Village, from where he issued reports which were circulated by radio worldwide.

In 1965, Peter Stuart Willett was transferred to New York City. He loved "Costello's", a favorite haunt of New York City journalists, the "Players' Club," and the old United Press crowd. They resided at 54 Stuyvesant Avenue, Larchmont, New York. He likes to fish and cross-country ski, and loves nothing better than to prepare a huge feast for a large crowd. Presently (1991), he has a consulting business in connection with media syndication and computer applications.

Peter S. Willett's children were raised mainly at Larchmont, New York, where the family lived at 54 Stuyvesant Avenue. The children attended nearby Chatsworth Avenue School, and then Hommocks Middle School and Mamaroneck High School.

He has become a pretty fair saltwater fisherman and spends a lot of his time aboard his fishing boat, the *Wampanand*, looking for bass and blues. He lives in Oak Bluff, Massachusetts, where he is a member of the Rod and Gun Club.

1. **Peter Sabin WILLETT**: b March 6, 1957, Raleigh, North Carolina; m 1st in Oyster Bay, Long Island, New York, June 14, 1986, Leonie Glen (divorced); m 2nd in Christ the King Lutheran Church, Holliston, Massachusetts, on September 26, 1998, to Marta Thodal Willey. See next I.1.1.7.6.3.1.2.1.

2. **Wade Stuart WILLETT**: b April 25, 1959, Atlanta, Georgia; m June 26, 1988, Ming Lee Han (divorced); resides Taipei, Taiwan. See next I.1.1.7.6.3.1.2.2.

3. **Errol Stanley WILLETT**: b July 26, 1960, Chicago, Illinois; 1983, B. A. University of Colorado; Master of Fine Arts, Penn State University, 1993; resides (1993) Aspen, Colorado, as part of an artist in residence program; an artist, writer, editor, and teacher; m on October 21, 1995, Mary Kellie Madigan (divorced). See next I.1.1.7.6.3.1.2.3.

4. **Mary Kate WILLETT**: b July 12, 1964; 198?, B.S.A. New York University; resided (1990) New York and worked in film production; (1990) assisted in the production of "Reversal of Fortune". Resided (1993) in Boulder, Colorado; currently (1998) resides in Seattle, Washington, where she works as a film editor.

I.1.1.7.6.3.1.2.1a
PETER SABIN WILLETT and **LEONIE GLEN**
Of Sherborn, Middlesex County, Massachusetts

Peter Sabin Willett was born March 6, 1957, in Raleigh, North Carolina where his father and mother were reporters for the old (now defunct) United Press International (UPI). Most of his youth was spent at Larchmont, New York, where he lived about a mile and a half from Long Island Sound. He swam at the Manor Beach Club virtually every day with his brothers. On Sundays they attended St. John's Episcopal Church. He was a Boy Scout, and summers were spent at Camp Siwanoy near Pawling, New York. Troop One spent every other weekend hiking, usually on the Appalachian Trail. Peter began skiing at an early age at Mad River Glen at Waitsfield, Vermont.

The family lived at 54 Stuyvesant Avenue. He attended nearby Chatsworth Avenue School, and then Hommocks Middle School and Mamaroneck High School. In the summer of 1973, Peter sailed aboard the *S.S. France* to England where he became an exchange student at Gresham's School, Holt, Norfolk, England. At Gresham's, he boarded at Howson's, shivered through cold winters, became a School Prefect, sat A-Level examinations in English, mathematics, and history, and played on the school, county and Eastern Counties Schoolboy Rugby sides. He was able to travel through France, Morocco, Spain and Italy during this time. He left ("one doesn't graduate from an English public school") in the summer of 1975, and entered Harvard College in the fall.

He spent his freshman year in Massachusetts Hall, where, legend has it, George Washington had put up 200 years before. According to the yearbooks, Bill Gates, the Microsoft billionaire, was a classmate, but Sabin doesn't recall him. After freshman year, Sabin was a resident of Eliot House. He studied Latin and Greek, and played rugby.

In 1979, Peter Sabin Willett was graduated from Harvard University with an A. B. in Classics magna cum laude. On June 7, 1979, Peter Sabin Willett delivered the Latin Oration at the Harvard Commencement to an audience of 15,000. He spoke concerning recent Massachusetts legislation raising the drinking age, and the students, each of whom had been provided with a translation, laughed uproariously, in order to convince their parents that they understood Latin. Peter Sabin Willett got a big hand for his efforts.

He spent 1980 at the Greenville (S. C.) News where he was a police beat reporter. Hurricane David came and went; 7-11 holdups (a regular occurrence) were the "big" local news.

In the fall of 1981, he entered Harvard Law School. Still a rugby player, he played NCAA final (NCAA rules were still a bit soft on eligibility and graduate students could play for club sides) against the University of California. On a rain-soaked pitch in Dayton, Ohio, Harvard lost to California, by a penalty goal in sudden death overtime. Still muddy from the playing field, Sabin raced for a cab and the airport. The following Monday, he sat for his first-year contracts examinations. In 1983, he was graduated with a J. D. from Harvard Law School, cum laude. He joined Bingham, Dana, and Gould, of Boston, Massachusetts.

Peter Sabin Willett married in Oyster Bay, Long Island, New York, on June 14, 1986, Leonie Glen. For a while they lived in New Hampshire were he worked for Orr and Reno as an associate, then in the town of Canterbury; in 1987, it was back to Bingham, Dana, and Gould, and Boston city life.

They resided (1991) at 67 Brush Hill Road, Sherborn, Massachusetts. He is a partner and attorney with the firm of Bingham, Dana, and Gould, Boston, Massachusetts, where he is a commercial litigator, a trier of civil corporate cases. Most of his clients are banks or corporations, with much of his present time spent in bankruptcy court.

On the side, Peter Sabin Willett has written a novel *The Deal*, May, 1996, published by Random House Publishers. *The Deal* is about a client, John Shepard a bright young associate in an old corporate law firm, and his attorney, Ed Mulcahy, in a first rate thriller about power play and skullduggery in Boston. *The Deal* was published in England as *The Mortgage*. His second novel, another thriller, *The Betrayal*, was published by Villard (an imprint of Random House) in 1998.

Children of Peter Sabin Willett and his 1st wife, Leonie Glen:

1. **Claire Dulaney WILLETT**: b January 25, 1988, Concord, New Hampshire.

2. **Hugh Maxwell WILLETT**: b October 25, 1989, Brookline, Massachusetts.

3. **Peter WILLETT**: b July 29, 1991, Sherborn, Middlesex County, Massachusetts.

4. **Catherine WILLETT**: b November 23, 1993, Boston, Middlesex County, Massachusetts.

I.1.1.7.6.3.1.2.1b
PETER SABIN WILLETT
And **MARTHA THODAL WILLEY**
Of Sherborn, Massachusetts

Peter Sabin Willett married 2nd at Christ the King Lutheran Church, Holliston, Massachusetts, September 26, 1998, to Mrs. Marta Thodal Willey.

Stepchildren of Peter Sabin Willett are the children of his 2nd wife, Martha Thodal Willey:

A. **Gordon WILLEY** (stepson):

B. **Hannah WILLEY**(stepdaughter):

I.1.1.7.6.3.1.2.2
WADE STUART WILLETT and MING LEE HAN
Of Larchmont, New York, and Taipei, Taiwan

Wade Stuart Willett was born on April 25, 1959, in Atlanta, Georgia. In 1981, he was graduated with a B.S. from Rice University.

Wade Stuart Willett married June 26, 1988, Ming Lee Han (divorced).

They resided in (1990) Taiwan, and (1991) at Larchmont, New York. They later returned to reside in Taipei, Taiwan.

He is a born-again Christian, having been saved as a college student at Rice University. He has lived in west Texas and for a number of years in Taipei. His religious faith is central to his life and his belief in the absolute truth and wisdom of the Bible is the essential precept of his personal knowledge (Peter Sabin Willett, August 3, 1993).

Wade Willett now (1998) lives in New York City were he is a discount broker at Waterhouse Securities. His children continue to live with their mother in Taiwan.

1. **Gurion Seal WILLETT**: b April 10, 1989, Taipei, Taiwan.

2. **Poiema Seeson WILLETT** (daughter): b August 25, 1990, Taipei, Taiwan.

I.1.1.7.6.3.1.2.3
ERROL STANLEY WILLETT
And MARY KELLIE MADIGAN
Of Boulder, Colorado

Errol Stanley Willett was born July 26, 1960, in Chicago, Cook County, Illinois.
Errol S. Willett studied German, Eastern European history, contour maps of back country ski regions, and the "Grateful Dead" while at college. He spent a year as an exchange student at the University of Regensburg, Federal Republic of Germany. While there he bought a motorcycle and toured Czechoslovakia, Hungary, Romania, and Bulgaria, among other European countries. This was of course much more exciting and daring than in the present era since his tour through Communist countries was before the Berlin Wall came down, and while the Cold War was still in progress, and while Communism was still "The Evil Empire". Errol S. Willett found the Romanians the most forbidding and repressive of the communist countries to visit, Bulgaria the warmest.

At Colorado University, he discovered ceramics, which have become his passion.

In 1983, he earned a B. A. from the University of Colorado. He has resided (1991) in Layton, New Jersey. In 1993, he received his Master of Fine Arts from Penn State University.

He resided (1993) Aspen, Colorado, as part of an artist in residence program. This is a fortuitous happening, since Errol is a superior skier, a gifted telemarketeer, and happiest on a steep pitched-slope with snow waist deep and rooster tails behind.

He is an artist, writer, editor, and teacher.

Errol Stanley Willett married in Oak Bluff, Massachusetts, on October 21, 1995, to Mary Kellie Madigan (divorced).

Errol is an Associate Professor of ceramic arts at Syracuse University and resides (1998) in Syracuse, New York.

CHAPTER TWELVE

ANN WILLETT (1813-1874)

OF IONIA COUNTY, MICHIGAN

I.1.1.8
ANN WILLETT and GEORGE CASE
Of Lyons, Ionia County, Michigan

Ann Willett was born in 1813, Onondaga County, New York.

Miss Ann Willett married about 1830, George Case (b 1807, New York). They removed to Ionia County, Michigan, about 1848.

In 1850, George W. Case and family are listed in the Town of Lyons, Ionia County, Michigan census, page 156, dwelling 457-457, as follows:

Case	George W.	head	43	NY	farmer, $2,000
	Ann	wife	33	NY	
	Alexander	son	11	MI	
	Jane	daughter	2	MI	
	William	son	2	MI	

In 1870, George W. Case and family are listed in the Ionia County, Michigan census, house 15, family 1150, as follows:

Case	George W.	head	63	NY	ret. Farmer
	Ann	wife	57	NY	keeping house
	Eliza	daughter	21	MI	at home
	Ray	son	19	MI	painter-laborer

Mrs. Anna (Willett) Case died on April 28, 1874, age 59 years, 4 months, 7 days, in Ionia County, Michigan.

1. **Alexander CASE**: b 1839, Michigan.

2. **Jane CASE**: b 1848, Michigan.

3. **William CASE**: b 1848, Michigan.

4. **Eliza CASE:** b 1849, Lyons, Ionia County, Michigan; d November 23, 1870, age 29 years, 20 days, Ionia County, Michigan (daughter of George Case).

5. **Ray CASE:** b 1851, Michigan.

CHAPTER THIRTEEN

WILLIAM WILLETT (1809-1853)

OF ONONDAGA COUNTY, NEW YORK

I.1.1.9
WILLIAM WILLETT and **TRYPHOSA JACKSON**
Of Onondaga County, New York

William Willett, Jr., was born in 1809 (1811) in Onondaga Township, Onondaga County, New York. (The census calculation and his age at death would indicate a birth year of 1811). He was born, reared, and died on the same clearing made by his father.

In considering the life of William Willett, one must realize that when he was born, western New York State was a wilderness. The first road through the region was not cut until 1791 when the earliest emigrants opened a road from Whitesboro (near Utica) to Canandaigua. The first stage coach over this road did not leave Utica until September 3, 1799.

In 1824, William Willett was still a young man. In the same year the Erie Canal was opened and General Lafayette made his triumphal American tour through the region.

On March 5, 1832, William Willett, Sr., of the town of Onondaga sold for $1,000.00, "lot 217 (late Onondaga Reservation) to William Willett, Junior and Alfred F. Smith containing 42 acres and 32/100 of an acre." (*Onondaga County Court House Land Record*, Syracuse, New York, Deed Book 134, page 375)

On April 12, 1836, Alfred F. Smith and wife, Hannah, sold for $671.00 "Lot 217 in the Onondaga Reservation now in the town and County of Onondaga ..." 42 acres and 32/100 of an acre, to William Willett, Junior, the brother of Mrs. Hannah [Willett] Smith. (Onondaga County Deed Book 63, page 208)

On April 18, 1836, William Willett, Senior, of the town of Onondaga sold for $1,500 "lot 209 (late Onondaga Reservation) and part of lot 217, being 42 acres and 32/100 of an acre (bordered on south and west by land owned by William Willett, Junior) to William Willett, Junior." (*Onondaga*

WILLIAM WILLETT (1769-1844)

County Court House Land Record, Syracuse, New York, Deed Book 63, page 209)

William Willett married about 1836, Miss Tryphosa (Triphosa/Triphena) Jackson (b 1817, New York; d August 4, 1895, age 78, buried Onondaga County, New York), the daughter of James Jackson and Triphosa (Howe) Bull. Miss Tryphosa Howe was born in 1779, at Hudson, New York, and was the daughter of Samuel Howe and Sarah Rose. Mrs. Triphosa (Howe) Jackson died on December 13, 1860, age 81 years, 10 months.

On April 1, 1837, William Willett, Junior, and Triphosa, his wife, of the town of Onondaga sold for $465.00 part of lot 217 *(late Onondaga Reservation)* 15 acres of land to Charles Rowe. (*Onondaga County Court House Land Record*, Syracuse, New York, Deed Book 67, page 49)

TRYPHOSA (JACKSON) WILLETT
(1815-1895)
(Photograph courtesy of Judy Gorham)
copied from a daguerreotype

In 1840, William Willett and family are listed in the Onondaga County, New York census, page 105, as follows:

1 male	60-70	1770-1780	William (father)	
1 female	60-70	1770-1780	Susan (stepmother)	
1 female	20-30	1810-1820	William	age 29 b 1811
1 male	20-30	1810-1820	Triphosa	age 23 b 1817
1 male	10-15	1825-1830		
1 female	0-5	1835-1840	Elizabeth	age 2 b 1838

The above reconstruction is speculative, but appears to fit the facts as known of this family.

WILLIAM WILLETT
(1809/1811-1853)
(Photograph courtesy of Judy Gorham)
copied from a daguerreotype

In the 1850 Onondaga Township, Onondaga County, New York census, page 265, dwelling 616-638, is listed William Willet and family, as follows:

Willet	William	39	m	NY	farmer, $4,000
	Triphosa	35	f	NY	
	Elisabeth	12	f	NY	
	Consider	9	m	NY	
	Mary L	3	f	NY	
Bull	Timothy	21	m	NY	laborer
Jackson	Triphosa	71	f	CN	

In 1850, William Willett was a fairly well-to-do farmer of Onondaga, Onondaga County, New York.

William Willett died August 27, 1853, age 42, in Onondaga County, New York, and is buried in the Pine Ridge Cemetery, Navarino, Onondaga County, New York.

On August 27, 1853, Tryphosa Willett, widow of William Willett, petitioned to act as administrator of the estate of William Willett, deceased. Survivors were Lucia E. Willett, Consider H. Willett, and Mary L. Willett.

Mrs. Triphosa (Jackson) Willett, widow, married 2d about 1855, Warren Rowe (b abt 1810, New York).

Mrs. Triphosa (Willett) Rowe died on August 4, 1895, in her 79th year, and is buried in the Pine Ridge Cemetery, Navarino, Onondaga County, New York, near her 1st husband, William Willett, Jr.

(Bookstaver, 1907, page 67; *The Willett Families*, 1985, page 170).

1. **Lucia Elizabeth** ("Etta"/"Laurette") **WILLETT**: b 1838; m abt 1860, Theodore ("Charles") Lord (b 1840; d September 13, 1918, age 78); d August, 1933, age 95. (Had one son who had a son, Charles Willett Lord).

2. **Consider Heath WILLETT**: b December 12, 1840, in Onondaga Township, Onondaga County, New York; m in Washtenaw County, Michigan, November 5, 1867, Lois Adelaide Wilder; d 1912, Chicago, Cook County, Illinois. See next I.1.1.9.2.

3. **Mary L. WILLETT**: b 1847, New York; m abt 1870, Fish.

1. **Willett FISH**:

CHAPTER FOURTEEN

CONSIDER H. WILLETT (1840-1912)

OF CHICAGO, ILLINOIS

I.1.1.9.2
CONSIDER HEATH WILLETT
And LOIS ADELAIDE WILDER
Of Chicago, Cook County, Illinois

Consider Heath Willett was born December 12, 1840, in Onondaga Township, Onondaga County, New York.

NOTE: One possible theory on how he received his name is that he was named after a cousin Consider Heath (one of Hannah Foster Willett's nieces married a Heath).

Consider Heath Willett's father died when he was only 11. His mother soon remarried, but through a disagreement with his stepfather at age 13, Consider "found himself afloat upon the sea of life" (*Chicago and Its Distinguished Citizens*, 1881, page 260).

As a teenager and young man, Consider Willett worked with his hands with farmers, in a sawmill, as a house painter, in a country store, and in a post office.

In 1855, Consider H. Willet is listed in the Marcellus, Onondaga County, New York State census (not copied).

With help from his mother, he managed to attend Onondaga and Cortlandville Academies.

Consider H. Willett was a Class of 1862 graduate of the New York State Normal College, Albany, Chautaugua County, New York.

On August 12, 1862, with the Union split asunder by Southern rebellion, Consider H. Willett volunteered as a private in Company E (originally made up of graduates from the New York State Normal School), 44th New York Infantry, Army of the Potomac. By vote, he became orderly Sergeant (*Chicago*, page 261).

Sergeant Willett caught up with his regiment just after the Battle of Antietam, Maryland. In October, 1862, the 44th New York was attached to the 5th Corps, Army of the

Potomac, and camped just southwest of Sharpsburg, Maryland. Sergeant Willett was a participant in the Battle of Fredericksburg.

1ST SERGEANT CONSIDER H. WILLETT
(Photograph Courtesy of the Mr. and Mrs. Robert Willett Collection at the US Army Military History Institute)

During the battle of Fredericksburg, December 13, 1862, Willett described the action in a letter sent to a friend in New York:

> Today I am on my knapsack for a seat, on the brick sidewalk of Main Street, Fredericksburg. The batteries (cannons) are playing around us, and the musketry occasionally throws in its voice to make the din of war complete. The boys of Company E crossed the Rappahannock on Saturday at 3 P.M. We were marched directly through the town along or near the railroad. As we neared the outskirts of town, a destructive fire poured upon us. Many of the 44th fell wounded and our Color Sergeant was killed. We are having a terrible battle here, but have high hopes in

the Ruler of all things that we shall ultimately succeed. I remain as true and firm in battle, as I hope to be in the battle of life. Yours truly, C. H. Willett. ("Gallantry at Gettysburg," Richard E. Clem, article in *North South Trader's Civil War*, Special Gettysburg Edition, Vol. XV, No. 4, May-June, 1988, pages 21-22)

1st Sergeant Consider H. Willett was at the Battle of Chancellorsville, Virginia, on May 2-3, 1863.

Gen. Lee broke contact with the Federal Army and screening his movement began moving the whole Confederate Army of Northern Virginia behind the Blue Ridge Mountains and down the Shenandoah Valley towards the Potomac River and Maryland. As soon as it was determined that the Confederate Army was on the march, the Federal Army was put into motion to keep it between Washington and the Confederate Army. Sergeant Consider H. Willett was part of this race and northward movement of the Federal Army. And during the race of blue against gray, Sergeant Willett lost his silver shield identification pin.

Still a 1st Sergeant, Consider H. Willett arrived at Little Round Top, Gettysburg, Pennsylvania, on the morning of July 2, 1863.

During the first three days in July, 1863, the greatest battle in the American Civil War was fought at the little town of Gettysburg, Pennsylvania. The aftermath of the first day's fighting left a landscape covered with countless bloated forms of Blue and Gray: now the two armies were in position to continue the struggle.

Defended by a force of seasoned veterans, the Union's extreme left flank rested on a small rocky knoll known as Little Round Top. This was Colonel Strong Vincent's Brigade of the 5th Corps, combining regiments of the 20th Maine, 83rd Pennsylvania, 44th New York, and the 16th Michigan. Late in the afternoon of July 2d, a portion of Major-General John Bell Hood's Confederate Division launched a furious attack against Vincent's Brigade. The notorious "Rebel Yell" filled the hot, humid air as Southern troops from Alabama and Texas stormed the heights of Little Round Top. The boys in blue were concealed behind a well-fortified breastwork of stone, and in a matter of minutes gray granite turned crimson red - stained with the life-giving substance of Rebel dead and dying. This violent assault cost General Hood an arm, while

Colonel Vincent paid the ultimate price ... his life. "I pray to God that I may never witness such a scene again," wrote one Union soldier who participated in this blood bath.

Scores of Confederates out of ammunition hugged the ground or crawled behind boulders to stay out of the line of fire. To prevent "needless slaughter," a Union commander requested several volunteers to go forward and round up or capture these unfortunate battle-weary souls. Under heavy musket and artillery fire, Sergeant Willett of the 44th New York was one of the first to vault the stone breastworks and start downhill on this "mission of mercy."

The regimental history of the 44th New York Volunteers gives the following account: "Sergeant Willett found a large number of the enemy (mostly Texans) concealed behind the rocks and the depression in the field, lying prone upon the ground. They were taken by surprise at his appearance among them and he quickly had them in motion and conducted to the rear. From his standpoint he counted 97 prisoners." In an article, "Incidents at Gettysburg," Willett wrote, "Our musketry firing left the dead piled so thick that it was almost impossible to walk over the ground without stepping on the Rebel dead."

Willett's capture of 97 prisoners on Little Round Top was more an act of compassion than capture, considering that these Confederate soldiers were out of ammunition, barefoot and completely demoralized. This brave act was only one of many performed during those three tragic days at Gettysburg.

Heavy rain soaked both man and beast as the armies withdrew from the Gettysburg field of battle - one massive sea of humanity, covered with mud and blood, slowly drifted through Pennsylvania into Maryland. These days of misery and grief found the 44th New York camped near Jones Crossroads in southern Washington County, Maryland.

For Sergeant Willett, the events of the past few days would be engraved on his memory. The nightmare of Gettysburg would be carried into eternity - even the long trek from the muddy fields of Pennsylvania could not erase that horrible scene ... ("Gallantry at Gettysburg," Richard E. Clem, article in *North South Trader's Civil War*, Special Gettysburg Edition, Vol. XV, No. 4, May-June, 1988, pages 18-19)

NOTE: An interesting aside to the story of 1st Sergeant Willett's silver identification pin is that on November 28, 1986, a collector, Mr. Clem, found the silver shield identification pin lost by 1st Sergeant Consider H. Willett. For over 133 years, it had lain buried and forgotten at a Civil War campsite near Lappans Crossroads, Maryland.

SILVER SHIELD IDENTIFICATION PIN
SERGT / C. H. WILLETT / CO. E
44TH REGT / N Y I VOL

On August 8, 1863, Sergeant Willett was promoted to Captain, in Command of Company G, Second U. S. Colored Infantry.

By mid-August, 1863, Captain Willett and the Second Colored Regiment were ordered to report to duty in Florida.

In February, 1865, after a Confederate raid on Fort Myers and Cedar Key, on Florida's southwest coast, an expedition was sent out by steamer to chase the Rebel raiders. Included in the force was Captain C. H. Willett and his Company G, 2nd U.S. Colored Infantry. They skirmished with the enemy in the St. Mark's area, Port Leon, East River, Natural Bridge, and St. Mark's River, all south of Tallahassee. The 2nd Colored Infantry lost 10 killed and 47 wounded.

As a result of this action, Brigadier General John Newton, commanding District of Key West and Tortugas, made recommendations for gallant and distinguished services, including Captain C. H. Willett, 2nd U.S. Colored Infantry. Captain Willett was recommended for brevet of major.

CAPTAIN CONSIDER H. WILLETT
(Photograph Courtesy of the Barrett Collection At the US Army Military History Institute)

In June, 1865, Captain Willett contracted yellow fever in the swamps of Key West, Florida, and was admitted to an Army hospital at Fort Taylor and placed on the disabled list. He was discharged on September 12, 1865, and transported back to New York were he recuperated.

In 1866, Consider H. Willett was granted an army pension due to "physical disability" caused by the yellow fever.

On May 29, 1866, Consider H. Willett sold to his mother, Mrs. Tryphosa W. (Willett) Rowe, for $1000.00 "two undivided ninths of all that part of Lots Number 209 and 217 of the Onondaga Reservation" about 94 acres "which William Willett died seized of" as a life right, reversion to Consider H. Willett on death of his mother (Onondaga County, New York, Deed Book 160, pages 319-320).

Consider Willett attended Bellevue Medical Hospital College in New York. He entered Albany Law School, and was admitted to the Bar in April, 1866. Later, he attended and was graduated from the University of Michigan.

Consider Heath Willett married at Ann Arbor, Washtenaw County, Michigan, on November 5, 1867, Lois Adelaide ("Addie") Wilder (b 1849, in Oswego County, New York; d July 12, 1936, at La Grange, Cook County, Illinois), the daughter of Edwin Wilder and Charlotte Barnard. They resided in Chicago, Illinois where he practiced law.

The Chicago fire of October 8, 1871 ("O'Leary's Cow") impoverished Consider Heath Willett. However, by October 11, 1871, he was counseling clients at Dr. F. M. Wilder's office on 22d Street.

In April, 1875, he was appointed Village Attorney of Hyde Park, Cook County, Illinois. He was reappointed for 1876-1877. In January, 1879, he was appointed County Attorney, Cook County, and reappointed for 1880-1881.

In the 1880, University Place, Chicago City, Cook County, Illinois census, 8-27-31-39, is listed Consider H. Willett and family, as follows:

Willett	Consider H.	m	39	NY	NY	NY
	L. Addie	f	31	NY	NY	NY
	Lucile	f	11	IL	NY	NY
	Pearl	f	9	IL	NY	NY
	Grace	f	7	IL	NY	NY
	Myrtle	f	5	IL	NY	NY
	Elouise (sic)	f	4	IL	NY	NY
	Mabelle	f	1	IL	NY	NY
Rowe	Tryphosa	f	63	NY	mother	
Casey	Johanna	f	21	IRE	servant/house	
	Helen	f	19	IRE	servant/house	

In 1880, his mother, Mrs. Tryphosa (Willett) Rowe, age 63, was living with him (1880 Cook County census).

WILLIAM WILLETT (1769-1844)

The sketch below is from
Chicago and Its Distinguished Citizens, 1881

In the 1900, Hyde Park, Chicago City, Cook County, Illinois census, 1-1022-13, is listed Consider H. Willett and family, as follows:

Willett	Consider H.	m	Dec 1840	59 NY NY NY M-32
	Lois A.	f	Jan 1849	51 NY NY NY M-32
				8 chn - 8 living
	Grace A.	f	Aug 1872	27 IL NY NY
	Mabelle	f	Feb 1879	21 IL NY NY
	William R.	m	Apr 1881	19 IL NY NY

Consider Willett died in Chicago October 12, 1912, and is buried in Oak Woods Cemetery in Chicago, along with his wife.

WILLETT SISTERS 1891
HELEN – GRACE – LUCILLE
PEARL – MAYBELLE – MYRTLE
(Photograph courtesy of Judy Gorham)

(Bookstaver, 1907, page 69; *The Willett Families*, 1985, page 171; *Chicago and Its Distinguished Citizens or the Progress of Forty Years*, 1881, pages 260-263).

1. **Adelaide** ("Adie") **Lucille WILLETT**: b August 12, 1868, Chicago, Cook County, Illinois; m William Burnay (Burnap); no issue; d 195x, Glencoe, Cook County, Illinois.

2. **Florence Pearl WILLETT**: b July 6, 1870, Chicago, Cook County, Illinois; m Harry Simons; he was with the Chicago Board of Trade; d 195x, Glencoe, Cook County, Illinois. See next I.1.1.9.2.2.

3. **Grace Annette WILLETT**: b August 24, 1872, Chicago, Cook County, Illinois; m Ernest Dillon; no issue; d 1960, Glencoe, Cook County, Illinois.

4. **Myrtle Geneveve WILLETT**: b June 22, 1874, Chicago, Cook County, Illinois; m abt 1895, Sidney S. Gorham (b 1874, Vermont; d December 23, 1935, Chicago, Cook County, Illinois); d January, 1968, Glencoe, Cook County, Illinois. See next I.1.1.9.2.4.

5. **Helen Eloise WILLETT**: b February 29, 1876,

Chicago, Cook County, Illinois; m Edwin T. Franklin; d 197x, Peoria, Peoria County, Illinois. See next I.1.1.9.2.5.

6. **Carlotta Maybelle WILLETT**: b 1880, Chicago, Cook County, Illinois; m in Chicago, Cook County, Illinois, in 1901, Henry Whitwell Wales (b October 8, 1875, Lanark, Carroll County, Illinois; d March, 1934, Winnetka, Cook County, Illinois); d 1939, Winnetka, Cook County, Illinois. See next I.1.1.9.2.6.

7. **William Roscoe WILLETT**: b April 7, 1881, Chicago, Cook County, Illinois; m in Louisville, Jefferson County, Kentucky, June 9, 1909, Philura Comnock (b September 29, 1886, Henderson, Henderson County, Kentucky; d June 3, 1963, Louisville, Jefferson County, Kentucky); d October, 1947, Louisville, Jefferson County, Kentucky, and is buried in the Cave Hill Cemetery, Louisville, Kentucky. See next I.1.1.9.2.7.

8. **Consider Heath WILLETT, Jr.**: b August 10, 1889, Chicago, Cook County, Illinois (he is the youngest son); m in Louisville, Jefferson County, Kentucky, on April 4, 1917, Margaret Meldrum Munn; d January 4, 1944, Louisville, Jefferson County, Kentucky. See next I.1.1.9.2.8.

WILLETT SISTERS CIRCA 1929
HELEN - GRACE - LUCILLE
PEARL - MAYBELLE - MYRTLE
(Photograph courtesy of Judy Gorham)

I.1.1.9.2.2
FLORENCE PEARL WILLETT and HARRY SIMONS
Of Cook County, Illinois

Florence Pearl Willett was born July 6, 1870, Chicago, Cook County, Illinois.

Miss Florence Pearl Willett married Harry Simons. He was with the Chicago Board of Trade.

Florence Pearl Willett died in 195x, Glencoe, Cook County, Illinois.

1. **Irving SIMONS**: died young as a teenager.

I.1.1.9.2.4
MYRTLE GENEVEVE WILLETT
And SIDNEY SMITH GORHAM
Of La Grange, Cook County, Illinois

Myrtle Geneveve Willett was born June 22, 1874, Chicago, Cook County, Illinois.

Miss Myrtle G. Willett married about 1895, Sidney Smith Gorham (b 1874, Vermont; d December 23, 1935, Chicago, Cook County, Illinois).

Mrs. Myrtle (Willett) Gorham died in January, 1968, at Glencoe, Cook County, Illinois.

1. **Lucy Maybelle GORHAM:** b 1900; d 1903, Cook County, Illinois.

2. **Sidney Smith GORHAM, Jr:** b December 23, 1906, LaGrange, Cook County, Illinois; graduate of Princeton University and the University of Chicago Law School; m on September 22, 1928, Corinne Aymond McVoy (b October 5, 1906, Chicago, Cook County, Illinois; d July 16, 1977, Chicago, Cook County, Illinois, buried in the All Saints Cemetery, Cook County, Illinois); practiced law in Chicago; resided in Winnetka and Chicago, Cook County, Illinois; d August 18, 1978, Chicago, Cook County, Illinois, and is buried in the All Saints Cemetery, Des Plaines, Cook County, Illinois. See next I.1.1.9.2.4.2.

3. **Willett Noble GORHAM:** b August 11, 1909, LaGrange, Cook County, Illinois; m in Winnetka, Cook County, Illinois, on March 29, 1933, Lucie Truesdale Jacobs (b April 26, 1911, Chicago, Cook County, Illinois; d July 3, 1967. Skokie, Cook County, Illinois). Mrs. Lucie (Jacobs) Gorham married 2nd in Winnetka, Cook County, Illinois, in April, 1969, Garret Lawrence Bergen. See next I.1.1.9.2.4.3.

I.1.1.9.2.4.2
SIDNEY SMITH GORHAM, SR.
And **CORINNE AYMOND MCVOY**
Of Chicago, Cook County, Illinois

Sidney Smith Gorham, Jr., was born December 23, 1906, LaGrange, Cook County, Illinois. He was graduated from Princeton University and the University of Chicago Law School.

Sidney Smith Gorham married September 22, 1928, Corinne Aymond McVoy (b October 5, 1906, Chicago, Cook County, Illinois; d July 16, 1977, Chicago, Cook County, Illinois, buried in the All Saints Cemetery in Des Plaines, Cook County, Illinois). He practiced law in Chicago, and resided in Winnetka and Chicago, Cook County, Illinois.

Sidney Smith Gorham, Jr., died August 18, 1978, Chicago, Cook County, Illinois, and is buried in the All Saints Cemetery, Des Plaines, Cook County, Illinois.

1. **Sidney Smith GORHAM (III)**: b January 16, 1932, Chicago, Cook County, Illinois; m in Chicago, Cook County, Illinois, December 28, 1963, Jean Elizabeth Howell (b December 23, 1934). See next I.1.1.9.2.4.2.1.

2. **Eugene Timothy GORHAM**: b May 2, 1935, Chicago, Cook County, Illinois; m 1st 1962, in Pentwater, Oceana County, Michigan, Jane Weinberg (b 1937) (divorced); m 2nd in Winnetka, Cook County, Illinois, in November, 1967, Barbara Steinke (b August 20, 1941). See next I.1.1.9.2.4.2.2.

3. **Jeffrey Heath GORHAM**: b May 22, 1940; m 1st in Glenview, Cook County, Illinois, December 21, 1968, Leslie Rathburn (Vognild) (b 1939) (divorced October 30, 1972, no issue); m 2nd in Chicago, Cook County, Illinois, on May 18, 1973, DeAnn Mary Dougherty (Harris) (b March 12, 1942, Syracuse, New York) (divorced March 11, 1976, Jackson, Jackson County, Michigan, no issue); m 3rd in Jackson, Jackson County, Michigan, October 30, 1976, Mrs. Marcia Jayne (Jacobs) Verspoor (b April 15, 1939, Chatfield, Crawford County, Ohio). See next I.1.1.9.2.4.2.3.

4. **Anthony McVoy GORHAM**: b March 10, 1947, Chicago, Cook County, Illinois; d May 15, 1947, Winnetka, Cook County, Illinois, buried in All Saints Cemetery, Des Plaines, Cook County, Illinois.

I.1.1.9.2.4.2.1
SIDNEY SMITH GORHAM, III
And JEAN ELIZABETH HOWELL
Of Newport, Rhode Island

Sidney Smith Gorham (III) was born January 16, 1932, Chicago, Cook County, Illinois.

Sidney Smith Gorham married in Chicago, Cook County, Illinois, December 28, 1963, Jean Elizabeth Howell (b December 23, 1934).

They reside (1999) in Newport, Rhode Island. He is a graduate of the University of Illinois.

1. **Sidney Smith GORHAM, IV**: b August 12, 1966; m in San Francisco, California, April 26, 1997, Teron Park; resides (1999) in San Francisco, California.

I.1.1.9.2.4.2.2a
EUGENE TIMOTHY GORHAM and **JANE WEINBERG**
Of Chicago, Cook County, Illinois

Eugene Timothy Gorham was born May 2, 1935, Chicago, Cook County, Illinois.
Eugene Timothy Gorham married 1st 1962, in Pentwater, Oceana County, Michigan, Jane Weinberg (b 1937) (divorced).
Mrs. Jane (Weinberg) Willett married 2nd Shere.

1. **Jonathan L. GORHAM SHERE**: b August 12, 1964 (adopted by stepfather).

I.1.1.9.2.4.2.2b
EUGENE TIMOTHY GORHAM and **BARBARA STEINKE**
Of Winnetka, Cook County, Illinois

Eugene Timothy Gorham married 2nd in Winnetka, Cook County, Illinois, in November, 1967, Barbara Steinke (b August 20, 1941).
He is a graduate of the Stanford University School of Engineering, and works as a conveyor belt engineer in the Cook County, Illinois, area. They reside (1999) in Winnetka, Cook County, Illinois, and have a summer residence, McVoy Cottage, Pentwater, Oceana County, Michigan.

2. **Eugene Timothy GORHAM, II**: b June 11, 1968, Chicago, Cook County, Illinois; m in Winnetka, Cook County, Illinois, September 16, 1997, Kimberly Coll; graduate of Lehigh University School of Engineering, Bethlehem, Pennsylvania; works for Automations Conveyor Belts, Itasca, Cook County, Illinois; resides (1999) Northfield, Cook County, Illinois.

1. **Dillon Timothy GORHAM**: b June 16, 1998, Chicago, Cook County, Illinois.

3. **Brooke Lee GORHAM**: b September 3, 1973, Chicago, Cook County, Illinois; graduate of Wittenberg University, Springfield, Ohio; resides (1999) Chicago, Cook County, Illinois.

4. **Whitney Ann GORHAM**: b May 27, 1975, Chicago, Cook County, Illinois; resides (1999) Chicago, Cook County, Illinois.

I.1.1.9.2.4.2.3a
JEFFREY HEATH GORHAM and **LESLIE RATHBURN**

Jeffrey Heath Gorham was born May 22, 1940, Chicago, Cook County, Illinois. He is a graduate of Dickinson College, Carlisle, Pennsylvania. Jeffrey Heath Gorham married 1st in Glenview, Cook County, Illinois, December 21, 1968, Leslie Rathburn (Vognild) (b 1939) (divorced October 30, 1972, no issue).

I.1.1.9.2.4.2.3b
JEFFREY HEATH GORHAM
And **DEANN MARY DOUGHERTY**

Jeffrey Heath Gorham married 2nd in Chicago, Cook County, Illinois, May 18, 1973, DeAnn Mary Dougherty (Harris) (b March 12, 1942, Syracuse, New York) (divorced March 11, 1976, Jackson, Jackson County, Michigan, no issue).

I.1.1.9.2.4.2.3c
JEFFREY HEATH GORHAM
And Mrs. **MARCIA JAYNE** (JACOBS) **VERSPOOR**

Jeffrey Heath Gorham married 3rd in Jackson, Jackson County, Michigan, October 30, 1976, Mrs. Marcia Jayne (Jacobs) Verspoor (b April 15, 1939, Chatfield, Crawford County, Ohio). Jeffrey is retired from Consumers Energy. They reside (1999) in Fort Myers, Florida.

1. **Shelly Ann VERSPOOR** (stepdaughter): b March 11, 1961, Jackson, Jackson County, Michigan; m in 1995, Blake Mann Brown (resides Dunwoody, Georgia).

1. **William** ("Will") **Patrick BROWN**: b October 6, 1995, Atlanta, Georgia.

2. **Kelly Ann VERSPOOR** (stepdaughter): b May 6, 1966, Kalamazoo, Michigan; m December, 1990, Robert Clayton Gray (divorced June, 1998); resides Jackson, Michigan; gemologist (GG).

1. **Andrew Clayton GRAY**: b April 25, 1991, Jackson, Jackson County, Michigan.

I.1.1.9.2.4.3
WILLETT NOBLE GORHAM
And LUCIE TRUESDALE JACOBS
Of Illinois

Willett Noble Gorham was born August 11, 1909, LaGrange, Cook County, Illinois. He was graduated from Exeter, Princeton University and in 1932, from the University of Chicago Law School.
Willett Noble Gorham married in Winnetka, Cook County, Illinois, on March 29, 1933, Lucie Truesdale Jacobs (b April 26, 1911, Chicago, Cook County, Illinois).
Willett Noble Gorham died on July 3, 1967, Skokie, Cook County, Illinois.
Mrs. Lucie (Jacobs) Gorham married 2nd in Winnetka, Cook County, Illinois, in April, 1969, Garret Lawrence Bergen. She is widowed for the second time, and resides (1999) in Manchester, Connecticut.

1. **Willett Noble GORHAM, Jr**: b June 21, 1934, Evanston, Cook County, Illinois; m in Chicago, Cook County, Illinois, on September 2, 1961, Judith Suzanne Mullins (b August 14, 1938, Coleraine, Itasca County, Minnesota); graduate of University of Arizona College of Agriculture; resides (1999) Norton Shores, Muskegon County, Michigan. See next I.1.1.9.2.4.3.1.

2. **Lucy ("Dale") Truesdale GORHAM**: b December 3, 1937, Evanston, Illinois; m in Winnetka, Illinois, September 7, 1957, Jeffrey Peter Carstern (b February 17, 1936, Evanston, Cook County, Illinois); graduate of Bennett Junior College; resides (1999) South Glastonbury, Connecticut. See next I.1.1.9.2.4.3.2.

I.1.1.9.2.4.3.1
WILLETT NOBLE GORHAM, JR.
And JUDITH SUZANNE MULLINS
Of Norton Shore, Muskegon, Michigan

Willett Noble Gorham, Jr., was born June 21, 1934, Evanston, Cook County, Illinois.

Willett Noble Gorham married in Chicago, Cook County, Illinois, September 2, 1961, Judith Suzanne Mullins (b August 14, 1938, Coleraine, Itasca County, Minnesota). He is a graduate of University of Arizona College of Agriculture. He has lived and worked on a leased ranch in Tucson, Arizona. He was a banker in Chicago, Dwight, and Belleville (all Illinois).

Presently, he is retired from Old Kent Bank-West, Grand Haven, Ottawa County, Michigan, and resides (1999) Norton Shores, Muskegon County, Michigan.

1. **Suzanne Willett GORHAM**: b March 31, 1962, Chicago, Illinois; m in Norton Shores, Muskegon County, Michigan, on August 20, 1990, Kris Long [Lindsey] Jennings (b May 12, 1962, Sandy, Salt Lake County, Utah); graduate of Colorado Mountain College, Leadville. See next I.1.1.9.2.4.3.1.1.

2. **Sandra Elizabeth GORHAM**: b April 5, 1965, Joliet, Will County, Illinois; m in Las Vegas, Nevada, on January 26, 1990, Billy Lee Hoopingarner (b May 30, 1962, Peoria, Peoria County, Illinois); graduate of the University of Colorado; presently (1999). a Master's degree candidate in early Childhood Education at Western Michigan University, Kalamazoo. See next I.1.1.9.2.4.3.1.2.

I.1.1.9.2.4.3.1.1
SUZANNE WILLETT GORGAM and KRIS LONG JENNINGS
Of Cumberland County, Maine

Suzanne Willett Gorham was born March 31, 1962, Chicago, Illinois.

Miss Suzanne Willett Gorham married in Norton Shores, Muskegon County, Michigan, August 20, 1990, Kris Long [Lindsey] Jennings (b May 12, 1962, Sandy, Salt Lake County, Utah).

She is a graduate of Colorado Mountain College, Leadville, and currently works for the City of Portland, Cumberland County, Maine, in the Assessors Office as a Data Clerk. They reside (1999) in Freeport, Cumberland County, Maine. Kris Lindsey had been adopted by his stepfather and assumed the surname Jennings.

1. **Maxwell Devereux JENNINGS**: b April 14, 1993, Portland, Cumberland County, Maine.

2. **Emily Willett JENNINGS**: b June 4, 1996, Portland, Cumberland County, Maine.

I.1.1.9.2.4.3.1.2
SANDRA ELIZABETH GORHAM
And **BILLY LEE HOOPINGARNER**
Of Colorado

Sandra Elizabeth Gorham was born April 5, 1965, Joliet, Will County, Illinois.

Miss Sandra Elizabeth Gorham married in Las Vegas, Nevada, January 26, 1990, Billy Lee Hoopingarner (b May 30, 1962, Peoria, Peoria County, Illinois).

She is a graduate of the University of Colorado, and is presently (1999) a Master's degree candidate in early Childhood Education at Western Michigan University, Kalamazoo, Michigan. They reside (1999) Otsego, Allegan County, Michigan.

1. **Alexander Redhed Gorham HOOPINGARNER**: b July 29, 1990, Thornton, Adam County, Colorado.

2. **Alicia Jacobs Gorham HOOPINGARNER**: b February 12, 1993, Wheatridge, Jefferson County, Colorado.

I.1.1.9.2.4.3.2
LUCY TRUESDALE GORHAM
And JEFFREY PETER CARSTENS
Of Hartford, Connecticut

Lucy Truesdale ("Dale") Gorham was born December 3, 1937, Evanston, Illinois. Miss Lucy Truesdale Gorham married in Winnetka, Cook County, Illinois, September 7, 1957, Jeffrey Peter Carstens (b February 17, 1936, Evanston, Cook County, Illinois). She is a graduate of Bennett Junior College, and Greater Hartford Community College with an RN Degree. She is a retired school nurse. They reside (1999) South Glastonbury, Hartford County, Connecticut.

1. **Julie Truesdale CARSTENS**: b March 5, 1959, Princeton, New Jersey; m in South Glastonbury, Hartford County, Connecticut, March 9, 1986, Edward Joseph Kamis, Jr. (b February 1, 1958, Hartford County, Connecticut); graduate of Lesley College and University of Connecticut (MA). See next I.1.1.9.2.4.3.2.1.

2. **Lucie Gorham CARSTENS**: b October 10, 1960, Hartford, Hartford County, Connecticut; m in South Glastonbury, Hartford County, Connecticut, June 18, 1988, Thomas Gerald Daly (b September 14, 1959). See next I.1.1.9.2.4.3.2.2.

3. **Willett Noble CARSTENS**: b February 28, 1967, Hartford, Hartford County, Connecticut; d accidentally by drowning on June 12, 1971, and is buried in South Glastonbury, Connecticut.

4. **Virginia Elizabeth CARSTENS**: b October 17, 1972, Hartford, Hartford County, Connecticut; graduate of Bryn Mawr College, Bryn Mawr, Pennsylvania; presently a law degree candidate; resides (1999) Boston, Massachusetts.

I.1.1.9.2.4.3.2.1
JULIE TRUESDALE CARSTENS
And EDWARD JOSEPH KAMIS
Of Hartford County, Connecticut

Julie Truesdale Carstens was born March 5, 1959, Princeton, New Jersey.

Miss Julie Truesdale Carstens was married in South Glastonbury, Hartford County, Connecticut, March 9, 1986, Edward Joseph Kamis, Jr. (b February 1, 1958, Hartford County, Connecticut).

She is a graduate of Lesley College, Cambridge, Massachusetts, and University of Connecticut (MA), Hartford, Connecticut; resides (1999) South Glastonbury, Hartford County, Connecticut.

1. **Meredith Katherine KAMIS**: b June 14, 1987, Hartford, Hartford County, Connecticut.

2. **Julia Hahn KAMIS**: b July 5, 1989, Hartford, Hartford County, Connecticut.

I.1.1.9.2.4.3.2.2
LUCIE GORHAM CARSTENS
And THOMAS GERALD DALY
Of Hartford County, Connecticut

Lucie Gorham Carstens was born October 10, 1960, Hartford, Hartford County, Connecticut.

Miss Lucie Gorham Carstens married in South Glastonbury, Hartford County, Connecticut, June 18, 1988, Thomas Gerald Daly (b September 14, 1959). They reside (1999) South Glastonbury, Hartford County, Connecticut.

1. **Virginia ("Genna") Elizabeth DALY**: b March 30, 1990, Hartford, Hartford County, Connecticut.

2. **Lila Margaret DALY**: b October 31, 1991, Hartford, Hartford County, Connecticut.

3. **Thomas Jeffrey DALY**: b February 26, 1997, Hartford, Hartford County, Connecticut.

I.1.1.9.2.5
HELEN ELOISE WILLETT and EDWIN T. FRANKLIN

Helen Eloise Willett was born on February 29, 1876, Chicago, Cook County, Illinois.
Miss Helen Eloise Willett married Edwin T. Franklin.
Mrs. Helen Eloise (Willett) Franklin died in 197x, Peoria, Peoria County, Illinois.

1. **William Henry FRANKLIN**: b January 30, 1909, Cook County, Illinois; was graduated from Princeton University; m on April 19, 1938, Mary; retired as President of Caterpillar, Inc; resided Peoria, Peoria County, Illinois. See next I.1.1.9.2.5.1.

I.1.1.9.2.5.1
WILLIAM HENRY FRANKLIN and MARY
Of Illinois

William Henry Franklin was born January 30, 1909, Cook County, Illinois. He was graduated from Princeton University.
William Henry Franklin married April 19, 1938, Mary. He retired as President of Caterpillar, Inc. They resided in Peoria, Peoria County, Illinois.

1. **William Henry FRANKLIN, Jr**: b November 21, 1941; m Gloria Jean Jacobs (b June 9, 1942). See next I.1.1.9.2.5.1.1.

2. **Ann Elizabeth FRANKLIN**: b June 4, 1944.

3. **Mary Josephine FRANKLIN**: b March 2, 1946.

4. **Robert Edward FRANKLIN**: b November 10, 1949; m October 17, 1981, Sheri Lynn Brogan (b December 27, 1958). See next I.1.1.9.2.5.1.4.

I.1.1.9.2.5.1.1
WILLIAM HENRY FRANKLIN, JR.
And GLORIA JEAN JACOBS

William Henry Franklin, Jr., was born November 21, 1941.

William Henry Franklin, Jr., married Gloria Jean Jacobs (b June 9, 1942).

1. **William Henry FRANKLIN, III**: b February 21, 1966; m November 4, 1989, Lisa Marie Goetz (b June 6, 1966).

    1. **Cassidy Marie FRANKLIN**: b September 9, 1991.

    2. **Andrew Jacob FRANKLIN**: b January 11, 1994.

I.1.1.9.2.5.1.4
ROBERT EDWARD FRANKLIN and SHERI LYNN BROGAN

Robert Edward Franklin was born November 10, 1949.

Robert Edward Franklin married October 17, 1981, Sheri Lynn Brogan (b December 27, 1958).

1. **Jennifer Lynn FRANKLIN**: b June 1, 1983.

2. **Daniel Robert FRANKLIN**: b March 2, 1988.

I.1.1.9.2.6
CARLOTTA MAYBELLE WILLETT
And HENRY WHITWELL WALES

Carlotta Maybelle Willett was born in 1879, Chicago, Cook County, Illinois (or 1880, depending on reference). Miss Carlotta Maybelle Willett married in Chicago, Cook County, Illinois, in 1901, Henry Whitwell Wales (b October 8, 1875, Lanark, Carroll County, Illinois; d March, 1934, Winnetka, Cook County, Illinois). He was a graduate of the University of Chicago Law School LLB.

The year 1937 was known as the year of the "Great Flood" in Louisville, Kentucky. Maybelle was very much alive then and experienced this event as attested by several of her grandchildren.

Mrs. Carlotta Maybelle (Willett) Wales died in 1939, in Winnetka, Cook County, Illinois.

1. **Henry Whitwell WALES, Jr**: b August 4, 1903, LaGrange, Cook County, Illinois; m Nancy Barbee Wilson (b October 23, 1901, Paris, Bourbon County, Kentucky; d May 31, 1993, Palo Alto, Santa Clara County, California); resided Louisville, Jefferson County, Kentucky; d August 2, 1975, Louisville, Jefferson County, Kentucky. See next I.1.1.9.2.6.1.

2. **Robert Willett WALES**: b December 23, 1906, Cook County, Illinois; m in Columbus, Franklin County, Ohio, October 10, 1931, Frances Solace Huntington (b June 20, 1907, Columbus, Ohio; d May 5, 1998, Southport, Fairfield County, Connecticut); was graduated in 1927, from Princeton University, A. B., and Harvard Law School; d April 18, 1983, in Southport, Fairfield County, Connecticut. See next I.1.1.9.2.6.2.

3. **Lois Elizabeth** ("Betty") **WALES**: b May 13, 1909, Chicago, Cook County, Illinois; m in Winnetka, Cook County, Illinois, June 20, 1934, Robert Taylor Porter (b April 9, 1903, in Chicago, Cook County, Illinois; d March 19, 1980, Memphis, Shelby County, Tennessee); d September 20, 1978, in Glenview, Cook County, Illinois. See next I.1.1.9.2.6.3.

I.1.1.9.2.6.1
HENRY WHITWELL WALES, JR.
And NANCY BARBEE WILSON
Of Louisville, Jefferson County, Kentucky

Henry Whitwell Wales, Jr., was born August 4, 1903, LaGrange, Cook County, Illinois.

Henry Whitwell Wales married Nancy Barbee Wilson (b October 23, 1901, Paris, Bourbon County, Kentucky; d May 31, 1993, Palo Alto, Santa Clara County, California). He was a 1925, graduate of Princeton University, A. B. He was President of the Consider Willett Furniture Company, Louisville, Kentucky, and resided Louisville, Jefferson County, Kentucky.

H. WHITWELL WALES, JR.
CIRCA 1955
(Courtesy of H. Whitwell Wales, III)

Henry Whitwell Wales died August 2, 1975, in Louisville, Jefferson County, Kentucky.

1. **Henry Whitwell WALES, III**: b August 26, 1935, Louisville, Jefferson County, Kentucky; 1957 graduate of Princeton University A. B; m 1st April 15, 1959, Katherine Wakefield Cohn (b February 14, 1941, Louisville, Jefferson County, Kentucky) (divorced); m 2nd December 22, 1971, Roxana Currie (b September 21, 1946). See next I.1.1.9.2.6.1.1.

I.1.1.9.2.6.1.1a
HENRY WHITWELL WALES, III
And **KATHERINE WAKEFIELD COHN**

Henry Whitwell Wales, III, was born August 26, 1935, Louisville, Jefferson County, Kentucky. He is a 1957 graduate of Princeton University, A. B.

Henry Whitwell Wales married 1st April 15, 1959, Katherine Wakefield Cohn (b Louisville, Jefferson County, Kentucky) (divorced).

1. **Henry Whitwell WALES, IV**: b November 23, 1959, Manhattan, New York City, New York; graduate of Amherst College, B.A., and Southern Methodist University, M. A; m 1st in Louisville, Jefferson County, Kentucky, on May 30, 1987, Robin Jane Pierce (b July 1, 1956, Mansfield, Richland County, Ohio) (divorced on March 15, 1995); 2nd at Hancock, Hillsboro County, New Hampshire, on August 26, 1995, Leslie Warfield Thatcher (b October 13, 1965, Palo Alto, Santa Clara County, California). See next I.1.1.9.2.6.1.1.1.

2. **Robert Willett WALES**: b November 15, 1961, Manhattan, New York City, New York; resides (1999) Fremont, California; sells wire and cable in the Silicon Valley.

3. **Sidney Wakefield WALES**: b March 28, 1963, Manhattan, New York City, New York; graduate of University of Virginia, B. A; U. C. L. A., M. B. A; resides (1999) Foster City, San Mateo County, California.

I.1.1.9.2.6.1.1b
HENRY WHITWELL WALES, III and **ROXANA CURRIE**

Henry Whitwell Wales married 2nd in Manhattan, New York City, New York, on December 22, 1971, Roxana Currie (b September 21, 1946). Roxana is a scientist at NASA.

He retired from Banking and Real Estate Development. They currently (1999) reside in Foster City, San Mateo County, California.

4. **Allison Currie WALES**: b November 22, 1975, Wilmington, New Castle County, Delaware; 1997 graduate of Princeton University, A. B; consultant to Non-Profit foundations; resides (1999) Manhattan, New York City, New York.

I.1.1.9.2.6.1.1.1a
HENRY WHITWELL WALES, IV, and ROBIN JANE PIERCE

Henry Whitwell Wales, IV, was born November 23, 1959, Manhattan, New York City, New York. He is a graduate of Amherst College, B.A., Amherst, Massachusetts, and Southern Methodist University, M. A.., Dallas, Texas

Henry Whitwell Wales married 1st in Louisville, Jefferson County, Kentucky, May 30, 1987, Robin Jane Pierce (b July 1, 1956, Mansfield, Richland County, Ohio) (divorced March 15, 1995).

1. **Zachary Pierce WALES**: b December 14, 1988, Fitchburg, Worcester County, Massachusetts.

I.1.1.9.2.6.1.1.1b
HENRY WHITWELL WALES, IV, And LESLIE WARFIELD THATCHER

Henry Whitwell Wales married 2nd at Hancock, Hillsboro County, New Hampshire, August 26, 1995, Leslie Warfield Thatcher (b October 13, 1965, Palo Alto, Santa Clara County, California).

Presently (1999) he is a teacher at Cushing Academy.

2. **Henry Whitwell WALES, V**: b July 2, 1997, Gardner.

I.1.1.9.2.6.2
ROBERT WILLETT WALES
And FRANCES SOLACE HUNTINGTON

Robert Willett Wales was born December 23, 1906, Cook County, Illinois.

Robert Willett married in Columbus, Ohio, October 10, 1931, Frances Solace Huntington (b June 20, 1907, Columbus, Franklin County, Ohio; d 1998, Southport, Fairfield County, Connecticut). He was graduated in 1927, from Princeton University, A. B., and Harvard Law School, and practiced law in Chicago and New York City.

Robert Willett Wales died April 18, 1983, in Southport, Fairfield County, Connecticut.

1. **Gwynne Huntington WALES**: b April 18, 1933, Evanston, Cook County, Illinois; m in January, 1958, Janet McCobb (b September, 1935); resides (1999) Ankara, Turkey. See next I.1.1.9.2.6.2.1.

2. **Ann Elizabeth WALES**: b May 2, 1935, Evanston, Cook County, Illinois; m on June 15, 1957, John David Kirkland (b June 6, 1933, in McAllen, Hidalgo County, Texas) (divorced February 27, 1985, in Houston, Harris County, Texas, and assumed her maiden name). See next I.1.1.9.2.6.2.2.

3. **Solace ("Sally") Huntington WALES**: b November 12, 1938, Cook County, Illinois; is a graduate of Smith College; m William Lionel Sheets (b August 25, 1937); William is a professional artist; resides (1999) Kentfield, Marin County, California, and Italy.

   1. **Gwyndolen Blanche SHEETS**: b July 17, 1973.

I.1.1.9.2.6.2.1
GWYNNE HUNTINGTON WALES and JANET MCCOBB
Of Ankara, Turkey

Gwynne Huntington Wales was born April 18, 1933, Evanston, Cook County, Illinois. He was graduated from Princeton University and Harvard Law School.

Gwynne Huntington Wales married in January, 1958, Janet McCobb (b September, 1935).

They currently (1999) reside in Ankara, Turkey.

1. **Thomas** ("Todd) **Gwynne WALES**: b March, 1959.

2. **Katherine Anne WALES**: b April, 1962; m James Lokay; they reside (1999) in Middletown, Middlesex County, Connecticut.

    1. Thomas LOKAY:

    2. **Allison LOKAY:**

3. **Louise WALES**: b April, 1969; m 1st William Reynolds (divorced); m 2nd Marshall Field.

    1. **Chloe FIELD:**

I.1.1.9.2.6.2.2
ANN ELIZABETH WALES and JOHN DAVID KIRKLAND

Ann Elizabeth Wales was born May 2, 1935, Evanston, Cook County, Illinois. She was graduated from Smith College and the University of St. Thomas, Houston, Texas, as a Certified Public Accountant. Miss Ann Elizabeth Wales married June 15, 1957, John David Kirkland (b June 6, 1933, McAllen, Hidalgo County, Texas) (divorced in Houston, Texas, on February 27, 1985, and assumed her maiden name). Currently (1999) she resides in Houston, Harris County, Texas.

1. **John David KIRKLAND, Jr**: b January 29, 1958, in New Haven, New Haven County, Connecticut; m August 21, 1982, Ann Ellen Ainsworth (b December 7, 1958, in Hong Kong); was graduated from Yale University and Yale Law School, and is practicing law in Houston, Texas; resides (1999) Houston, Harris County, Texas.

   1. **Diana Margaret KIRKLAND**: b March 22, 1988, Houston, Harris County, Texas.

   2. **William Daniel KIRKLAND**: b March 10, 1992, Houston, Harris County, Texas.

2. **Solace Huntington KIRKLAND**: b March 4, 1961, Houston, Harris County, Texas; m in Houston, Harris County, Texas, February 1, 1997, James Thurlow Southwick (b July, 1960); was graduated from Smith College, Northampton, Massachusetts, and the University of Texas Law School; practicing attorney in Houston, Texas; resides (1999) Houston, Texas.

   1. **James Morrell SOUTHWICK**: b April 22, 1998.

3. **Robert Wales KIRKLAND**: b May 10, 1964, Houston, Harris County, Texas; m in Houston, Harris County, Texas, March 1, 1996, Alicia Skiff Crawford (b January 12, 1962).

   1. **Pierce Wales KIRKLAND**: b March 11, 1997, in Houston, Harris County, Texas.

I.1.1.9.2.6.3
LOIS ELIZABETH WALES
And ROBERT TAYLOR PORTER

Lois Elizabeth ("Betty") Wales was born May 13, 1909, Chicago, Cook County, Illinois. She was a 1931 graduate of Smith College, Northampton, Massachusetts. Miss Lois Elizabeth Wales married in Winnetka, Cook County, Illinois, June 20, 1934, Robert Taylor Porter (b April 9, 1903, Chicago, Illinois; d March 19, 1980, Memphis, Shelby County, Tennessee).

Mrs. Elizabeth (Wales) Porter died September 20, 1978, in Glenview, Cook County, Illinois.

1. **Elizabeth** ("Betsy") **PORTER**: b August 9, 1937, Evanston, Cook County, Illinois; m in Winnetka, Cook County, Illinois, June 20, 1959, Phillip Boynton Bowman (b February 28, 1936, Ames, Story County, Iowa) (divorced July 21, 1992). See next I.1.1.9.2.6.3.1.

2. **Robert Taylor** ("Ty") **PORTER**: b January 23, 1940, Evanston, Cook County, Illinois; m in Grand Rapids, Kent County, Michigan, October 2, 1965, Sarah Lee Webber (b July 17, 1940, Grand Rapids, Kent County, Michigan); resides (1999) in Germantown, Shelby County, Tennessee. See next I.1.1.9.2.6.3.2.

3. **Pamela Lucy PORTER**: b October 21, 1943, Evanston, Cook County, Illinois; m in Northfield, Cook County, Illinois, August 8, 1970, Dr. William F. Gee (b August 28, 1941, Milwaukee, Milwaukee County, Wisconsin); homemaker and gift shop buyer; resides (1999) Lexington, Fayette County, Kentucky. See next I.1.1.9.2.6.3.3.

4. **William Wales PORTER**: b April 24, 1946, Evanston, Cook County, Illinois; m in Denver, Denver County, Colorado, April 27, 1973, Deborah Rath (b August 11, 1949, Morristown, Morris County, New Jersey); was graduated from Hanover College, Hanover, Indiana, and University of Denver with a Ph.D. in Psychology. See next I.1.1.9.2.6.3.4.

I.1.1.9.2.6.3.1
ELIZABETH PORTER and PHILLIP BOYNTON BOWMAN

Elizabeth ("Betsy") Porter was born August 9, 1937, Evanston, Cook County, Illinois. She is a graduate of National Louis University, Evanston, Illinois. Miss Elizabeth Porter married in Northfield, Cook County, Illinois, June 20, 1959, Phillip Boynton Bowman (b February 28, 1936, Ames, Story County, Iowa) (divorced July 21, 1992). She resides (1999) in Northbrook, Cook County, Illinois.

1. **Susan Foxworthy BOWMAN**: b December 5, 1962, in Chicago, Cook County, Illinois; m in Northfield, Cook County, Illinois, August 20, 1988, Russell Craig Flom (b February 10, 1963, Minneapolis, Hennepin County, Minnesota). She was graduated from Northwestern University, Evanston, Illinois; resides (1999) Mequon, Ozaukee County, Wisconsin.

   1. **Emily Porter FLOM**: b April 6, 1993, in Chicago, Cook County, Illinois.

   2. **Benton Taylor FLOM**: b December 3, 1996, in Minneapolis, Hennepin County, Minnesota.

2. **William Porter BOWMAN**: b October 15, 1965, in Chicago, Cook County, Illinois; m in Nantucket, Nantucket County, Massachusetts, September 23, 1995, Catherine Roberts (b January 6, 1966, Greenwich, Fairfield County, Connecticut); graduate of Princeton University; resides (1999) San Carlos, San Mateo County, California. Catherine works in commercial real estate.

   1. **Porter Roberts BOWMAN**: b January 7, 1999, in San Mateo, San Mateo County, California.

3. **Peter Wales BOWMAN**: b May 8, 1968, in Chicago, Cook County, Illinois; m in Bernardsville, Somerset County, New Jersey, June 8, 1996, Laura Forster (b June 25, 1970, in New York City, New York); graduate of Kenyon College, Gambier, Ohio; works in computer software; resides (1999) in Mill Valley, Marin County, California.

I.1.1.9.2.6.3.2
ROBERT TAYLOR PORTER and SARAH LEE WEBBER

Robert Taylor ("Ty") Porter was born January 23, 1940, Evanston, Cook County, Illinois. He was graduated from Lake Forest College, Lake Forest, Illinois. Robert Taylor Porter married in Grand Rapids, Kent County, Michigan, October 2, 1965, Sarah Lee Webber (b July 17, 1940, Grand Rapids, Kent County, Michigan). They reside (1999) in Germantown, Shelby County, Tennessee, where he works in fleet leasing of automobiles.

1. **Erik Webber PORTER** (twin): b September 8, 1971, Grand Rapids, Kent County, Michigan; graduate of Auburn University, Atlanta, Georgia; resides (1999) Atlanta, Georgia; works as an industrial designer.

2. **Ann Elizabeth PORTER** (twin): b September 8, 1971, Grand Rapids, Kent County, Michigan; graduate of Oklahoma State University, Stillwater, Oklahoma; resides (1999) in Dallas, Texas.

I.1.1.9.2.6.3.3
PAMELA LUCY PORTER and WILLIAM F. GEE

Pamela Lucy Porter was born October 21, 1943, Evanston, Cook County, Illinois. She is a graduate of Skidmore College, Saratoga Springs, New York.
Miss Pamela Lucy Porter married in Northfield. Cook County, Illinois, August 8, 1970, Dr. William F. Gee (b August 28, 1941, Milwaukee, Milwaukee County, Wisconsin). She is a homemaker and gift shop buyer. They reside (1999) Lexington, Fayette County, Kentucky.

1. **Robert Warren GEE**: b May 2, 1972, Seattle, King County, Washington; graduate of Northwestern University; works as newspaper reporter; resides (1999) McAllen, Texas.

2. **Lucy Wales GEE**: b July 16, 1974, Seattle, Washington; graduate of Northwestern University; works as benefits consultant; resides (1999) Chicago, Cook County, Illinois.

I.1.1.9.2.6.3.4
WILLIAM WALES PORTER and DEBORAH RATH

William Wales Porter was born April 24, 1946, Evanston, Cook County, Illinois.

William Wales Porter married in Denver, Denver County, Colorado, April 27, 1973, Deborah Rath (b August 11, 1949, Morristown, Morris County, New Jersey). He graduated from Hanover College, Hanover, Indiana and University of Denver with a Ph.D. in Psychology. He is the Director of Cherry Creek School District special Education Program. They reside (1999) Denver, Colorado.

1. **Elizabeth** ("Lisa") **Ann PORTER**: b July 19, 1975, in Colorado; was graduated from the University of Colorado, Boulder, Colorado; teacher assistant; resides (1999) Denver, Colorado.

2. **Marna Wales PORTER**: b January 21, 1978, in Denver, Colorado; student at University of Redland, Redlands, California.

3. **Lara Taylor PORTER**: b February 14, 1980, in Denver, Colorado; student in Brussels, Belgium.

I.1.1.9.2.7
WILLIAM ROSCOE WILLETT and PHILURA COMNOCK
Of Louisville, Jefferson County, Kentucky

William Roscoe Willett was born April 7, 1881, Chicago, Cook County, Illinois.

William Roscoe Willett married in Louisville, Jefferson County, Kentucky, June 9, 1909, Philura Comnock (b September 29, 1886, Henderson, Henderson County, Kentucky). In 1912, they moved to Louisville, Kentucky.

In 1920, Roscoe W. Willett and family are listed in the Ten Mile House Precinct, Jefferson County, Kentucky census, 5-17-26, as follows:

Willett	Roscoe W.	head	33	IL NY NY
	Philura C.	wife	32	KY SCOT KY
	Elizabeth N.	daughter	6	KY IL KY
	William R.	son	3	KY IL KY
Orller?	Mary C.	cook	42	PA FRA GER
Klie?	Alma	nurse	21	IN IN IN
Smothers?	French?	Servant	25	IN KY KY

William Roscoe Willett founded the W. R. Willett Lumber Company.

William Roscoe Willett died in October, 1947, at Louisville, Jefferson County, Kentucky, and is buried in the Cave Hill Cemetery, Louisville, Kentucky.

1. **Elizabeth** ("Dixie") **Priest WILLETT**: b September 20, 1911; m 1st in Louisville, Jefferson County, Kentucky, May 7, 1935, William Kenneth Browne (b March 19, 1911, Memphis, Shelby County, Tennessee; d March 10, 1972, Louisville, Jefferson County, Kentucky); m 2nd Kenneth Welch. See next I.1.1.9.2.9.7.1.

2. **William** ("Buddy") **Roscoe WILLETT, Jr**: b April 7, 1916, Louisville, Jefferson County, Kentucky; m in Louisville, Kentucky, October 19, 1946, Fayette McDowell (b October 29, 1921, Louisville, Kentucky), the daughter of Louise and Robert McDowell; resides (1998) at 150 West Wind Road, Louisville, Jefferson County, Kentucky, 40207. See next I.1.1.9.2.9.7.2.

I.1.1.9.2.9.7.1a
ELIZABETH PRIEST WILLETT
And WILLIAM KENNEDY BROWNE

Elizabeth ("Dixie") Priest Willett was born September 20, 1911, in Louisville, Jefferson County, Kentucky. Miss Elizabeth Priest Willett married 1st in Louisville, Jefferson County, Kentucky, May 7, 1935, William Kennedy Browne (b March 19, 1911, Memphis, Shelby County, Tennessee; d March 10, 1972, Louisville, Jefferson County, Kentucky).

1. **William Kennedy BROWNE, Jr**: b February 16, 1937, Louisville, Jefferson County, Kentucky; graduate of Yale University; m 1st in Orlando, Orange County, Florida, April 16, 1966, Sarah Colledge (b August 9, 1944, Orlando, Orange County, Florida) (divorced August 4, 1979); m 2nd in Orlando, Orange County, Florida, November 16, 1979, Lisa Mandell (b November 9, 1956, Rockville Center, Nassau County, New York) (divorced in Orlando May 9, 1986). See next I.1.1.9.2.9.7.1.1.

2. **Roscoe Willett BROWNE**: b May 1, 1939 Louisville, Jefferson County, Kentucky; resided in Louisville, and Sydney, N. S. W., Australia; d June 3, 1985, Louisville, Jefferson County, Kentucky, and is buried in the Cave Hill Cemetery, Louisville, Jefferson County, Kentucky.

3. **Alexander Cumnock BROWNE**: b June 25, 1941 Louisville, Jefferson County, Kentucky; attended the University of Arizona, Tucson; m 1st in Wilmore, Jassimine County, Kentucky, April 16, 1968, Mary Francis Jewell; m 2nd in Louisville, Jefferson County, Kentucky, August 25, 1994, Gloria Gadjen; d June 10, 1995 Louisville, Jefferson County, Kentucky, and is buried in the Cave Hill Cemetery, Louisville, Jefferson County, Kentucky.

4. **Robert Mallory BROWNE**: b March 11, 1948 Louisville, Jefferson County, Kentucky; graduate of Princeton University; MBA from Harvard University; realtor; resides (1999) New York City, New York.

I.1.1.9.2.9.7.1b
ELIZABETH PRIEST WILLETT and KENNETH WELCH

Mrs. Elizabeth Priest (Willett) Browne married 2nd Kenneth Welch. She resides (1999) in Louisville, Jefferson County, Kentucky.

I.1.1.9.2.9.7.1.1a
WILLIAM KENNEDY BROWNE, JR., and SARAH COLLEDGE

William Kennedy Browne, Jr., was born February 16, 1937, Louisville, Jefferson County, Kentucky. He is a graduate of Yale University.

William Kennedy Browne, Jr., married 1st in Orlando, Orange County, Florida, on April 16, 1966, Sarah Colledge (b August 9, 1944, Orlando, Orange County, Florida) (divorced August 4, 1979).

1. **James Slaughter BROWNE** (adopted): b October 13, 1968, Gainesville, Florida; graduate of Furman University, Greenville, South Carolina; resides (1999). Groveland, Lake County, Florida.

2. **Alexander Duncan BROWNE** (adopted): b December 12, 1970, Gainesville, Florida; m in Orlando, Orange County, Florida, April 17, 1999, Jenifer Leigh Brown (b May 5, 1974, Titusville, Brevard County, Florida).

I.1.1.9.2.9.7.1.1b
WILLIAM KENNEDY BROWNE, JR., and LISA MANDRELL

William Kennedy Browne, Jr., married 2nd in Orlando, Orange County, Florida, on November 16, 1979, Lisa Mandell (b November 9, 1956, Rockville Center, Nassau County, New York) (divorced in Orlando on May 9, 1986). He resides (1999) Orlando, Orange County, Florida.

3. **Keene McEwan BROWNE**: b June 24, 1980, Orlando, Orange County, Florida.

4. **William Kennedy BROWNE, III**: b November 19, 1981, Orlando, Orange County, Florida.

5. **Baldwin Willett BROWNE**: b April 9, 1983, Orlando, Orange County, Florida.

I.1.1.9.2.9.7.2
WILLIAM ROSCOE WILLETT, JR.
And FAYETTE MCDOWELL
Of Louisville, Kentucky

William ("Buddy") Roscoe ("Buddy") WILLETT, Jr., was born April 7, 1916, Louisville, Jefferson County, Kentucky. During World War II, Buddy served in the US Navy. William Roscoe Willett, Jr., married in Louisville, Kentucky, October 19, 1946, Fayette McDowell (b October 29, 1921, Louisville, Kentucky), the daughter of Louise and Robert McDowell. Buddy worked in wholesale lumber at the W. R. Willett Lumber Company. The Willett Lumber Company has remained in the family until the present. Buddy has since retired. They reside (1998) at 150 West Wind Road, Louisville, Jefferson County, Kentucky, 40207.

1. **Louise McDowell WILLETT**: b September 25, 1947, Louisville, Kentucky; resides (1998) Maitland, Florida.

2. **William Roscoe WILLETT (III)**: b June 9, 1949, Louisville, Kentucky; m 1st Holis Hibbs (divorced); m 2nd at the home of his parents May 26, 1996, Sally McCracken (b June 21, 1950), the daughter of Mr. And Mrs. John McCracken. Graduate of University of Virginia, Charlottesville; Stock Broker; resides Louisville, Kentucky.

    1. **William Roscoe WILLETT (IV)**: b September 5, 1984, Louisville, Kentucky.

3. **Robert ("Mac") McDowell WILLETT**: b February 25, 1953, Louisville, Kentucky; m in Statesville, Iredell County, North Carolina, April 26, 1983, Catherine Templeton (b August 26, 1954), the daughter of Dr. and Mrs. Thomas Templeton; resided Statesville, North Carolina; resides (1998) Louisville, Kentucky.

    1. **Thomas WILLETT**: b February 15, 1985, Louisville, Kentucky.

    2. **Clay WILLETT**: b May 19, 1987, Louisville, Kentucky.

I.1.1.9.2.8
CONSIDER HEATH WILLETT, JR.,
And MARGARET MELDRUM MUNN
Of Louisville, Jefferson County, Kentucky

Consider Heath Willett, Jr., was born August 10, 1889, Chicago, Cook County, Illinois. He was the youngest of the family.

Consider Heath Willett married in Louisville, Jefferson County, Kentucky, on April 4, 1917, Margaret Meldrum Munn.

Consider founded the Willett Furniture Company in Louisville, Kentucky. In 1941, it was a going concern with factories at 30th and Kentucky Streets, and 31st and Magazine Streets, Louisville, Kentucky. There was also a permanent exhibit of Willett Furniture at the 314 American Furniture Mart, Chicago, Illinois. Willett Furniture Company specialized in the manufacturer of Early American Reproductions in "Golden Beryl" Sugar Tree Hard Maple and American Wild Cherry.

From a 1941 Willett Furniture Catalog:

> What Will the Heirlooms of Our Future Generations be?
>
> The furniture of today has all been inspired by our Early American Cabinet Makers. Golden Beryl Solid Hard Sugar Tree Maple, Solid Wild Cherry, simplicity of design, beauty and grace of proportion, strength and durability, beauty and simplicity of finish, faithful reproductions of the Early American are what we offer you in this catalog.
>
> The latest and most up-to-date equipment, care, time, and effort in preparing the raw lumber, machine sanding, plus each and every piece hand sanded, proper time in drying finish and sanding between coats, hand rubbing throughout, proper packing for safe delivery, we offer you the finest commercial furniture of today [1941].
>
> Consider H. Willett, Inc.

The Willett Furniture Company was eventually sold out of the family, but continued under the Willett name until at least 1959. It went out of business in the 1960s.

Consider Heath Willett, Jr., died January 4, 1944, at Louisville, Jefferson County, Kentucky.

CICRA 1950
CONSIDER HEATH WILLETT, JR.
FOUNDER OF THE WILLETT FURNITURE COMPANY
(Photograph courtesy of Judy Gorham

1. **Lois Wilder WILLETT:** b September 11, 1918, Louisville, Jefferson County, Kentucky, m in Louisville, Jefferson County, Kentucky, September 23, 1939, Robert Danforth Ross (b October 15, 1911; d 1996). See next I.1.1.9.2.8.1.

2. **Margaret Munn WILLETT:** b January 28, 1925, Louisville, Jefferson County, Kentucky; m 1st at home, Chenoweth Lane, Louisville, Jefferson County, Kentucky, May 24, 1944, Edwin Babbitt Weir (b December 22, 1922, Louisville, Jefferson County, Kentucky) (divorced 1960); m 2nd September, 1978, Henry French Wallace (divorced 1989); m 3rd on June 22, 1990, John Hunt Stitesi (b June 22, 1922). See next I.1.1.9.2.8.2.

I.1.1.9.2.8.1
LOIS WILDER WILLETT and ROBERT DANFORTH ROSS
Of Louisville, Jefferson County, Kentucky

Lois Wilder Willett was born September 11, 1918, Louisville, Jefferson County, Kentucky.

Miss Lois Wilder Willett married in Louisville, Jefferson County, Kentucky, September 23, 1939, Robert Danforth Ross (b October 15, 1911; d 1996).

Mrs. Lois Wilder (Willett) Ross resides (1999) in Louisville, Jefferson County, Kentucky. She is planning to remove soon to Lake Forest, Cook County, Illinois.

1. **Consider Willett ROSS**: b May 10, 1942, Louisville, Jefferson County, Kentucky; m at St. Igid Roman Catholic Church, in Tyrol, Austria, October 2, 1965, Elizabeth Charlotte Giner (b August 13, 1943, Worbis, Thuringen, East Germany), the daughter of Romed Giner and Edeltrud Erdglmann. See next I.1.1.9.2.8.1.1.

2. **Sarah ("Sally") Henshaw ROSS**: b January 12, 1948, Louisville, Jefferson County, Kentucky; m in Louisville, Jefferson County, Kentucky, April 17, 1971, Robert Earl Allgyer (b October 1, 1944), the son of Kenneth Eugene Allgyer and Dorothy Irene Renninger. See next I.1.1.9.2.8.1.2.

I.1.1.9.2.8.1.1
CONSIDER WILLETT ROSS
And ELIZABETH CHARLOTTE GINER

Consider Willett Ross was born May 10, 1942, Louisville, Jefferson County, Kentucky. Consider Willett Ross married at St. Igid Roman Catholic Church, in Tyrol, Austria, October 2, 1965, Elizabeth Charlotte Giner (b August 13, 1943, Worbis, Thuringen, East Germany), the daughter of Romed Giner and Edeltrud Erdglmann.

1. **Elisabeth Charlotte ROSS**: b August 10, 1967, Landstuhl, Federal Republic of Germany; m in Chicago, Cook County, Illinois, July 13, 1991, Daniel Ivankovich.

    1. **Sophie Chaccone IVANKOVICH**: b May 5, 1993, Chicago, Cook County, Illinois.

    2. **Anthony Francis IVANKOVICH**: b November 4, 1994, Chicago, Cook County, Illinois.

    3. **Lukas Alexander IVANKOVICH**: b July 17, 1996, Chicago, Cook County, Illinois.

    4. **Katarina Gabriala IVANKOVICH**: b January 26, 1998, Chicago, Cook County, Illinois.

2. **Stephan Alexander ROSS**: b December 30, 1970, Evanston, Cook County, Illinois; graduate of Washington and Lee University, Lexington, Virginia; Stock Broker; resides (1999) Chicago, Cook County, Illinois.

3. **Katherine Margaret ROSS**: b December 28, 1973, Evanston, Cook County, Illinois; graduate of University of Michigan, Ann Arbor, Michigan; English Teacher; resides (1999) Santiago, Chile.

I.1.1.9.2.8.1.2
SARAH HENSHAW ROSS and ROBERT EARL ALLGYER

Sarah ("Sally") Henshaw Ross was born January 12, 1948, Louisville, Jefferson County, Kentucky.

Miss Sarah Henshaw Ross married in Louisville, Jefferson County, Kentucky, April 17, 1971, Robert Earl Allgyer (b October 1, 1944), the son of Kenneth Eugene Allgyer and Dorothy Irene Renninger.

1. **Sarah Scott ALLGYER** (adopted November 26, 1976): b November 25, 1976, Chicago, Cook County, Illinois; graduate of Furman University, Greenville, South Carolina; fund raiser for Boys and Girls Clubs; resides (1999) Chicago, Cook County, Illinois.

2. **Robert Earl ALLGYER, Jr**: b November 6, 1978, Lake Forest, Cook County, Illinois; attends Dartmouth College, Hanover, New Hampshire.

3. **Kenneth Ward ALLGYER**: b September 7, 1980, Lake Forest, Cook County, Illinois; attends Colby College, Waterville, Maine.

I.1.1.9.2.8.2a
MARGARET MUNN WILLETT
And EDWIN BABBITTE WEIR
Of Louisville, Jefferson County, Kentucky

Margaret Munn Willett was born January 28, 1925, at Louisville, Jefferson County, Kentucky. Miss Margaret Munn Willett married 1st at home, Chenoweth Lane, Louisville, Jefferson County, Kentucky, May 24, 1944, Edwin Babbitt Weir (b December 22, 1922, Louisville, Jefferson County, Kentucky) (divorced 1960).

1. **Margaret Willett WEIR:** b September 6, 1947, Louisville, Jefferson County, Kentucky; m at Crestwood, Fayette County, Kentucky, July, 1968, John Bruce Franck (b February 1, 1947) (divorced 1989).

   1. **John Rumsey FRANCK:** b June 13, 1970, Louisville, Jefferson County, Kentucky.

   2. **David Garnett FRANCK:** b April 11, 1974, Louisville, Jefferson County, Kentucky.

2. **James Rumsey WEIR:** b April 10, 1949, Louisville, Jefferson County, Kentucky; d at Louisville, Jefferson County, Kentucky, June 18, 1965, in an automobile accident.

3. **Heath Babbitt WEIR:** b March 23, 1951, Louisville, Jefferson County, Kentucky; m at Crestwood, Fayette County, Kentucky, September 23, 1971, Courtney Ward Ball.

   1. **Courtney Lee BALL:** b April 6, 1977, Louisville, Jefferson County, Kentucky.

I.1.1.9.2.8.2b
Mrs. MARGARET MUNN (WILLETT) WEIR
And HENRY FRENCH WALLACE

Mrs. Margaret (Willett) Weir married 2nd September, 1978, Henry French Wallace (divorced 1989).

I.1.1.9.2.8.2a
Mrs. MARGARET MUNN (WILLETT, WEIR) WALLACE
And JOHN HUNT STITESI

Mrs. Margaret (Willett, Weir) Wallace married 3rd June 22, 1990, John Hunt Stitesi (b June 22, 1922).

CHAPTER FIFTEEN
THE CONSIDER H. WILLETT FURNITURE COMPANY

CONSIDER H. WILLETT FURNITURE COMPANY, 1941 CATALOG, PLANT NO. 1, 30TH AND KENTUCKY STREETS, COURTESY H. WHITWELL WALES, III

CONSIDER H. WILLETT FURNITURE COMPANY, 1941 CATALOG, PLANT NO. 2, 31ST AND MAGAZINE STREETS. COURTESY H. WHITWELL WALES, III

CATALOG COURTESY H. WHITWELL WALES, III
FROM 1941 CATALOG

CATALOG COURTESY H. WHITWELL WALES, III
FROM 1941 CATALOG

CATALOG COURTESY H. WHITWELL WALES, III
FROM 1942 C. H. WILLETT FURNITURE
COMPANY CATALOG

WILLIAM WILLETT (1769-1844)

CATALOG COURTESY H. WHITWELL WALES, III FROM 1942 C. H. WILLETT FURNITURE COMPANY CATALOG

CATALOG COURTESY H. WHITWELL WALES, III
FROM 1958-1959 CATALOG

CATALOG COURTESY H. WHITWELL WALES, III
FROM 1958-1959 CATALOG

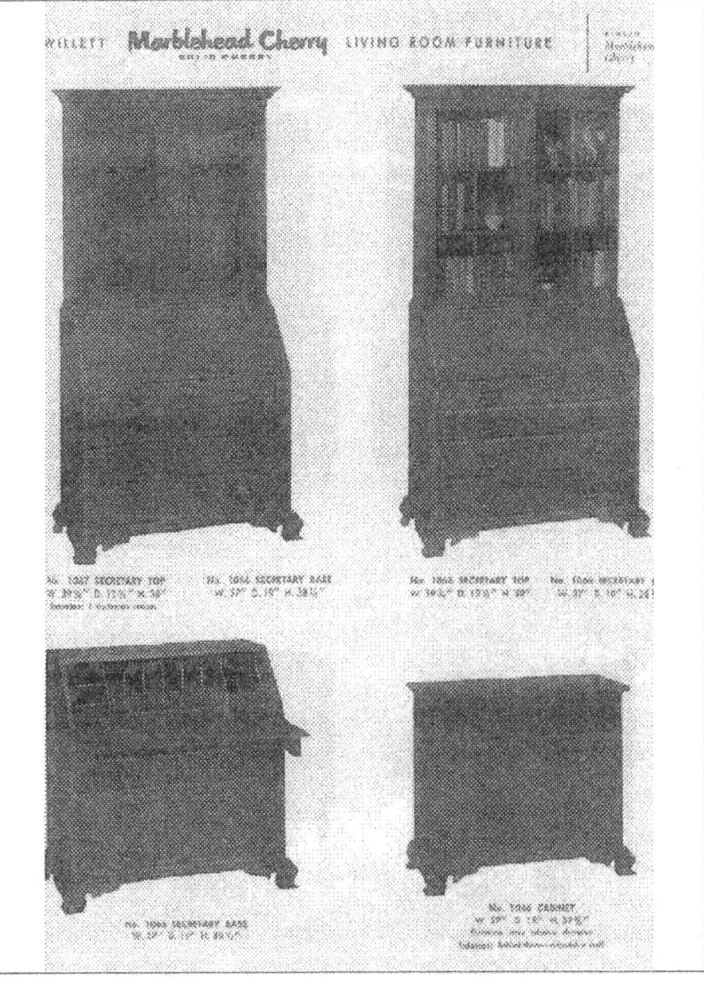

CATALOG COURTESY H. WHITWELL WALES, III
FROM 1958-1959 CATALOG

BIBLIOGRAPHY

Newspaper articles, obituaries, and short biographical notices are cited internally.

Bookstaver, J. E., *Willet-Willets-Willett-Willits Genealogy*, 1906, 142 hand-written pages, 17 Roman Numeral pages, Index.

Goss, Warren Lee, *Recollections of a Private, A Story of the Army of the Potomac*, Thomas Y. Cromwell & Company, New York, 1890, 354 pages.

Marcot, Roy M., *Civil War Chief of Sharpshooters, Hiram Berdan, Military Commander, and Firearms Inventor*, Northwood Heritage Press, Irvine California, 1989, hard bound.

The *Photographic History of the Civil War, in Ten Volumes*, Francis Trevelyan Miller, Editor in Chief, Robert S. Lanier, Managing Editor, Eaton Press Edition, 1995.

Stevens, Capt. C. A., *Berdan's United States Sharpshooters, in the Army of the Potomac, 1861-1865*, 1892, Morningside Bookshop, Dayton, Ohio, reprinted 1984, 597 pages.

Townsend, George Alfred, *Campaigns of a Non-Combatant*, Blelock & Company, 1866, 368 pages.

Willett, Albert James, *The Willett Families of North America*, Southern Historical Press, 1985, 1040 pages.

Willett, Herbert Lockwood, *The Corridor of Years*, privately printed, 1967; access to and permission to quote from is courtesy of Herbert Lockwood Willett, III, of Massachusetts.

Willett, Herbert Lockwood, *Further Corridor of Years*, privately printed, no date; access to and permission to quote from is courtesy of Herbert Lockwood Willett, III, of Massachusetts.

Diary: Mrs. Mary E. (Yates) Willett extracts May 29, 1862, to April 14, 1863, 7 typescript pages; access to and permission to quote from is courtesy of Robert and Donna Willett of Florida.

Diary: Copy of Original Diary of Alfred Milan Willett beginning date August 5, 1860, ending date April 12, 1862, 118 unnumbered original pages; access to and permission to quote from is courtesy of Robert and Donna Willett of Florida.

Letters: Transcription of Letters send by or received by A. W. Smith (1833-1868) beginning October 29, 1849, last entry November 28, 1859, 104 typescript unnumbered pages, access to and permission to quote from is courtesy of Robert and Donna Willett of Florida..

INDEX

ALLGYER
  Kenneth Ward, 216
  Robert Earl, 216
  Robert Earl, Jr., 216
  Sarah Scott, 216

BALL
  Courtney Lee, 217

BOWMAN
  Peter Wales, 205
  Philip Boynton, 205
  Porter Roberts, 205
  Susan Foxworthy, 205
  William Porter, 205

BROGAN
  Sherri Lynn, 196

BROWN
  William Patrick, 189

BROWNE
  Alexander Cumnock, 209
  Alexander Duncan, 210
  Balwin Willett, 210
  James Slaughter, 210
  Keene McEwan, 210
  Robert Mallory, 209
  Roscoe Willett, 209
  William Kennedy, 209
  William Kennedy, Jr., 209, 210
  William Kennedy, III, 210

BUGSBY
  Betsey, 13

CARSTENS
  Jeffrey Peter, 193
  Julie Truesdale, 193, 194
  Lucie Gorham, 193, 194
  Virginia Elizabeth, 193
  Willett Noble, 193

CASE
  Alexander, 168
  Eliza, 169
  George, 168
  Jane, 168
  Ray, 169
  William, 168

COHN
  Katherine Wakefield, 199

COLLEDGE
  Sarah, 210

COMNOCK
  Philura, 208

CUMMINGS
  Asher T., 11
  Lydia, 12
  George O., 12
  James R., 12, 148
  Willard T., 12

CURRIE
  Roxanna, 199

DALY
  Lila Margaret, 194
  Thomas Gerald, 194
  Thomas Jeffrey, 194
  Virginia Elizabeth, 194

DASEF
  Margaret Elizabeth, 157

DAVIS
  Sophia, 16

DAY
  Sylvia, 142

DOAN
  Edith, 141

DOUGHTERTY
  Deann Mary, 189

ETHRIDGE
  Abigail MacKenzie, 141
  Paul James, 141
  Philip Austin, 141

FIELD
  Chloe, 202

FISH
  Willett, 173

FLOM
  Benton Porter, 205
  Emily Roberts, 205

FOSTER
  Hannah, 4

FRANCK
  David Garnett, 217
  John Ramsey, 217

FRANKLIN
  Andrew Jacob, 196
  Ann Elizabeth, 195
  Cassidy Marie, 196
  Daniel Robert, 196
  Edwin T., 195
  Jennifer Lynn, 196
  Mary Josephine, 195
  Robert Edward, 195, 196
  William Henry, 195
  William Henry, Jr., 195, 196
  William Henry, III, 196

GEE
  Lucy Wales, 206
  Robert Warren, 206
  William F., 206

GERMAIN
  Mary Annette, 150

GINER
  Elizabeth Charlotte, 215

GLEN
  Leonie, 163

GORHAM
  Anthony McVoy, 186
  Brooke Lee, 188
  Dillon Timothy, 188
  Eugene Timothy, 186, 188
  Eugene Timothy, II, 188

Jeffrey Heath, 186, 189
Lucy Maybelle, 185
Lucy Truesdale, 190, 193
Sandra Elizabeth, 191, 192
Sidney Smith, 185
Sidney Smith, Jr., 185, 186
Sidney Smith, III, 186, 187
Sidney Smith, IV, 187
Suzanne Willett, 191, 192
Whitney Ann, 188
Willett Noble, 185, 190
Willett, Noble, Jr., 190, 191

GORHAM SHERE
  Jonathan L., 188

GROVES
  Pearl, 146

GRAY
  Andrew Clayton, 189

HAN
  Ming Lee, 166

HOOPINGARNER
  Alexander Redhed Gorham, 192
  Alicia Jacobs Gorham, 192
  Billy Lee, 192

HOSKINS
  Clara Bradley, 127

HOWELL
  Jean Elizabeth, 187

HUNTINGTON
  Frances Solace, 201

IVANKOVICH
  Anthony Francis, 215
  Katarina Gabriala, 215
  Lucas Alexander, 215
  Sophie Chaccone, 215

JACKSON
  Tryphosa, 170

JACOBS
  Lucie Truesdale, 190

JENNINGS
   Kris Long, 192
   Maxwell Devereux, 192

JONES
   Mary Haskell, 132

KAMIS
   Edward Joseph, 194
   Julia Hahn, 194
   Meredith Katherine, 194

KIRKLAND
   Diana Margaret, 203
   John David, 203
   John David, Jr., 203
   Pierce Wales, 203
   Robert Wales, 203
   Solace Huntington, 203
   William Daniel, 203

KOCHTITZKY
   Lucy Carolyn, 161

LESLEY
   Susan (Foster), 9

LOKAY
   Allison, 202
   Thomas, 202

MACPHERSON
   Margery, 158

MADIGAN
   Mary Kellie, 167

MCCOBB
   Janet, 202

MCDOWELL
   Fayette, 211

MINER
   Anna Howell, 106

MULLINS
   Judith Suzanne, 191

MUNN
   Margaret Meldrum, 212

NORTHRUP
   Harriet J., 105

PIERCE
   Robin Jane, 200

PORTER
   Ann Elizabeth, 206
   Elizabeth, 204, 205
   Elizabeth Ann, 206
   Erik Webber, 206
   Lara Taylor, 207
   Marna Wales, 207
   Pamela Lucy, 204, 206
   Robert Taylor, 204, 206
   William Wales, 204, 207

PRICE
   Emma Augusta, 120

RATHBURN
   Leslie, 189

ROSS
   Consider Willett, 214, 215
   Elizabeth Charlotte, 215
   Katherine Margaret, 215
   Robert Danforth, 214
   Sarah Henshaw, 214, 216
   Stephan Alexander, 215

SAMSON
   Blake Anthony, 160
   Charles Felix, 160
   David, 160
   Hugh, 160
   Peter, 160

SHEETS
   Gwendolen Blanche, 201

SIMONS
   Harry, 184
   Irving, 184

SMITH
   Abigail Jane, 24, 148
   Abram Willett, 24, 106

Alfred Floyd, 18
Carrie H., 104
Eva M., 104
Gordon Arthur, 24, 111
James Willett, 24, 150
Jane, 23
Milan Willett, 23, 99

SOUTHWICK
 James Morrell, 203

STANLEY
 Margaret Long, 131

STEINKE
 Barbara, 188

STITESI
 John Hunt, 217

SUMMERS
 Clay, 156
 Esther, 156
 Germain, 156
 Helen, 156
 Marion, 156

THATCHER
 Leslie Warfield, 200

VERSPOOR
 Kelly Ann, 189
 Marcia Jayne, 189
 Shelly Ann, 189

WALES
 Allison Currie, 199
 Ann Elizabeth, 201, 203
 Gwynne Huntington, 201, 202
 Henry Whitwell, 197
 Henry Whitwell, Jr., 197, 198
 Henry Whitwell, III, 198, 199
 Henry Whitwell, III, 199
 Henry Whitwell, IV, 199, 200
 Henry Whitwell, V, 200
 Katherine Anne, 202
 Lois Elizabeth, 197, 204
 Louise, 202
 Robert Willett, 197, 199, 201
 Sidney Wakefield, 199

Solace Huntington, 201
Zachary Pierce, 200

WALLACE
 Henry French, 217
 Margaret Munn, 217

WEBBER
 Sarah Lee, 206

WEINBERG
 Jane, 188

WEIR
 Edwin Babbitte, 217
 Heath Babbitt, 217
 James Rumsey, 217
 Margaret Munn, 217
 Margaret Willett, 217

WELCH
 Kenneth, 210

WILDER
 Lois Adelaide, 174

WILLETT
 Abraham, 1, 8, 13
 Adelaide Lucille, 182
 Alice J., 104
 Alfred Milan, 23, 99, 105
 Ann, 9, 168
 Arthur Floyd, 119, 142
 Arthur Floyd, Jr., 144, 145
 Betsey, 8
 Carlotta Maybelle, 183, 197
 Carrie, 104
 Catherine, 164
 Charles Adrian, 17
 Claire Dulaney, 164
 Clay, 211
 Consider Heath, 173, 174
 Consider Heath, Jr., 183, 212
 Edith, 158, 160
 Edith A., 155, 156
 Elizabeth Priest, 208, 209, 210
 Enoch Furman, 15, 16
 Enos Hale, 119
 Errol Stanley, 162, 167
 Errol William, 157, 158

Eva, 104
Experience, 9
Fern H., 156
Florence Woodford, 141
Floyd Abram, 24, 106
Florence Pearl, 182, 184
Genevra A., 155
George Germaine, 155
Gordon Arthur, 24, 111
Grace A., 156
Grace Annette, 182
Gurion Seal, 166
Hannah, 9, 18
Helen Eloise, 182, 195
Herbert Lockwood, 119, 120
Herbert Lockwood, Jr., 126, 127, 131
Herbert Lockwood, III, 132
Hellen M., 17
Hugh Maxwell, 164
James W., 24, 150
Jane F., 109
John, 9
Leslie Gordon, 119, 142
Lois Wilder, 213, 214
Louise McDowell, 211
Lucia Elizabeth, 173
Margaret Munn, 213, 217
Mary A., 110
Mary Kate, 162
Mary L., 173
Myrtle Geneveve, 182, 185
Patience, 9
Paul Yates, 126
Permelia, 8, 11
Peter, 164
Peter Sabin, 162, 163, 165
Peter Stuart, 159, 161
Polema Seeson, 166
Robert Leslie, 126
Robert McDowell, 211
Thomas, 211
Wade Stuart, 162, 166
William, 3, 4, 9, 170
William George, 155, 157
William Roscoe, 183, 208
William Roscoe, Jr., 208, 211
William Roscoe, III, 211
William Roscoe, IV, 211

WILLEY
Gordon, 165
Hannah, 165
Martha Thodal, 165

WILSON
Nancy Barbee, 198

YAGER
Julia, 99

YATES
Mary Elizabeth, 111

Heritage Books by Albert James Willett, Jr.:

Abraham Willett (c1735–c1805) of Onondaga County, New York

The Martin Family of the Poquoson District, York County, Virginia
Albert James Willett, Jr. and Dr. Fred William Martin, Ph.D.

*Poquoson Families, Volume I: The Forrest Family
of the Poquoson District, York County, Virginia*

*Poquoson Families, Volume II: The Holloway, Messick, and Linton Families
of the Poquoson District, York County, Virginia*

*Poquoson Families, Volume III: The Topping, Rollins, and Carmines Families
of Poquoson District, York County, Virginia*

*Poquoson Families, Volume IV: The Amory, Insley, Firman, and Firth Families
of the Poquoson District, York County, Virginia*

*Poquoson Families, Volume V: The Gilbert and Hopkins Families
of the Poquoson District, York County, Virginia*

*Poquoson Families, Volume VI: The Patrick, Evans and Lawson Families
of the Poquoson District, York County, Virginia*

CD: *Willett Family of Pennsylvania*

Willett House Collection [Willett Family of Pennsylvania]

About The Author

ALBERT JAMES WILLETT, JR., is a husband, father, grandfather, author, historian, genealogist, US Army Master Aviator, Instructor Pilot and Test Pilot, and veteran of the Vietnam War and the Saudi-Iraqi War. His earliest Willett ancestor, William Willett (1645-1719) settled in Accomack County in 1666, and his family has remained in Virginia ever since. Albert is the son of Albert James Willett, Sr., and Mamie Rose Gilbert.

During his years in the military, Chief Warrant Officer Willett saw extended service in Vietnam, South Korea, Germany, and Saudi Arabia. After retiring from the US Army in 1996, after 28-years of aviation service, he began a new full-time career at the Army Materiel Command, Alexandria, Virginia, first as a Budget Officer and currently as a Program Analyst in the Logistics Civil Augmentation Program (LOGCAP).

Albert Willett has published three Willett surname volumes *The Willett Families of North America, Being a Comprehensive guide encompassing Willett, Willet, Willette, Willit, Willot, Willets, Willetts, Willits, and other variations and early spellings of the Willett Surname*, 1985, 1040 pages, 2 vol., *The Willett Family of Pennsylvania*, 1998, 454 pages; *Abraham Willett (c1735-c1805) of Onondaga County, New York*, 2000, 233 pages, and hopes to publish several more Willett surname volume that are currently in various stages of draft and research.

Albert Willett has published five volumes on the families of Poquoson, Virginia. They are *Poquoson Watermen, A Guide to Messick District, Poquoson, Virginia, Families of Martin, Holloway, Forrest, Topping, Messick, Rollins,*

Carmines, Insley, Firth, Evans, Hopkins, Page, Pauls, Ferguson, Firman, Huggett, Linton, Thomas, Gilbert, 1988, 392 pages; and co-authored with Dr. Fred William Martin, Ph.D., *The Martin Family of Poquoson District, York County, Virginia, with additional Martin notes on Portsmouth, Virginia, and Grafton District, York County, Virginia,* 1994, 317 pages; and is the author of a continuing series *Poquoson Families, Volume I: The Forrest Family of the Poquoson District, York County, Virginia,* 2001, 256 pages; *Poquoson Families, Volume II: The Holloway, Messick, and Linton Families of the Poquoson District, York County, Virginia,* 2002, 379 pages; *Poquoson Families, Volume III: The Topping, Rollins, and Carmines Families of the Poquoson District, York County, Virginia,* 2002, 480 pages. Mr. Willett hopes to continue the Poquoson series into several additional volumes covering the families of Amory, Firman, Firth, Gilbert, Insley, Hopkins, Evans, Page, Pauls, Ferguson, Huggett, Thomas, Begor, Cox, Moore, Weston, Quinn and Ward

Albert Willett has been married for 40 years to the former Miss Diane Lynn Myers, the daughter of Raymond Otis Myers and Ruth Pugh and has two children, Albert James Willett, Jr., of Stafford, Virginia, and Mrs. Karen Diane (Willett) Crowley, of Hampton, Virginia.

Albert hopes to leave a legacy of history to his children, grandchildren, and those who read his volumes of family histories that are rich in stories and examples of family heritage, family loyalty, and of service to family and country.

www.ingramcontent.com/pod-product-compliance
Lightning Source LLC
Chambersburg PA
CBHW050138170426
43197CB00011B/1887